THE FUNDAMENTALS OF ECONOMICS

VEERAREDDY PRABHAKAR REDDY,
MURALIDHAR RAO AKKALADEVI

Contents

Preface

Economics is more than just numbers, graphs, and financial policies—it is the study of human behavior, decision-making, and the forces that shape societies. From understanding the impact of inflation on household budgets to analyzing how international trade agreements influence global markets, economics provides a structured way to interpret and navigate the complexities of the modern world.

This book, ***The Fundamentals of Economics,*** is designed to serve as a comprehensive and analytical guide for students, educators, policymakers, and anyone seeking to develop a strong foundation in economic principles. It is structured to provide a balanced exploration of both microeconomic and macroeconomic concepts, while also covering contemporary issues such as **global trade, monetary and fiscal policies, technological innovations, and sustainable development**.

The book is divided into **fifteen systematically arranged chapters**, ensuring a logical flow from fundamental economic theories to real-world applications. It begins by introducing the **core principles of economics,including demand and supply dynamics, market structures, and national income accounting**, before expanding into critical topics like **monetary policy, inflation, exchange rates, and financial markets**. The latter sections delve into emerging economic trends, such as blockchain technology, artificial intelligence in economic forecasting, and the future of global trade and finance.

A distinctive feature of this book is its emphasis on practical applications and case studies, with detailed discussions on Indian economic reforms, the 2008 global financial crisis, and contemporary fiscal and monetary challenges. These insights help bridge the gap between economic theory and real-world policymaking, enabling readers to grasp the significance of economic principles in shaping national and global economies.

We have taken great care to ensure that the content is academically rigorous yet accessible, maintaining clarity without oversimplifying key concepts. Whether you are an undergraduate student exploring economics for the first time, a policymaker seeking data-driven insights, or a professional looking to refine your understanding of economic frameworks, this book is structured to provide valuable perspectives for all readers.

We express our gratitude to friends, students, and scholars whose insights have enriched this work. We also acknowledge the contributions of economists and policymakers whose research continues to inspire new discussions in economic theory and practice.

It is our sincere hope that this book will serve as a valuable resource in your exploration of economics, providing you with the knowledge and analytical skills needed to understand and navigate the evolving economic landscape.

Happy Reading!

Veerareddy Prabhakar Reddy & Muralidhar Rao Akkaladevi

Chapter Wise Contents

CHAPTER 1: ECONOMICS AND ITS ROLE IN THE MODERN WORLD
1.1 What is Economics?

- Definitions and Scope
- Microeconomics vs. Macroeconomics
- The Importance of Economics in Everyday Life

1.2 Evolution of Economic Thought

- Classical, Keynesian, and Modern Schools of Thought

1.3 Why Economics Matters Today

- Decision-Making in Households, Businesses, and Governments
- Economics as a Tool for Policy and Strategy

CHAPTER 2: UNDERSTANDING NATIONAL ECONOMIES
2.1 National Income Accounting

- Definitions: GDP, GNP, NNP
- Differences and Methods of Calculation
- Real GDP vs. Nominal GDP

2.2 Per Capita Income

- Importance in Measuring Economic Growth
- Applications in Policy-Making

2.3 Key Indicators of Economic Health

- Consumer Price Index (CPI)
- Wholesale Price Index (WPI)
- GDP Deflator

CHAPTER 3: INFLATION, DEFLATION, AND ECONOMIC STABILITY

3.1 Inflation

- Types: Demand-Pull, Cost-Push
- Measurement: CPI, WPI

3.2 Deflation and Disinflation

- Causes and Economic Impacts
- Policies for Mitigation

3.3 Advanced Concepts

- Stagflation: Definition and Case Studies
- Hyperinflation: Examples and Lessons

CHAPTER 4: MONEY, BANKING, AND MONETARY POLICY
4.1 Role of Money and Banking

- Functions of Money
- Structure of Modern Banking Systems

4.2 Key Tools of Monetary Policy

- Repo Rate, Reverse Repo Rate
- CRR, SLR, Bank Rate
- Open Market Operations (OMO)

4.3 Money Supply

- Components: M1, M2, M3, M4

4.4 Inflation Targeting and Monetary Transmission

- Role of the Monetary Policy Committee (MPC)
- Challenges in Monetary Transmission

CHAPTER 5: FISCAL POLICY AND PUBLIC FINANCE
5.1 Understanding Fiscal Policy

15.3 Emerging Trends in Global Trade and Finance

- Opportunities and Challenges

ONE

ECONOMICS AND ITS ROLE IN THE MODERN WORLD

1.1 What is Economics?

Economics is a field of study that examines how societies allocate scarce resources to satisfy unlimited wants and needs. It delves into the production, distribution, and consumption of goods and services, forming the backbone of modern civilization's functioning. Rooted in practicality and theoretical analysis, economics extends its influence from government policies to individual decision-making, and its significance has grown exponentially in the contemporary world.

Definitions and Scope

The term "economics" originates from the Greek word *oikonomia*, meaning household management. Historically, it referred to managing resources within a household or a small community. Today, its scope has expanded to encompass national and global systems. A widely accepted definition, given by Lionel Robbins, describes economics as "the science which studies human behavior as a relationship between ends and scarce means which have alternative uses." This definition emphasizes scarcity and the need for prioritization and efficient resource allocation.

Economics can be broadly divided into two core approaches: normative economics and positive economics. Normative economics involves value judgments and prescribes what ought to be, whereas positive economics focuses on objective analysis and explains what is. For instance, while positive economics might analyze the effects of increasing taxes, normative economics debates whether raising taxes is the right policy for equitable wealth distribution.

The scope of economics is vast and multifaceted, addressing issues like inflation, unemployment, poverty, trade, resource depletion, and technological advancements. It also incorporates subfields such as environmental economics, behavioral economics, and development economics, each offering specialized insights into pressing global challenges.

Microeconomics vs. Macroeconomics

Understanding the Divide

Economics operates on two primary levels: **microeconomics** and **macroeconomics**. Microeconomics examines individual agents, such as households, firms, and industries, focusing on how they make decisions to allocate resources. Macroeconomics, on the other hand, analyzes the economy as a whole, investigating aggregate indicators such as GDP, inflation, and employment levels.

For example, microeconomics would study how a bakery decides the price of its bread based on costs and market demand. In contrast, macroeconomics would explore how changes in national interest rates influence overall consumer spending and economic growth.

Principles of Microeconomics

1. **Demand and Supply**: Microeconomics heavily relies on the laws of demand and supply. For instance, if the price of apples rises due to a drought, consumers might switch to oranges, showcasing price elasticity.
2. **Utility Maximization**: Consumers aim to achieve the highest satisfaction from limited resources. Calculating marginal utility helps understand

why consumers buy one product over another.

3. **Cost Structures and Production**: Firms analyze fixed and variable costs to determine optimal production levels, employing methods such as break-even analysis.

Principles of Macroeconomics

1. **Economic Growth**: Tracking GDP growth helps measure a nation's economic health. For instance, emerging economies like India prioritize increasing industrial output to boost GDP.
2. **Monetary Policy**: Central banks, such as the Reserve Bank of India, use tools like interest rate adjustments to control inflation and stabilize currency.
3. **Fiscal Policy**: Governments influence the economy through spending and taxation. For example, public infrastructure projects can stimulate job creation and consumption.

Microeconomics vs. Macroeconomics

The Importance of Economics in Everyday Life

Individual Decision-Making

Economics plays a critical role in shaping personal choices, from selecting a career to managing household budgets. For instance, an individual deciding between purchasing a car or saving for retirement weighs opportunity costs—foregoing one benefit to gain another. Tools like budgeting apps or investment calculators stem from economic principles, guiding consumers toward informed financial decisions.

Business Strategies

Businesses thrive on economic insights. Firms conduct market analysis to understand consumer behavior, price elasticity, and competition. For instance, e-commerce giants like Amazon use data-driven economic models to optimize pricing strategies, ensuring profit maximization while maintaining customer satisfaction. Similarly, cost-benefit analyses inform decisions on expanding operations or launching new products.

National Policy Development

Governments use economics to address societal challenges, such as unemployment, inequality, and resource allocation. For example, public distribution systems in India ensure food security for underprivileged populations. Moreover, economic indicators like inflation rates or fiscal deficits influence policy-making, shaping initiatives like the **Mahatma Gandhi National Rural Employment Guarantee Scheme (MGNREGS).**

Global Trade and Cooperation

Economics underpins international trade, fostering globalization. Principles of comparative advantage explain why countries specialize in producing certain goods. For instance, India exports software services due to its skilled workforce, while importing crude oil to meet energy demands. Institutions like the World Trade Organization (WTO) ensure fair trade practices and economic cooperation among nations.

Challenges in Applying Economics

Despite its utility, economics faces challenges in addressing complex, real-world scenarios. Assumptions like rational behavior or perfect competition often diverge from reality. Behavioral economics, which studies psychological influences on decision-making, seeks to bridge this gap. For example, people might prefer immediate rewards over long-term gains, contrary to traditional economic predictions.

Economic forecasting also encounters limitations, such as unforeseen global events like pandemics or natural disasters disrupting models. During the COVID-19 pandemic, traditional supply-chain theories were upended, highlighting the need for adaptable and resilient economic strategies.

Practical Applications

Economics is not confined to theoretical constructs; its principles have practical applications that enhance societal well-being.

Addressing Poverty

Economic policies targeting poverty alleviation focus on job creation, education, and skill development. Microfinance institutions, such as Grameen Bank in Bangladesh, empower low-income individuals by providing small loans, fostering entrepreneurship.

Sustainable Development

Environmental economics promotes sustainable practices by factoring in externalities, such as pollution, into cost analyses. Policies like carbon taxes incentivize businesses to reduce emissions, aligning economic growth with environmental conservation.

Healthcare Economics

Healthcare resource allocation, particularly during crises, relies on economic efficiency. For instance, cost-effectiveness analysis determines whether investing in vaccines or hospital infrastructure yields better public health outcomes.

1.2 Evolution of Economic Thought

The field of economics has undergone remarkable transformation over centuries, reflecting the changing dynamics of societies, markets, and political structures. From its origins in classical philosophy to the advent of Keynesian theories and modern approaches, economic thought has evolved to address the complexities of human needs, resource allocation, and global interdependence. Each school of thought has contributed unique perspectives and tools, shaping the discipline into what it is today.

Classical School of Thought

The Classical School of economics emerged during the 18th and 19th centuries, primarily influenced by the works of Adam Smith, David Ricardo, and John Stuart Mill. This school laid the foundation of economic theory, emphasizing the role of free markets, individual self-interest, and minimal government intervention.

Core Principles of the Classical School

1. **Invisible Hand and Market Efficiency**: Adam Smith, often regarded as the father of economics, introduced the concept of the "invisible hand" in his seminal work, *The Wealth of Nations* (1776). He argued that when individuals pursue their self-interest, markets achieve optimal allocation of resources. For instance, a baker producing bread for profit inadvertently contributes to society's welfare by ensuring food availability.

2. **Law of Comparative Advantage**: David Ricardo introduced the principle of comparative advantage, emphasizing that countries should specialize in producing goods where they have a relative efficiency. For example, if India excels in software development while the US excels in automobile manufacturing, both nations benefit by trading these goods.

3. **Labor Theory of Value**: Classical economists posited that the value of a commodity is determined by the labor required to produce it. While this theory laid important groundwork, it later faced criticism for overlooking factors like utility and consumer preferences.

4. **Say's Law**: This principle, proposed by Jean-Baptiste Say, asserts that "supply creates its own demand." It implies that production inherently generates enough income to purchase the output, negating the possibility of long-term economic slumps.

Challenges and Criticism

While the Classical School championed the virtues of laissez-faire economics, it failed to adequately address market failures, inequality, and cyclical unemployment. The Industrial Revolution highlighted the plight of factory workers and the environmental consequences of unchecked industrialization, revealing the limitations of classical doctrines.

Keynesian School of Thought

The Keynesian revolution, spearheaded by John Maynard Keynes during the 1930s, marked a paradigm shift in economic thinking. Keynes' groundbreaking work, *The General Theory of Employment, Interest, and Money* (1936), responded to the Great Depression, challenging classical assumptions and advocating active government intervention to stabilize economies.

Core Principles of the Keynesian School

1. **Aggregate Demand and Economic Output**: Keynes argued that aggregate demand—comprising consumption, investment, government spending, and net exports—drives economic output and employment levels. During recessions, insufficient demand leads to unemployment and stagnation, necessitating policy measures to boost spending.
2. **Role of Fiscal Policy**: Keynes emphasized the importance of government spending and taxation as tools to influence aggregate demand. For instance, during the Great Depression, public works programs were used to create jobs and stimulate consumption.
3. **Multiplier Effect**: This concept illustrates how an initial injection of government spending multiplies throughout the economy. For example, building a highway not only employs construction workers but also increases demand for materials and ancillary services, amplifying the economic impact.
4. **Liquidity Preference and Interest Rates**: Keynes introduced the idea of liquidity preference, explaining that people prefer holding liquid cash, especially during uncertain times. Central banks, therefore, play a crucial role in regulating interest rates to encourage borrowing and investment.

Practical Applications and Legacy

Keynesian principles underpinned post-World War II economic policies, contributing to rapid growth and stability in Western economies. However, the stagflation crisis of the 1970s, characterized by high inflation and unemployment, exposed the limitations of Keynesian models, paving the way for new approaches.

Modern Schools of Thought

Economic thought has further diversified in the modern era, encompassing various approaches that address globalization, technological advancement, and environmental sustainability. Prominent among these are monetarism, new classical economics, behavioral economics, and ecological economics.

Monetarism

Developed by Milton Friedman, monetarism emphasizes the role of money supply in influencing inflation and economic stability. Friedman critiqued Keynesian over-reliance on fiscal policy, arguing that stable monetary growth is essential for long-term economic health. The "quantity theory of money," expressed as $MV = PQ$, links money supply (M) and velocity (V) to price level (P) and output (Q). For example, excessive money printing can lead to hyperinflation, as witnessed in Zimbabwe during the early 2000s.

Behavioral Economics

Challenging the classical assumption of rational behavior, behavioral economics integrates psychology into economic models. Researchers like Daniel Kahneman and Richard Thaler have demonstrated how cognitive biases influence decision-making. For instance, the "endowment effect" explains why individuals overvalue their possessions, even if selling them would yield greater economic benefits.

Ecological Economics

In response to global environmental crises, ecological economics examines the interplay between economic systems and ecosystems. It advocates sustainable development, emphasizing that GDP growth should not come at the cost of ecological degradation. Concepts like carbon pricing and green GDP have gained traction as policymakers grapple with climate change.

Game Theory and Strategic Interactions

Modern economics has also embraced game theory, analyzing strategic interactions among rational agents. For instance, in international trade negotiations, countries employ game-theoretic models to anticipate and counteract each other's moves, aiming for mutually beneficial outcomes.

Challenges in Synthesizing Economic Thought

The evolution of economic thought reflects the discipline's dynamic nature, but it also highlights inherent tensions and trade-offs. Integrating insights from diverse schools requires balancing theoretical rigor with practical applicability. For instance, while Keynesian policies may effectively combat recessions, long-term reliance on deficit spending risks unsustainable debt levels. Similarly, ecological economics advocates for green policies that may conflict with immediate economic growth objectives.

Practical Applications of Economic Theories

1. **Macroeconomic Stabilization**: Central banks worldwide employ Keynesian and monetarist tools to manage inflation, unemployment, and economic growth. For example, the Federal Reserve's quantitative easing measures during the 2008 financial crisis were rooted in modern economic principles.
2. **Policy Design and Evaluation**: Governments use a blend of classical and modern theories to design policies addressing poverty, inequality, and environmental challenges. For instance, universal basic income proposals draw on behavioral insights to reduce income disparities while maintaining incentives for work.
3. **Corporate Strategies**: Businesses leverage game theory and behavioral economics to optimize pricing, marketing, and consumer engagement. Companies like Google and Amazon utilize data-driven models to predict customer behavior, enhancing profitability and market share.

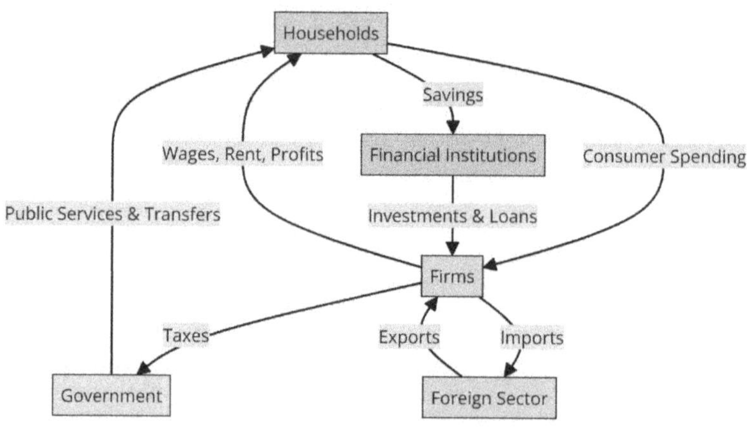

Circular Flow of Income Model

1.3 Why Economics Matters Today

Economics plays an indispensable role in the modern world, influencing decisions at every level of society, from individual households to global organizations. Its principles and methodologies provide critical tools for navigating complexities, optimizing resources, and achieving both personal and collective goals. By applying economic reasoning, individuals, businesses, and governments can make informed choices, adapt to changing circumstances, and plan for the future with precision and insight.

Decision-Making in Households, Businesses, and Governments

Households: Managing Limited Resources

Economics profoundly impacts household decision-making by offering frameworks for allocating limited resources effectively. Families regularly face trade-offs—choosing between saving for education, purchasing a home, or investing in healthcare. Concepts like **opportunity cost** help households evaluate the benefits and drawbacks of alternative choices.

For instance, a middle-income family may need to decide between enrolling a child in a private school or saving for retirement. By calculating potential returns on each option, such as long-term career benefits of quality education versus financial security, the family can make an informed decision. Economic principles also guide budgeting and consumption. Tools like marginal utility analysis help individuals understand diminishing returns—why a third car might add less value to life than a long-awaited vacation.

Businesses: Strategic Planning and Market Competitiveness

Businesses rely heavily on economics to formulate strategies, manage risks, and remain competitive. Economic theories guide pricing, production, and investment decisions. For instance, understanding **elasticity of demand** enables companies to set optimal prices. A firm selling luxury goods, for example, might recognize that a small price increase leads to a significant drop in demand, while a manufacturer of essentials like salt can afford minimal price sensitivity.

Businesses also use cost-benefit analysis for investment decisions. Consider a tech company planning to launch a new product. By estimating production costs, market demand, and potential revenue, the firm can decide whether to proceed. Moreover, game theory helps corporations anticipate competitors' moves, such as how rival airlines adjust fares during peak seasons to gain market share.

Economic forecasting further aids in risk management. Multinational corporations analyze global trends—like currency fluctuations or trade regulations—to adapt their supply chains. During the COVID-19 pandemic, many companies utilized such insights to pivot toward e-commerce and digital solutions, mitigating losses from disrupted traditional operations.

Governments: Balancing Growth and Equity

For governments, economics is fundamental to policymaking, enabling the balancing of growth, stability, and equity. Policymakers must allocate resources across diverse sectors such as infrastructure, education, and healthcare while addressing deficits and public debt. Tools like **cost-effectiveness analysis** guide such decisions, ensuring maximum societal benefit per unit of expenditure.

For instance, governments facing unemployment may adopt Keynesian principles, implementing stimulus packages to boost aggregate demand and job creation. India's Mahatma Gandhi National Rural Employment Guarantee Scheme (MGNREGS) is a prime example, providing rural employment while improving infrastructure.

Economic models also help governments combat inflation and recession. Central banks employ monetary policies, such as adjusting interest rates, to control inflation or stimulate growth. Similarly, trade policies based on comparative advantage theory foster international cooperation, ensuring access to critical resources and markets.

Economics as a Tool for Policy and Strategy
Shaping Effective Policies

Economics provides a scientific foundation for crafting policies that address pressing societal issues. For example, in combating climate change, governments use carbon pricing—an economic tool that internalizes the environmental costs of pollution into production and consumption. This approach incentivizes businesses to adopt cleaner technologies while generating revenue for green initiatives.

Healthcare is another area where economics enhances policy design. Through cost-utility analysis, policymakers can determine which interventions yield the highest health outcomes relative to cost. For instance, during vaccine rollouts, governments prioritize populations based on economic and epidemiological factors, ensuring maximum societal impact.

Driving Corporate Strategies

Corporate leaders integrate economic insights into decision-making to adapt to market dynamics. For example, during economic downturns, businesses may adopt strategies like downsizing non-essential operations or focusing on core competencies to maintain profitability. Conversely, in periods of economic growth, firms might expand investments, diversify offerings, and tap into new markets.

The use of behavioral economics has become particularly prevalent in shaping consumer behavior. Companies leverage insights from this field to design nudges, such as loyalty programs or limited-time offers, that encourage specific purchasing patterns. For instance, e-commerce platforms often use algorithms to recommend products based on user preferences, boosting sales by aligning consumer psychology with economic goals.

Global Strategy and Cooperation

On the global stage, economics drives international cooperation and conflict resolution. Institutions like the International Monetary Fund (IMF) and World Trade Organization (WTO) rely on economic principles to mediate trade disputes, stabilize currencies, and support development in low-income nations.

For example, during financial crises, the IMF provides conditional loans, requiring recipient nations to implement structural reforms. While these reforms can be politically contentious, they often stabilize economies by reducing fiscal deficits and encouraging private sector growth. Similarly, trade agreements built on economic models ensure mutual benefits, fostering peaceful international relations.

Practical Applications and Challenges

While economics offers powerful tools, its application is not without challenges. Uncertainty and behavioral complexities often complicate predictions, as seen during global shocks like the COVID-19 pandemic or the 2008 financial crisis. Despite these limitations, the discipline continues to evolve, integrating advancements like big data analytics and machine learning to refine forecasting accuracy.

In everyday life, economics empowers individuals, businesses, and governments to navigate an increasingly interconnected and dynamic world. Whether managing personal finances, optimizing corporate strategies, or crafting national policies, its relevance has never been greater. By applying economic reasoning, societies can achieve sustainable growth, equitable development, and resilience in the face of uncertainty.

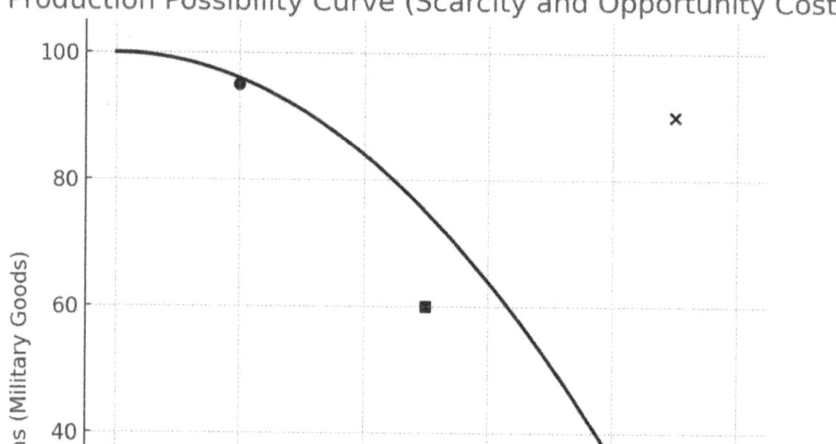

Scarcity & Trade-offs

The PPC illustrates the concept of scarcity: resources are limited, so producing more of one good (e.g., butter) means sacrificing the production of another (e.g., guns).

TWO
UNDERSTANDING NATIONAL ECONOMIES

2.1 National Income Accounting

National income accounting is a vital framework used to measure the economic activity of a nation. It provides a systematic way to record, analyze, and interpret the income generated within an economy, enabling policymakers, businesses, and researchers to assess the health of the economy and make informed decisions. The cornerstone of this system lies in key metrics such as Gross Domestic Product (GDP), Gross National Product (GNP), and Net National Product (NNP). These indicators serve as tools for understanding economic growth, development, and productivity at the national level.

Definitions: GDP, GNP, NNP

Gross Domestic Product (GDP)

Gross Domestic Product (GDP) is the total monetary value of all final goods and services produced within a country's borders over a specific period, typically a year or a quarter. It serves as the primary indicator of economic performance and is used to compare the economic strength of nations.

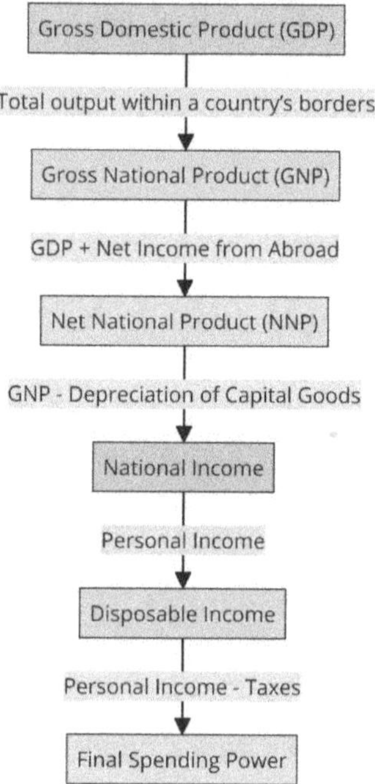

National Income Framework: GDP, GNP, and NNP

GDP is calculated using three main approaches:

1. **Production Approach**: This method sums up the value added at each stage of production across all industries. For instance, in manufacturing a car, the value added includes raw material processing, assembly, and final delivery.
2. **Income Approach**: This sums up all incomes earned in the economy, such as wages, rents, interest, and profits.
3. **Expenditure Approach**: This measures total spending on the economy's goods and services, expressed as: **GDP=C+I+G+(X−M)** where:

- **C = Consumption by households**
- **I = Investment by businesses**
- **G = Government spending**
- **X−M = Net exports (exports minus imports)**

For example, if India's GDP in a fiscal year is ₹300 trillion, it reflects the monetary value of goods and services produced within the country during that year.

Applications of GDP

GDP data guides government policy decisions, such as determining budget allocations or implementing stimulus packages. It also helps investors evaluate economic trends to predict market performance.

Challenges in GDP Measurement

While GDP provides a snapshot of economic activity, it does not account for non-market activities (like household work), environmental degradation, or income inequality, making it an imperfect measure of well-being.

Gross National Product (GNP)

Gross National Product (GNP) expands the scope of GDP by including the total monetary value of goods and services produced by a nation's residents, regardless of location. It captures the income generated by citizens and domestic companies operating abroad while excluding income earned by foreign entities within the country.

GNP=GDP+Net Factor Income from Abroad (NFIA)

For instance, if Indian companies and workers abroad generate ₹10 trillion, and foreign companies operating in India generate ₹5 trillion, the NFIA is ₹10T– ₹5T= ₹5T. If India's GDP is ₹300 trillion, the GNP becomes ₹300T+ ₹5T= ₹305T

Applications of GNP

GNP is particularly useful for countries with significant overseas operations or remittances. For example, countries like the Philippines heavily rely on remittances from citizens working abroad, which significantly contribute to their GNP.

Challenges in GNP Measurement

Calculating NFIA accurately can be challenging due to difficulties in tracking all cross-border income flows. Moreover, GNP may not reflect domestic economic conditions if a large portion of income comes from abroad.

Net National Product (NNP)

Net National Product (NNP) adjusts GNP by accounting for depreciation, which represents the wear and tear of capital assets like machinery, buildings, and infrastructure over time. It is a more refined measure of national income, as it indicates the net value available for investment and consumption.

NNP=GNP–Depreciation

For example, if India's GNP is ₹305 trillion and depreciation amounts to ₹15 trillion, the NNP is ₹305T–₹15T=₹290T .

Applications of NNP

NNP serves as an indicator of sustainable economic activity by highlighting the value of resources available after accounting for their degradation. It guides long-term planning and investment strategies.

Challenges in NNP Measurement

Depreciation is often difficult to quantify accurately, as it varies across sectors and depends on factors like technology and maintenance practices.

Comparative Insights

While GDP, GNP, and NNP are interrelated, each offers distinct insights:

- **GDP** focuses on domestic production, making it ideal for measuring short-term economic performance.
- **GNP** emphasizes national income, capturing the economic contributions of a nation's residents globally.
- **NNP** reflects the sustainability of growth by considering asset depreciation.

These metrics collectively provide a comprehensive view of a nation's economic activity, aiding governments and institutions in crafting policies for development and growth.

Differences and Methods of Calculation

Understanding the differences between GDP, GNP, and NNP, as well as their respective calculation methods, is crucial for analyzing national income comprehensively. Each metric serves a unique purpose, reflecting different aspects of economic performance and resource utilization.

Methods of Calculation

Gross Domestic Product (GDP)

GDP is calculated using three main approaches, each providing a unique perspective:

1. **Production Approach**:
   This method calculates GDP by summing the value added at each stage of production.

   GDP=$\sum$(Gross Output–Intermediate Consumption)
   For example, if the automobile sector produces ₹10 trillion worth of vehicles but consumes ₹6 trillion in raw materials, the value added is ₹4 trillion. Adding such values across sectors gives GDP.

1. **Income Approach**:
   This approach sums all incomes earned within the economy, including wages, rents, interest, and profits.

   GDP=Compensation of Employees+Gross Operating Surplus+Taxes on Production and Imports–
   Expenditure Approach:
   The most commonly used method, it aggregates spending by households, businesses, governments, and net exports.
   GDP=C+I+G+(X–M)

Example: In a given year, a country has ₹50 trillion in consumption, ₹20 trillion in investment, ₹15 trillion in government spending, ₹5 trillion in exports, and ₹3 trillion in imports. GDP = ₹50T+ ₹20T+ ₹15T+(₹5T– ₹3T)= ₹87T.

Gross National Product (GNP)

GNP accounts for the income earned by residents abroad and subtracts income earned by foreign entities within the domestic economy.

GNP=GDP+Net Factor Income from Abroad (NFIA)
Example Calculation:

- GDP = ₹300 trillion
- Income earned by residents abroad = ₹20 trillion
- Income earned by foreign entities within the country = ₹10 trillion

GNP= ₹300T+(₹20T– ₹10T)= ₹310T

GNP provides a broader perspective, particularly for nations with substantial international trade or expatriate workers. For instance, nations like India benefit significantly from remittances, contributing to a higher GNP relative to GDP.

Net National Product (NNP)
NNP adjusts GNP by subtracting depreciation, which represents the wear and tear of physical assets over time.

NNP=GNP–Depreciation
Example Calculation:

- GNP = ₹310 trillion
- Depreciation = ₹15 trillion

NNP= ₹310T– ₹15T= ₹295T

NNP reflects the net value available for consumption and reinvestment, making it an essential measure for assessing sustainable growth.

Illustrative Example Comparing All Metrics
Consider the following hypothetical data for a country in a fiscal year:

- GDP: ₹400 trillion

- Income earned by residents abroad: ₹30 trillion
- Income earned by foreign entities within the country: ₹20 trillion
- Depreciation: ₹25 trillion

Step-by-Step Calculation:

1. **GDP**: ₹400 trillion (domestic production).
2. **GNP**: GNP=₹400T+(₹30T–₹20T)=₹410T
3. **NNP**: NNP=₹410T–₹25T=₹385T The data highlights the transition from domestic production to global income contributions and finally to net sustainable resources.

Practical Implications of Differences

1. **Policy Insights**: A higher GNP compared to GDP suggests significant income from abroad, influencing policies on international trade and taxation.
2. **Economic Sustainability**: A declining NNP signals excessive depreciation, indicating the need for investments in infrastructure and maintenance.
3. **Investment Decisions**: Businesses analyze GDP trends to gauge market potential, while long-term strategies often rely on NNP for assessing sustainability.

Real GDP vs. Nominal GDP

Gross Domestic Product (GDP) is a fundamental measure of a nation's economic performance. It can be expressed in two forms: **Real GDP** and **Nominal GDP**. While both provide valuable insights into economic activity, they differ significantly in their approach to measuring and interpreting growth. Understanding these differences is crucial for accurate analysis and policy-making.

Definitions

Nominal GDP

Nominal GDP represents the total monetary value of all final goods and services produced within a country's borders in a given time period, measured using current market prices. It does not account for inflation or changes in price levels over time.

For example, if a country produces 10,000 units of a commodity at ₹ 500 each in 2023, the nominal GDP is:

Nominal GDP=10,000× ₹500= ₹5,000,000

Nominal GDP provides a snapshot of the economy's output based on prevailing market conditions but can be misleading when comparing different time periods due to the impact of price changes.

Real GDP

Real GDP adjusts nominal GDP for inflation, using constant prices from a base year to eliminate the effect of price level changes. This adjustment provides a more accurate reflection of an economy's actual production and growth over time.

For example, if the same 10,000 units were valued at ₹450 per unit in 2020 (base year prices), the real GDP for 2023 would be:

Real GDP=10,000× ₹450= ₹4,500,000

Real GDP offers a clear picture of an economy's performance, focusing on production rather than price fluctuations.

Aspect	Nominal GDP	Real GDP
Definition	Measures GDP at current market prices.	Measures GDP at constant base-year prices.
Inflation Adjustment	Not adjusted for inflation.	Adjusted for inflation to reflect actual growth.
Purpose	Reflects current economic conditions.	Reflects real production levels over time.
Comparison Over Time	Can be distorted by price changes.	Enables accurate comparisons over time.
Usage	Useful for understanding short-term trends.	Useful for analyzing long-term economic growth.

Key Differences

Calculating Real GDP from Nominal GDP

Real GDP is derived from nominal GDP using a price index, such as the GDP deflator, which measures the change in prices over time.

$$\text{Real GDP} = \frac{\text{Nominal GDP}}{\text{GDP Deflator}} \times 100$$

Real GDP

For example:
Nominal GDP in 2023 = ₹5,000,000
GDP Deflator = 111 (where the base year is indexed at 100)

$$\text{Real GDP} = \frac{₹5,000,000}{111} \times 100 = ₹4,504,504.50$$

This calculation eliminates the effects of inflation, providing a clearer view of economic output.

Practical Implications of Real and Nominal GDP

Understanding Inflation's Impact

One of the primary distinctions between real and nominal GDP is their treatment of inflation. Nominal GDP may overstate growth if prices rise sharply, even when actual production remains constant. For example, during hyperinflation, nominal GDP might surge without any increase in goods or services produced, leading to misinterpretation of economic performance.

Real GDP, by isolating price changes, allows policymakers to focus on actual productivity. A consistent rise in real GDP indicates genuine economic growth, making it a reliable measure for long-term planning.

Policy Applications

Governments and central banks rely on real GDP to formulate fiscal and monetary policies. For instance, if nominal GDP increases significantly but real GDP remains stagnant, it signals inflationary pressures. This information might prompt a central bank to tighten monetary policy by raising interest rates to control inflation.

Conversely, if both real and nominal GDP grow simultaneously, it suggests robust economic expansion, encouraging investment in infrastructure and public services.

Illustrative Example

Consider the following data for a hypothetical economy:

- Year 1: Nominal GDP = ₹1,000 billion, Real GDP = ₹1,000 billion (base year).
- Year 2: Nominal GDP = ₹1,200 billion, GDP Deflator = 120.

Step-by-Step Calculation for Real GDP in Year 2:

$$\text{Real GDP (Year 2)} = \frac{\text{Nominal GDP (Year 2)}}{\text{GDP Deflator}} \times 100$$

$$\text{Real GDP (Year 2)} = \frac{₹1,200}{120} \times 100 = ₹1,000 \text{ billion}$$

This example shows that while nominal GDP increased by 20%, real GDP remained constant, indicating that the apparent growth was due solely to inflation.

Challenges in Measurement

1. **Choice of Base Year**: Real GDP calculations depend on the selection of a base year, which may not accurately represent current economic conditions if it becomes outdated.
2. **Sectoral Shifts**: Changes in the structure of the economy, such as the growth of the services sector, can distort comparisons between real and nominal GDP.

3. **Informal Economy**: Both measures often exclude informal economic activities, leading to underestimation in developing nations.

Real GDP vs. Nominal GDP in Practice
Global Comparisons

Real GDP is essential for comparing economic performance across nations. For example, comparing India's and China's GDP in nominal terms can be misleading due to differences in price levels and currency values. Using real GDP adjusted for purchasing power parity (PPP) offers a more accurate comparison of living standards and productivity.

Business and Investment Decisions

Investors and corporations use real GDP to assess market potential and predict economic trends. A sustained rise in real GDP signals favorable conditions for expanding operations, while stagnation may indicate economic challenges requiring strategic adjustments.

2.2 Per Capita Income

Per capita income, often referred to as income per person, is a critical economic indicator that reflects the average income earned by individuals in a specific region, typically within a nation. It is calculated by dividing the total national income by the population. This measure is widely used to evaluate economic growth, compare living standards, and assess the overall development of countries.

Importance in Measuring Economic Growth

Per capita income plays a pivotal role in understanding the well-being of individuals and the economic performance of nations. Unlike aggregate income measures such as GDP, per capita income provides insights into how wealth is distributed among the population, making it a more nuanced indicator of economic prosperity.

Reflecting Living Standards

Per capita income is a direct measure of average living standards. Higher per capita income generally correlates with better access to essential services such as healthcare, education, and infrastructure. For example, countries like Switzerland and Norway, with high per capita incomes, often rank among the highest in human development indices, indicating the strong link between income and quality of life.

However, it is crucial to note that per capita income does not capture income inequality. For instance, a nation with high income disparity might report a high per capita income, while a significant portion of its population remains impoverished.

Indicator of Economic Development

Economic growth is often assessed through the growth rate of per capita income. A steady increase in this metric suggests that an economy is generating sufficient income to improve individual welfare. For example, between 2000 and 2020, India's per capita income more than doubled, reflecting the country's economic transformation and rising living standards.

Furthermore, per capita income is used to classify nations into income groups—low-income, middle-income, and high-income—by organizations like the World Bank. Such classifications influence global trade, investment decisions, and eligibility for international aid.

International Comparisons

Per capita income allows for meaningful comparisons between countries, adjusting for population size. For instance, while the United States has a larger GDP than Luxembourg, Luxembourg's per capita income is significantly higher, indicating greater wealth distribution among its smaller population.

To enhance the comparability of per capita income across countries with differing price levels, economists often use **Purchasing Power Parity (PPP)** adjustments. PPP accounts for variations in the cost of living, providing a more accurate representation of individual purchasing power.

Policy Implications

Per capita income is a crucial metric for policymakers to design and evaluate development strategies. For example:

- **Taxation Policies**: Governments in high per capita income countries can implement progressive taxation systems to reduce inequality, while those in low-income nations might focus on expanding the tax base.
- **Investment in Public Services**: A rise in per capita income often translates into greater fiscal capacity for governments to invest in healthcare, education, and infrastructure.
- **Poverty Alleviation**: Tracking per capita income growth helps identify regions or populations that lag behind, enabling targeted interventions to reduce poverty.

Challenges and Limitations

1. **Income Inequality**: Per capita income averages can mask disparities. For example, despite high per capita income, the United States faces significant income inequality compared to countries like Sweden.
2. **Non-Monetary Factors**: Per capita income does not account for non-economic contributors to well-being, such as environmental

sustainability or social cohesion.

3. **Informal Economy**: In many developing countries, a substantial portion of income is generated in informal sectors, which are often excluded from official calculations, leading to underestimation.

4. **Currency and Price Level Variations**: Without adjustments like PPP, cross-country comparisons of per capita income may be misleading.

Illustrative Example of Calculation

Consider a hypothetical country with the following data for a given year:

- **Total National Income**: ₹5,000 billion

Population: 1 billion

$$\text{Per Capita Income} = \frac{\text{Total National Income}}{\text{Population}}$$

$$\text{Per Capita Income} = \frac{₹5,000 \text{ billion}}{1 \text{ billion}} = ₹5,000$$

This figure represents the average income earned by each individual in the nation.

Practical Applications
Assessing Regional Disparities

Within countries, per capita income helps identify economic disparities among states or regions. For instance, in India, states like Goa and Kerala have higher per capita incomes than Bihar or Uttar Pradesh, highlighting the need for targeted developmental policies.

Business Decisions

Multinational corporations use per capita income to assess market potential. High-income regions are likely to support demand for luxury goods, while low-income areas may require affordable products or basic services.

Economic Planning

Rising per capita income often signals an economy's readiness for structural shifts, such as transitioning from agriculture to industry or services. Policymakers can use this insight to allocate resources effectively and foster balanced growth.

Applications of Per Capita Income in Policy-Making

Per capita income plays a significant role in shaping public policy by providing valuable insights into economic growth, living standards, and resource allocation. Policymakers use this metric to design, implement, and evaluate strategies aimed at achieving sustainable development, reducing inequality, and fostering economic stability. By analyzing per capita income alongside other indicators, governments and institutions can craft targeted interventions that address specific challenges and opportunities within their economies.

Economic Classification and Planning

Per capita income is a key determinant for categorizing countries into income groups, such as low-income, middle-income, and high-income economies, as defined by global organizations like the World Bank. These classifications guide national governments in formulating economic strategies tailored to their developmental stage.

For instance, low-income countries may prioritize poverty alleviation and basic infrastructure, while middle-income countries focus on industrialization and technological advancements. High-income countries, on the other hand, often concentrate on innovation, sustainability, and wealth redistribution.

Budget Allocation and Fiscal Policies

Governments use per capita income data to allocate budgets efficiently across sectors such as education, healthcare, and infrastructure. Higher per capita income levels may enable greater public spending on advanced social programs, while lower levels necessitate prioritization of essential services.

Example:

In India, regions with lower per capita income, such as Bihar and Jharkhand, receive greater central government funding for poverty reduction schemes and rural development projects compared to higher-income states like Maharashtra or Karnataka.

Assessing Inequality and Targeting Poverty

Although per capita income measures the average income, its variations across regions or demographics reveal underlying inequalities. Policymakers use this insight to design targeted interventions aimed at reducing disparities.

Policy Example:

- **Direct Benefit Transfers (DBT)**: In India, per capita income data is used to identify economically weaker sections for schemes like PM-KISAN, where eligible farmers receive direct financial support.
- **Subsidized Services**: Governments may introduce subsidies for healthcare, education, and food in low-income regions, ensuring access to basic necessities for the underprivileged.

Trade and Foreign Investment Policies

Per capita income is a critical factor for shaping trade and foreign investment policies. Countries with rising per capita incomes become attractive markets for international businesses, prompting policymakers to facilitate foreign direct investment (FDI) through regulatory reforms.

Example:

China's rapid increase in per capita income over the last three decades has attracted multinational corporations to invest heavily in sectors like technology and manufacturing. This influx of FDI has further boosted economic growth, creating a virtuous cycle of development.

Infrastructure Development

Policymakers rely on per capita income data to identify regions with developmental gaps and channel investments into infrastructure projects such as roads, electricity, and internet connectivity. These investments are aimed at enhancing productivity and economic opportunities in underserved areas.

Example:

In India, programs like the Pradhan Mantri Gram Sadak Yojana (PMGSY) focus on improving rural road connectivity in low-income regions to bridge developmental divides and stimulate economic activity.

International Aid and Development Assistance

Per capita income also influences eligibility for international aid and concessional financing. Low-income nations often receive preferential treatment in accessing funds from organizations like the International Monetary Fund (IMF) or World Bank to address developmental challenges.

Example:

- Countries classified as "low-income" by the World Bank often qualify for grants or low-interest loans under the International Development Association (IDA) framework.
- Humanitarian aid during crises is often prioritized for regions with low per capita income to mitigate the impact of disasters on vulnerable populations.

Monitoring Economic Growth and Sustainability

Per capita income serves as a benchmark for tracking economic progress over time. Policymakers use trends in this metric to evaluate the effectiveness of existing policies and make adjustments as needed.

Example:

In Southeast Asia, countries like Vietnam have leveraged per capita income growth data to transition from agriculture-based economies to manufacturing and services, aligning their development trajectory with long-term sustainability goals.

Stimulating Consumer Demand

As per capita income rises, consumer behavior shifts, creating opportunities for policymakers to encourage domestic consumption as a driver of growth. Policies that enhance disposable income, such as tax cuts or wage subsidies, are often designed based on per capita income trends.

Example:

In the United States, stimulus packages during economic downturns, such as the COVID-19 pandemic, were aimed at boosting household incomes and stimulating demand for goods and services.

Challenges in Policy-Making Using Per Capita Income

1. **Ignoring Inequality**: Average income figures can obscure income disparities, leading to policies that overlook marginalized populations.
2. **Exclusion of Informal Economy**: In developing nations, significant portions of income are generated in informal sectors, which are not accurately captured in per capita income.
3. **Non-Economic Indicators**: Per capita income does not account for non-monetary factors like environmental quality or social well-being, which are equally important for comprehensive policy-making.

2.3 Key Indicators of Economic Health

One of the most critical indicators of a nation's economic health is the **Consumer Price Index (CPI)**. It reflects changes in the price level of a basket of goods and services commonly purchased by households, serving as a measure of inflation. By tracking how prices change over time, CPI provides valuable insights into purchasing power, cost of living, and economic stability. Policymakers, businesses, and individuals rely on CPI to make informed decisions in areas like wage adjustments, investment strategies, and monetary policies.

Consumer Price Index (CPI)

Definition and Purpose

The **Consumer Price Index (CPI)** measures the average change in prices over time for a fixed basket of consumer goods and services, including food, housing, transportation, healthcare, and other essentials. It acts as a barometer of inflation, helping to determine the rate at which the purchasing power of money declines.

For example, if the CPI increases by 5% in a year, it indicates that, on average, the cost of living has risen by 5%, requiring households to spend more for the same goods and services.

How CPI is Measured

CPI is calculated using the following formula:

$$CPI = \frac{\text{Cost of Basket in Current Year}}{\text{Cost of Basket in Base Year}} \times 100$$

Example Calculation:

- Cost of basket in base year: ₹1,000
- Cost of basket in current year: ₹1,200

$$\text{CPI} = \frac{\text{₹}1,200}{\text{₹}1,000} \times 100 = 120$$

A CPI value of 120 means prices have increased by 20% since the base year.

Components of CPI

CPI is typically broken down into various categories, each representing a share of household spending. Common categories include:

- **Food and Beverages**: Basic necessities such as grains, vegetables, and dairy products.
- **Housing**: Rent, maintenance costs, and utilities.
- **Transportation**: Fuel prices, public transit fares, and vehicle maintenance.
- **Healthcare**: Costs of medicines, hospital services, and insurance.

The relative weight assigned to each category depends on consumer spending patterns, which are determined through surveys conducted by statistical agencies.

CPI as an Inflation Measure

Headline vs. Core Inflation

CPI is often used to calculate two types of inflation:

1. **Headline Inflation**: Measures the total change in CPI, including all categories. This is the most commonly reported inflation figure.
2. **Core Inflation**: Excludes volatile components like food and fuel prices to provide a clearer picture of underlying inflation trends.

For instance, if food prices spike due to a poor harvest, headline inflation might rise sharply, but core inflation would remain stable, indicating that the overall economy is not overheating.

Impact of Inflation

- **Positive Inflation**: A moderate level of inflation (typically 2–3%) is considered healthy, as it encourages spending and investment.
- **High Inflation**: Excessive inflation erodes purchasing power, making goods and services unaffordable.
- **Deflation**: A sustained decline in prices can lead to reduced consumer spending, slowing economic growth.

Applications of CPI
Policy Formulation

CPI plays a crucial role in shaping monetary and fiscal policies. Central banks, such as the Reserve Bank of India (RBI), monitor CPI to set interest rates. For instance, if CPI indicates high inflation, the RBI may increase interest rates to reduce borrowing and curb spending, thereby stabilizing prices.

Wage and Pension Adjustments

CPI is used to adjust wages, pensions, and social security benefits to account for rising living costs. This process, known as **indexation**, ensures that workers and retirees maintain their purchasing power despite inflation.

Example:

If CPI increases by 4% in a year, government and private sector employees may receive a 4% wage hike to keep pace with inflation.

Guiding Investment Decisions

Investors use CPI trends to predict economic stability and plan their portfolios. For example, during periods of high inflation, they might shift investments to inflation-protected assets like gold or inflation-indexed bonds.

Tracking Cost of Living

Governments and international organizations use CPI to compare living standards across regions or countries. For instance, a higher CPI in urban areas might prompt policies aimed at reducing urban-rural disparities.

Challenges and Limitations of CPI

1. **Substitution Bias**: CPI assumes a fixed basket of goods, ignoring the fact that consumers may switch to cheaper alternatives when prices rise.
2. **Exclusion of Quality Improvements**: CPI often fails to account for quality enhancements in goods and services, which can overstate inflation. For example, a car priced higher than its predecessor might offer better safety features, justifying the cost increase.

3. **Regional Variations**: Price trends vary widely between urban and rural areas, making national CPI figures less representative for localized policy-making.
4. **Informal Economy**: In developing countries, informal transactions constitute a significant portion of consumer spending but are often excluded from CPI calculations.

Practical Implications of CPI
Example of Real-World Application

During the COVID-19 pandemic, global CPI trends were closely monitored to assess the economic impact of lockdowns and supply chain disruptions. Sharp increases in food and fuel prices led to high headline inflation in many countries, prompting governments to provide subsidies and central banks to maintain accommodative monetary policies.

Sectoral Insights

CPI data can also guide industry-specific strategies. For instance:

- Rising healthcare CPI may encourage investment in medical infrastructure.
- Increasing fuel costs, reflected in transportation CPI, could drive innovation in electric vehicles and renewable energy.

Wholesale Price Index (WPI)

The **Wholesale Price Index (WPI)** is another critical economic indicator used to measure changes in the prices of goods at the wholesale level before they reach consumers. It tracks price movements in bulk transactions and provides insights into inflationary trends in an economy. While similar in purpose to the Consumer Price Index (CPI), WPI focuses on the wholesale market and excludes services, making it particularly relevant for industries, policymakers, and supply chain managers.

Definition and Purpose

The **Wholesale Price Index** measures the average change in prices of goods sold in bulk over a specific period. Unlike CPI, which focuses on retail prices affecting consumers, WPI assesses price fluctuations in goods traded among businesses or between producers and wholesalers.

WPI serves as an early indicator of inflation and helps in understanding supply-side price pressures. For instance, if the WPI increases, it often signals rising input costs for manufacturers, which could eventually translate into higher retail prices.

How WPI is Measured

Formula for WPI

$$WPI = \frac{\text{Current Price of Basket}}{\text{Price of Basket in Base Year}} \times 100$$

Example Calculation

- Cost of a basket of goods in the base year = ₹10,000
- Cost of the same basket in the current year = ₹11,500

$$WPI = \frac{₹11,500}{₹10,000} \times 100 = 115$$

A WPI value of 115 indicates a 15% increase in wholesale prices compared to the base year

Components of WPI

The composition of WPI varies by country but generally includes three broad categories:

1. **Primary Articles**: Agricultural products (grains, fruits, vegetables) and non-agricultural items (minerals).

   - Example: Rising prices of wheat due to poor monsoons significantly impact the WPI.

2. **Fuel and Power**: Prices of crude oil, coal, electricity, and related products.

   - Example: A surge in global crude oil prices increases the WPI for fuel.

3. **Manufactured Goods**: Industrial products such as textiles, machinery, chemicals, and pharmaceuticals.

Example: Higher steel prices influence the WPI for construction materials

WPI as an Inflation Indicator

Aspect	WPI	CPI
Scope	Measures wholesale prices of goods.	Measures retail prices of goods and services.
Focus	Tracks supply-side inflation.	Tracks consumer-level inflation.
Coverage	Excludes services.	Includes both goods and services.
Audience	Relevant for industries and businesses.	Relevant for consumers and policymakers.

Differences Between WPI and CPI

Significance of WPI in Inflation Measurement

WPI provides early warnings about inflationary trends. For example:

- If WPI shows consistent increases in manufacturing costs, retail inflation measured by CPI might rise shortly after as businesses pass costs to consumers.
- Conversely, a decline in WPI indicates reduced input costs, which may lead to lower consumer prices.

Applications of WPI
Policy Formulation

Policymakers use WPI as a tool for designing monetary and fiscal policies. Central banks monitor WPI to assess cost-push inflation, which occurs when rising production costs drive up prices.

Example:

If WPI shows a steep rise in fuel prices, the central bank might increase interest rates to curb inflation by reducing overall demand in the economy.

Industrial Decision-Making

Industries and businesses use WPI to forecast input costs and plan production strategies. For instance, manufacturers monitor WPI trends in raw materials like steel or cotton to anticipate price changes and adjust procurement schedules accordingly.

Deflating Economic Data

WPI is often used to adjust economic data for inflation, providing "real" measures of economic activity. For example, GDP or industrial output figures can be deflated using WPI to account for changes in price levels and reflect true growth.

Global Trade and Export Competitiveness

Exporters and importers use WPI to analyze international competitiveness. If domestic WPI rises faster than global prices, it may signal reduced competitiveness due to higher production costs.

Challenges and Limitations of WPI

1. **Exclusion of Services**: WPI focuses solely on goods, ignoring the growing importance of services in modern economies.
2. **Limited Consumer Relevance**: WPI does not reflect retail price movements or the cost of living for households, making it less useful for analyzing consumer welfare.
3. **Time Lag**: Changes in WPI may not immediately translate into retail price changes, complicating inflation analysis.
4. **Regional Variations**: National WPI figures may not account for price disparities across regions, which can lead to misinterpretations of localized inflation.

Practical Implications of WPI
Impact on Business Operations

WPI data allows businesses to identify supply chain inefficiencies and take corrective actions. For example, rising WPI for crude oil may prompt a transportation company to adopt fuel-efficient vehicles or explore alternative energy sources.

Sectoral Insights

WPI provides granular insights into specific industries, such as agriculture or manufacturing. Policymakers can use this information to offer subsidies or incentives to sectors facing inflationary pressures, ensuring price stability.

Example:

If the WPI for fertilizers rises sharply, governments may provide subsidies to farmers to prevent higher food prices.

WPI in a Global Context

Many countries use WPI to monitor inflation, though its importance varies. For instance:

- **India** relies heavily on WPI to track wholesale market trends and inform industrial policies.
- **United States**: The **Producer Price Index (PPI)**, a similar concept, has largely replaced WPI as a more detailed measure of price changes at different production stages.

GDP Deflator

The **GDP Deflator** is a crucial economic indicator that measures the overall level of price changes in an economy. Unlike specific price indices such as the Consumer Price Index (CPI) or Wholesale Price Index (WPI), the GDP deflator reflects the prices of all goods and services produced domestically. It serves as a broad measure of inflation, capturing how much of the change in nominal GDP is attributable to changes in price levels rather than output.

Definition and Purpose

The GDP deflator, also known as the implicit price deflator, is the ratio of nominal GDP to real GDP, expressed as a percentage. It accounts for price changes in a comprehensive basket of goods and services, including those consumed by households, businesses, and the government.

$$\text{GDP Deflator} = \frac{\text{Nominal GDP}}{\text{Real GDP}} \times 100$$

For instance, if nominal GDP increases significantly, the GDP deflator can determine how much of that growth is due to higher prices rather than increased production.

How GDP Deflator is Calculated

Step-by-Step Example

Consider the following data:

- **Nominal GDP**: ₹500 billion (current prices)
- **Real GDP**: ₹450 billion (constant base year prices)

Step 1: Apply the formula:

$$\text{GDP Deflator} = \frac{\text{Nominal GDP}}{\text{Real GDP}} \times 100$$

Step 2: Substitute the values:

$$\text{GDP Deflator} = \frac{₹500}{₹450} \times 100 = 111.11$$

This GDP deflator of 111.11 indicates that prices have risen by 11.11% since the base year.

Comparison with Other Inflation Measures

Aspect	GDP Deflator	Consumer Price Index (CPI)
Scope	Includes all domestically produced goods and services.	Focuses on goods and services consumed by households.
Exclusion	Excludes imports.	Includes imports consumed domestically.
Base Year Adjustments	Flexible; adjusts the basket of goods dynamically.	Fixed basket of goods and services over time.
Purpose	Broad measure of price level changes in the economy.	Tracks cost of living for households.

GDP Deflator vs. CPI

Aspect	GDP Deflator	Wholesale Price Index (WPI)
Focus	Reflects prices of all domestic production.	Focuses on wholesale prices of goods only.
Services	Includes services.	Excludes services.

GDP Deflator vs. WPI

Applications of the GDP Deflator
Measuring Inflation

The GDP deflator serves as a comprehensive inflation measure, particularly for policymakers and economists. It provides insights into the overall price level of the economy rather than specific consumer or wholesale prices.

Example:

If the GDP deflator increases significantly, central banks may tighten monetary policy by raising interest rates to curb inflation.

Distinguishing Between Nominal and Real GDP

The GDP deflator is essential for converting nominal GDP into real GDP, allowing for meaningful comparisons across time periods by adjusting for price changes.

Example:

A country's nominal GDP may rise by 8% in a year, but if the GDP deflator indicates 6% inflation, the real GDP growth is only 2%.

Evaluating Economic Policies

Governments use the GDP deflator to assess the effectiveness of fiscal and monetary policies. For instance, if stimulus measures lead to rapid inflation without proportional real GDP growth, the policy may require adjustments.

Advantages of the GDP Deflator

1. **Comprehensive Scope**: Includes a wide range of goods and services, making it a broad indicator of price level changes.
2. **Dynamic Basket**: Unlike CPI, the GDP deflator reflects changes in consumption and production patterns, ensuring greater accuracy over time.
3. **Policy Relevance**: Captures inflation at the macroeconomic level, directly linking to national income and output.

Challenges and Limitations

1. **Data Intensity**: Calculating the GDP deflator requires detailed and accurate GDP data, which may not always be timely.
2. **Exclusion of Imports**: By focusing solely on domestic production, the GDP deflator does not reflect price changes in imported goods, which are

significant in globalized economies.

3. **Limited Consumer Relevance**: It does not directly measure changes in household costs or living standards, unlike CPI.

Practical Implications
For Policymakers

The GDP deflator helps central banks and governments evaluate macroeconomic conditions and adjust monetary or fiscal policies accordingly. For example, a rising deflator may prompt interest rate hikes to control inflation.

For Businesses

Corporations use GDP deflator trends to gauge economic stability and predict changes in consumer purchasing power, aiding in strategic planning.

For International Comparisons

The GDP deflator provides a basis for comparing the price levels and economic stability of different countries, especially when evaluating exchange rates or trade competitiveness.

THREE
INFLATION, DEFLATION, AND ECONOMIC STABILITY

3.1 Inflation

Inflation refers to the sustained increase in the general price level of goods and services in an economy over a specific period. It erodes the purchasing power of money, meaning individuals and businesses need more money to purchase the same quantity of goods. Inflation is a natural economic phenomenon and, within moderate limits, is often considered a sign of economic growth. However, excessive inflation can destabilize economies, impacting savings, investments, and consumption patterns.

The two primary types of inflation are **demand-pull inflation** and **cost-push inflation**, each arising from different causes and having distinct implications for economic stability.

Types of Inflation

Demand-Pull Inflation

Demand-pull inflation occurs when the demand for goods and services in an economy exceeds its productive capacity. This imbalance between aggregate demand (AD) and aggregate supply (AS) drives prices upward. Often associated with periods of economic expansion, demand-pull inflation indicates robust economic activity but can become problematic if left unchecked.

Causes of Demand-Pull Inflation:

1. **Increased Consumer Spending**: Higher disposable incomes, often fueled by tax cuts or wage hikes, lead to greater consumption.
2. **Expansionary Monetary Policy**: Central banks may lower interest rates, making borrowing cheaper, which stimulates spending and investment.
3. **Government Spending**: Public expenditure on infrastructure or social programs can boost aggregate demand.
4. **Exports Surpassing Imports**: When exports increase significantly, foreign demand for domestically produced goods rises, creating upward price pressures.

Example:
Suppose a government implements a large-scale infrastructure project, creating jobs and increasing consumer incomes. The resulting rise in demand for construction materials, vehicles, and labor can lead to price hikes if supply cannot match the surge.

Economic Indicators:

- Rising GDP growth rates.
- Declining unemployment.
- Increasing retail and wholesale prices.

Challenges:
Demand-pull inflation, if excessive, can strain supply chains, lead to overheating of the economy, and push central banks to tighten monetary policy through interest rate hikes.

Cost-Push Inflation

Cost-push inflation arises when production costs increase, compelling businesses to pass these costs onto consumers in the form of higher prices. Unlike demand-pull inflation, this type of inflation is supply-side driven, occurring even when demand remains unchanged.

Causes of Cost-Push Inflation:

1. **Rising Raw Material Costs**: Increases in the price of essential inputs like oil, steel, or agricultural products directly raise production costs.
2. **Wage Increases**: Higher wages demanded by workers, often driven by labor unions, add to operational expenses.

3. **Supply Chain Disruptions**: Natural disasters, pandemics, or geopolitical conflicts can restrict supply, pushing up costs.
4. **Depreciation of Currency**: A weaker domestic currency makes imports more expensive, affecting industries reliant on imported inputs.

Example:

If crude oil prices surge due to geopolitical tensions, transportation and manufacturing industries face higher fuel costs. This ripple effect increases the prices of goods reliant on transportation, such as groceries and clothing.

Economic Indicators:

- Rising production costs.
- Stagnating or declining economic output (stagflation).
- Increasing input price indices, such as the Producer Price Index (PPI).

Challenges:

Cost-push inflation can reduce economic growth as higher production costs discourage investment and lower consumer purchasing power. It often leads to stagflation—a combination of inflation and stagnant economic growth.

Aspect	Demand-Pull Inflation	Cost-Push Inflation
Primary Cause	Excessive aggregate demand.	Rising production costs.
Economic Environment	Occurs during economic growth or expansion.	Occurs during supply-side disruptions.
Impact on Output	Increases output initially but risks overheating.	Decreases output due to higher costs.
Policy Solutions	Contractionary monetary or fiscal policies.	Supply-side reforms, subsidies, or cost controls.

Comparative Analysis: Demand-Pull vs. Cost-Push Inflation

Policy Responses to Inflation
Managing Demand-Pull Inflation

Policymakers often use contractionary measures to curb excessive demand:

1. **Raising Interest Rates**: Central banks increase borrowing costs to discourage consumption and investment.

2. **Reducing Government Spending**: By cutting public expenditure, the government lowers aggregate demand.
3. **Increasing Taxes**: Higher taxes reduce disposable incomes, moderating consumer spending.

Managing Cost-Push Inflation

Addressing cost-push inflation requires supply-side interventions:

1. **Subsidizing Key Inputs**: Governments may subsidize essential raw materials to lower production costs.
2. **Improving Supply Chains**: Investments in infrastructure and logistics reduce supply bottlenecks.
3. **Promoting Technological Advancements**: Innovations that enhance productivity can offset rising costs.

Real-World Examples of Inflation Types

1. **Demand-Pull Inflation**:

   - During the post-COVID-19 recovery, government stimulus packages and pent-up consumer demand in many countries led to a surge in aggregate demand, causing demand-pull inflation in sectors like housing and consumer electronics.

2. **Cost-Push Inflation**:

   - The 1970s oil crisis is a classic example of cost-push inflation. Rising crude oil prices drove up transportation and manufacturing costs globally, leading to widespread inflation despite stagnant economic growth.

Measurement of Inflation: CPI and WPI

Inflation is primarily measured using price indices, with the **Consumer Price Index (CPI)** and the **Wholesale Price Index (WPI)** being the most widely used metrics. Each serves a unique purpose, reflecting inflationary trends from different perspectives—consumer-level and wholesale-level price changes. Together, they provide a comprehensive understanding of inflation dynamics and their impact on the economy.

Consumer Price Index (CPI)

Definition

The **Consumer Price Index** measures the average change over time in the prices of goods and services consumed by households. It reflects the cost of living and is widely used to gauge inflation at the consumer level.

Scope and Coverage

The CPI includes a fixed basket of goods and services grouped into categories such as:

1. **Food and Beverages**
2. **Housing**
3. **Transportation**
4. **Healthcare**
5. **Clothing and Footwear**

The basket's composition and weights are determined based on household consumption patterns, which are periodically updated through surveys.

Formula

$$CPI = \frac{\text{Cost of Basket in Current Period}}{\text{Cost of Basket in Base Period}} \times 100$$

Example Calculation

- Cost of basket in base year: ₹1,000
- Cost of basket in current year: ₹1,200

$$\text{CPI} = \frac{\text{₹1,200}}{\text{₹1,000}} \times 100 = 120$$

A CPI of 120 indicates that prices have increased by 20% since the base year.

Applications

1. **Tracking Cost of Living**: CPI measures inflation directly affecting consumers.
2. **Adjusting Wages and Benefits**: It is used to index wages, pensions, and social security benefits to maintain purchasing power.
3. **Monetary Policy**: Central banks use CPI to monitor inflation and set interest rates accordingly.

Wholesale Price Index (WPI)
Definition
The **Wholesale Price Index** measures the average change in prices of goods sold in bulk at the wholesale level, before reaching consumers. It captures supply-side price pressures and is often used as an early indicator of inflation.

Scope and Coverage
The WPI focuses exclusively on goods and excludes services. It is categorized into:

1. **Primary Articles**: Agricultural and non-agricultural products like food grains, minerals, etc.
2. **Fuel and Power**: Crude oil, electricity, and other energy products.
3. **Manufactured Goods**: Textiles, chemicals, machinery, and other industrial products.

Formula

$$\text{WPI} = \frac{\text{Current Price of Basket}}{\text{Price of Basket in Base Year}} \times 100$$

Example Calculation

- Cost of basket in base year: ₹5,000
- Cost of basket in current year: ₹5,500

$$\text{WPI} = \frac{\text{Current Price of Basket}}{\text{Price of Basket in Base Year}} \times 100$$

A WPI of 110 indicates a 10% increase in wholesale prices since the base year.

Applications

1. **Tracking Supply-Side Inflation**: WPI reflects changes in production costs and input prices.
2. **Business Planning**: Industries use WPI to anticipate cost changes in raw materials and adjust production strategies.
3. **Policy Formulation**: WPI data aids governments in designing subsidies or interventions to stabilize supply chains.

Aspect	CPI	WPI
Focus	Retail prices paid by consumers.	Wholesale prices of goods.
Coverage	Includes both goods and services.	Focuses only on goods.
Audience	Relevant for households and consumers.	Relevant for industries and businesses.
Purpose	Tracks cost of living and consumer inflation.	Tracks supply-side inflation.
Volatility	Less volatile as it includes stable services.	More volatile due to commodity price fluctuations.

Comparison of CPI and WPI

CPI and WPI in Practice
CPI as a Consumer-Centric Tool

CPI reflects price changes that directly impact households. For example, during periods of high inflation, CPI increases, signaling reduced purchasing power. Governments may respond by raising wages or offering subsidies to ease the burden on consumers.

WPI as a Supply-Side Indicator

WPI tracks input cost changes for businesses. For instance, a sharp rise in WPI due to increased fuel prices signals higher production costs, which may later affect consumer prices, leading to inflation at the retail level.

Challenges in Measuring Inflation

1. **Basket Composition**: Both CPI and WPI rely on fixed baskets of goods that may not reflect current consumption or production patterns accurately.
2. **Exclusion of Informal Economy**: Informal transactions, common in developing economies, are often omitted, leading to underestimation of inflation.
3. **Regional Disparities**: National-level indices may not capture price variations across urban and rural areas effectively.
4. **Service Exclusion in WPI**: WPI's omission of services limits its comprehensiveness in modern service-driven economies.

3.2 Deflation and disinflation

Deflation and disinflation are two distinct economic phenomena that relate to price changes within an economy. **Deflation** refers to a sustained decrease in the general price level of goods and services, while **disinflation** denotes a slowdown in the rate of inflation. Both can have significant implications for economic stability, influencing consumption, investment, and overall growth.

Deflation

Causes of Deflation

Deflation occurs when there is a prolonged imbalance between supply and demand, typically caused by one or more of the following factors:

1. **Decrease in Aggregate Demand**

   - A decline in consumer spending, often triggered by economic uncertainty, rising unemployment, or wage stagnation, leads to reduced demand for goods and services.
   - Example: During the Great Depression of the 1930s, widespread unemployment and loss of income caused a sharp drop in consumer demand, resulting in deflation.

2. **Increase in Aggregate Supply**

   - Overproduction or advancements in technology can lead to an excess supply of goods, causing prices to fall.
   - Example: Rapid agricultural growth without corresponding demand can result in falling food prices.

3. **Tight Monetary Policy**

   - High interest rates can reduce borrowing and spending, contracting demand and creating downward pressure on prices.
   - Example: A central bank's aggressive monetary tightening to combat inflation may inadvertently trigger deflation.

4. Debt Deflation

- When debt burdens become unsustainable, individuals and businesses reduce spending to repay debts, further depressing demand.

Economic Impacts of Deflation

Deflation can have far-reaching consequences, often creating a vicious cycle that hampers economic growth:

1. Reduced Consumer Spending

- Consumers delay purchases in anticipation of lower future prices, leading to a further drop in demand and economic stagnation.
- Example: In Japan's "Lost Decade" (1990s), persistent deflation caused prolonged economic stagnation as consumers and businesses deferred spending.

2. Increased Real Debt Burden

- As prices fall, the real value of existing debt rises, making it harder for borrowers to repay loans. This increases defaults and financial instability.

3. Profit Margins and Investment

- Falling prices reduce corporate revenues, shrinking profit margins and discouraging investment in production and innovation.

4. Unemployment

- Lower revenues lead to cost-cutting measures, including layoffs, exacerbating economic challenges.

Disinflation
Causes of Disinflation

Disinflation refers to a slowdown in the rate of inflation and is often a deliberate outcome of monetary or fiscal policies aimed at stabilizing the economy. Common causes include:

1. **Contractionary Monetary Policy**

   - Central banks raise interest rates or reduce the money supply to curb excessive inflation.
   - Example: In the 1980s, the U.S. Federal Reserve, under Paul Volcker, implemented high interest rates to combat double-digit inflation, leading to disinflation.

2. **Fiscal Austerity**

   - Governments may reduce public spending or increase taxes to control inflation, slowing economic activity and inflation rates.

3. **Supply-Side Reforms**

   - Improved efficiency or technological advancements reduce production costs, slowing price increases.

4. **Global Factors**

   - Declines in international commodity prices, such as oil, can reduce inflationary pressures across economies.

Economic Impacts of Disinflation
While disinflation is less severe than deflation, it can still affect economic dynamics:

1. **Stabilized Price Levels**

   - Disinflation often restores price stability, benefiting consumers and long-term economic planning.
   - Example: Moderate disinflation helps central banks maintain inflation targets, typically around 2%.

2. **Reduced Growth in Short Term**

- Contractionary policies leading to disinflation can temporarily slow economic growth and increase unemployment.
- Example: During the Volcker disinflation of the 1980s, the U.S. economy experienced a recession as inflation fell sharply.

3. Positive Effects on Savings

- Disinflation preserves the purchasing power of savings, encouraging individuals to save and invest.

Aspect	Deflation	Disinflation
Definition	A sustained decrease in the general price level.	A slowdown in the rate of inflation.
Causes	Reduced demand, oversupply, or tight monetary policy.	Contractionary policies or global price reductions.
Economic Impact	Negative: Reduced spending, rising debt burdens.	Mixed: Short-term economic slowdown, but price stability.
Long-Term Effects	Economic stagnation, financial instability.	Stable inflation, better economic planning.

Comparison Between Deflation and Disinflation

Policy Responses to Deflation and Disinflation
Addressing Deflation

1. Expansionary Monetary Policy

- Central banks lower interest rates or implement quantitative easing to encourage borrowing and spending.
- Example: The European Central Bank (ECB) adopted negative interest rates during deflationary pressures in the 2010s.

2. Fiscal Stimulus

- Governments increase public spending or cut taxes to boost demand.
- Example: The U.S. implemented stimulus packages during the 2008 financial crisis to counteract deflationary risks.

3. Debt Relief Programs

- Reducing debt burdens through restructuring or forgiveness can restore financial stability and spending capacity.

Managing Disinflation

1. Gradual Policy Adjustments

- Central banks aim for gradual disinflation to avoid sharp economic contractions.
- Example: Inflation targeting policies ensure smooth transitions to lower inflation rates.

2. Supply-Side Investments

- Governments invest in infrastructure and technology to enhance productivity and reduce inflationary pressures naturally.

Real-World Examples

1. Deflation:

- Japan's "Lost Decade" is a classic case of deflation. Persistent price declines led to stagnation, unemployment, and a rising debt burden, forcing the government to adopt aggressive monetary easing.

2. Disinflation:

- The U.S. in the 1980s underwent disinflation due to the Federal Reserve's high interest rates. Inflation fell from 13.5% in 1980 to 3.2% in 1983, stabilizing the economy but causing a short-term recession.

Policies for Mitigating Deflation and Disinflation

Addressing deflation and managing disinflation require carefully designed policies to stabilize prices, encourage economic growth, and prevent long-term economic damage. Effective strategies involve a mix of monetary, fiscal, and structural policies that target the root causes while minimizing adverse effects.

Mitigation of Deflation

Deflation, characterized by a sustained decline in prices, can lead to reduced spending, rising debt burdens, and economic stagnation. Policies to counter deflation focus on stimulating demand and restoring price stability.

Monetary Policies

1. **Lowering Interest Rates**

   - Central banks reduce interest rates to make borrowing cheaper and savings less attractive, encouraging consumption and investment.
   - Example: During Japan's deflationary period in the 1990s, the Bank of Japan (BoJ) slashed interest rates to near-zero levels to stimulate demand.

2. **Quantitative Easing (QE)**

   - Central banks purchase government securities or other financial assets to inject liquidity into the economy, increasing money supply and boosting spending.
   - Example: The U.S. Federal Reserve implemented QE during the 2008 financial crisis to counteract deflationary pressures.

3. **Negative Interest Rates**

   - Central banks may adopt negative interest rates, effectively charging banks for holding reserves, to incentivize lending.
   - Example: The European Central Bank (ECB) introduced negative interest rates in 2014 to combat deflation in the Eurozone.

Fiscal Policies

1. **Increased Government Spending**

   - Public investment in infrastructure, healthcare, and education creates jobs, increases income, and boosts aggregate demand.
   - Example: The U.S. stimulus packages during the Great Recession included large-scale infrastructure projects to revitalize the economy.

2. **Tax Cuts and Subsidies**

   - Reducing taxes or offering subsidies increases disposable income for households and businesses, encouraging consumption and investment.

3. **Direct Cash Transfers**

   - Governments provide direct financial aid to individuals, particularly in lower-income groups, to stimulate spending.
   - Example: Cash transfer schemes in India, such as the PM-Kisan Yojana, aim to boost rural demand.

Structural Reforms

1. **Debt Restructuring**

   - Reducing or renegotiating debt burdens helps households and businesses regain financial stability, encouraging spending.

2. **Strengthening Supply Chains**

   - Ensuring smooth production and distribution of goods prevents deflation caused by supply-side bottlenecks.

Management of Disinflation

Disinflation, or the slowdown in inflation rates, often requires deliberate intervention to stabilize prices without causing economic disruptions. Policies focus on gradual adjustments and ensuring that the economy remains resilient during the transition.

Monetary Policies

1. **Gradual Interest Rate Adjustments**

   - Central banks carefully raise interest rates to slow inflation while avoiding sharp contractions in demand.
   - Example: The Federal Reserve uses inflation targeting, ensuring a gradual approach to achieve its 2% inflation goal.

2. **Inflation Targeting Frameworks**

- ○ Adopting explicit inflation targets ensures price stability and sets clear expectations for businesses and consumers.
- ○ Example: The Reserve Bank of India (RBI) maintains an inflation target of 4% (+/-2%) to guide its monetary policy.

Fiscal Policies

1. **Reducing Budget Deficits**

- ○ Governments may cut excessive public spending to control inflationary pressures without triggering deflation.

2. **Balancing Taxes**

- ○ A mix of indirect and direct tax adjustments ensures that fiscal consolidation does not stifle growth.

Structural Reforms

1. **Supply-Side Investments**

- ○ Investing in infrastructure, technology, and productivity enhancements reduces production costs and naturally moderates inflationary pressures.
- ○ Example: Technological advancements in renewable energy can reduce costs in energy-dependent industries.

2. **Trade and Global Integration**

- ○ Promoting international trade ensures access to competitively priced imports, helping reduce inflation without relying solely on domestic policy interventions.

Policy Challenges and Considerations

1. **Balancing Growth and Stability**

- Policies aimed at mitigating deflation or disinflation must balance stimulating demand with avoiding excessive price volatility.

2. **Coordination of Monetary and Fiscal Policies**

- Ensuring alignment between central banks and governments is essential to maximize the effectiveness of interventions.

3. **Global Factors**

- External shocks, such as commodity price fluctuations or geopolitical events, can limit the effectiveness of domestic policies.

Real-World Examples

1. **Mitigating Deflation in Japan**

- The Bank of Japan implemented zero interest rates, QE, and fiscal stimulus during its prolonged deflationary phase, though structural issues like aging demographics continued to pose challenges.

2. **Managing Disinflation in the U.S.**

- During the 1980s, the Federal Reserve under Paul Volcker raised interest rates sharply to reduce inflation. While this caused a short-term recession, it successfully stabilized prices and restored long-term growth.

3.3 Advanced Concepts: Stagflation

Stagflation is an unusual and challenging economic condition characterized by a combination of stagnant economic growth, high unemployment, and persistently high inflation. This paradoxical phenomenon contradicts the conventional economic theory that inflation and unemployment usually have an inverse relationship, as described by the **Phillips Curve**. Stagflation presents a severe challenge for policymakers because the tools used to address inflation can worsen unemployment, and vice versa.

Definition of Stagflation

Stagflation occurs when:

1. **Economic Growth Slows**: Measured by stagnant or negative growth in GDP, indicating a lack of productive activity.
2. **Unemployment Rises**: Reflecting weak labor markets and reduced job creation.
3. **Inflation Persists**: Prices continue to rise despite the economic slowdown, typically due to supply-side shocks or structural inefficiencies.

Key Characteristics:

- Persistent inflation coexisting with high unemployment.
- Weak consumer and business confidence.
- Decline in productivity and investment.

Causes of Stagflation

1. Supply-Side Shocks

Sudden disruptions in the supply of critical commodities, such as oil or food, lead to higher production costs and reduced output.

- **Example**: The 1973 oil crisis caused a sharp increase in global oil prices, disrupting production and triggering inflation across economies reliant on petroleum.

2. Misguided Economic Policies

- Excessive monetary expansion or fiscal stimulus in response to a supply-side shock can worsen inflation without addressing the underlying stagnation.
- Over-regulation of industries may hinder productivity and innovation, compounding the problem.

3. Structural Problems in the Economy

Structural inefficiencies, such as outdated infrastructure, skill mismatches in the labor market, or reliance on volatile sectors, can cause stagnation alongside inflation.

Economic Impacts of Stagflation

1. Erosion of Purchasing Power

Persistent inflation reduces the real value of wages and savings, leading to lower consumer spending and reduced economic activity.

2. Weak Business Environment

Stagflation discourages investment as businesses face higher input costs, lower consumer demand, and uncertainty about future profitability.

3. Policy Dilemmas

Policymakers face a catch-22: Tightening monetary policy to control inflation can exacerbate unemployment, while stimulating growth can further fuel inflation.

Case Studies of Stagflation

1. The 1970s Oil Crisis (Global)

One of the most well-known instances of stagflation occurred during the 1970s due to a series of oil price shocks:

- **Cause**: The Organization of the Petroleum Exporting Countries (OPEC) imposed an oil embargo in 1973, causing crude oil prices to quadruple.
- **Impact**:

  - Inflation soared as higher energy costs cascaded through the economy.
  - Industrial output declined due to rising production costs and reduced profitability.
  - Unemployment increased as businesses scaled back operations.

- **Policy Response**:

  - Central banks raised interest rates to combat inflation, further slowing growth and increasing unemployment.
  - Governments in affected countries adopted energy conservation policies and explored alternative energy sources to reduce reliance on imported oil.

2. India in the Late 1970s and Early 1980s

India experienced stagflation during this period, largely due to:

- **Cause**:

  - Global oil shocks significantly increased import bills, straining the balance of payments.
  - Inefficiencies in agricultural production led to food shortages and price hikes.

- **Impact**:

  - Inflation exceeded 15% at its peak, while GDP growth stagnated.
  - Rising unemployment and declining living standards fueled socio-economic tensions.

- **Policy Response**:

  - The government introduced rationing and subsidies to manage essential goods.
  - Long-term reforms were later initiated, focusing on industrial modernization and agricultural productivity.

3. Japan in the 1990s (Atypical Stagflation)

While not a textbook case of stagflation, Japan's "Lost Decade" exhibited similar characteristics:

- **Cause**:

- A financial bubble burst in the late 1980s, leading to economic stagnation.
- Deflationary pressures persisted, but specific sectors experienced inflation due to supply-side constraints.

- **Impact**:

  - Prolonged stagnation and high unemployment eroded economic growth.
  - Inflation in key sectors like real estate and healthcare created localized stagflationary effects.

- **Policy Response**:

  - Massive fiscal stimulus and near-zero interest rates failed to revive growth due to structural inefficiencies and demographic challenges.

Policy Responses to Stagflation
1. Supply-Side Solutions

- **Investing in Productivity**: Governments can invest in infrastructure, education, and technology to boost efficiency and reduce production costs.
- **Reducing Structural Barriers**: Deregulation and labor market reforms can encourage innovation and economic flexibility.

2. Balanced Monetary and Fiscal Policies

- **Targeted Interventions**: Policymakers may use targeted subsidies for essential goods to control inflation without suppressing demand.
- **Gradual Tightening**: Central banks can implement gradual interest rate hikes to avoid severe shocks to the economy.

3. Long-Term Energy and Resource Strategies

- Diversifying energy sources and investing in renewable energy can mitigate supply-side shocks, such as those caused by oil price spikes.

Hyperinflation: Examples and Lessons

Hyperinflation is an extreme and rapid increase in the general price level of goods and services, often exceeding 50% per month. Unlike regular inflation, which can occur as part of normal economic cycles, hyperinflation reflects a complete breakdown of a country's monetary system. It devastates purchasing power, erodes savings, and disrupts economic activity, often requiring drastic measures to restore stability.

Definition and Characteristics of Hyperinflation

Hyperinflation occurs when:

1. **Prices Increase Exponentially**: The cost of basic goods and services rises rapidly, often daily or even hourly.
2. **Currency Loses Value**: Money becomes almost worthless, driving people to seek alternative means of exchange, such as barter or foreign currency.
3. **Economic Collapse**: Production slows, unemployment rises, and basic economic functions deteriorate.

Key Characteristics:

- Inflation rates exceed hundreds or thousands of percent annually.
- Physical cash is often printed in ever-larger denominations.
- Citizens lose confidence in the government and central bank's ability to manage the economy.

Causes of Hyperinflation

1. **Excessive Money Printing**

   - When governments finance spending by printing large quantities of money without corresponding increases in economic output, the supply of money far outpaces demand, causing hyperinflation.
   - Example: Germany's Weimar Republic (1921–1923) printed money to pay war reparations, leading to catastrophic inflation.

2. **Collapse in Public Confidence**

- Loss of faith in a currency's stability drives people to hoard tangible assets or foreign currencies, reducing demand for the domestic currency and accelerating its decline.

3. **Severe Supply-Side Shocks**

- Wars, political instability, or natural disasters that disrupt production and supply chains can trigger hyperinflation.

4. **Exchange Rate Collapse**

- Depreciation of a country's currency in international markets leads to skyrocketing import prices, exacerbating inflation.

Examples of Hyperinflation
1. Germany: Weimar Republic (1921–1923)

- **Cause**: Post-World War I reparations demanded by the Treaty of Versailles strained Germany's economy. The government printed excessive amounts of money to meet its obligations and support domestic spending.
- **Impact**:

  - Prices doubled every few days. A loaf of bread that cost 250 marks in January 1923 rose to 200 billion marks by November 1923.
  - Savings became worthless, and the middle class lost its wealth.
  - Bartering replaced monetary transactions, and foreign currencies like the U.S. dollar were widely used.

- **Resolution**: The introduction of the **Rentenmark**, backed by tangible assets like land and industrial goods, stabilized the economy.

2. Zimbabwe (2007–2008)

- **Cause**: Land reform policies and political instability reduced agricultural output, leading to economic collapse. The government financed deficits by printing money.
- **Impact**:

- ◦ Inflation peaked at 79.6 billion percent in November 2008.
- ◦ Basic goods, like bread and milk, became unaffordable for most citizens.
- ◦ People abandoned the Zimbabwean dollar in favor of the U.S. dollar and South African rand.

- **Resolution**: Zimbabwe abandoned its currency and officially adopted foreign currencies to restore stability.

3. Venezuela (2016–2021)

- **Cause**: A combination of declining oil revenues, corruption, and mismanagement of public finances led to hyperinflation.
- **Impact**:

  - ◦ Annual inflation exceeded 1,000,000% at its peak in 2018.
  - ◦ Citizens resorted to barter, cryptocurrencies, and U.S. dollars as the bolívar became worthless.
  - ◦ Emigration surged as millions fled economic hardship.

- **Resolution**: Limited reforms, dollarization, and increased oil revenues have reduced hyperinflation, but long-term stability remains uncertain.

Lessons from Hyperinflation
1. Monetary Discipline is Crucial
Excessive money printing without corresponding economic growth leads to currency devaluation and hyperinflation. Governments must maintain disciplined fiscal and monetary policies to preserve currency stability.
2. Confidence in Institutions is Key
Economic stability depends on public trust in the government and central bank. Transparency, accountability, and sound policy-making are essential to avoid hyperinflation.
3. Importance of Economic Diversification
Overreliance on a single sector, such as oil in Venezuela, makes economies vulnerable to external shocks. Diversified economies are more resilient against hyperinflationary pressures.
4. Hyperinflation is Hard to Reverse

Restoring stability after hyperinflation requires drastic measures, such as introducing a new currency, dollarization, or implementing strict monetary reforms. However, these measures can take years to produce results.

5. Impact on Society

Hyperinflation erodes wealth, exacerbates inequality, and undermines social cohesion. It disproportionately affects the most vulnerable, worsening poverty and human suffering.

Policy Measures to Prevent Hyperinflation

1. **Prudent Monetary Policy**

   - Central banks must ensure that money supply growth aligns with economic output to maintain price stability.

2. **Fiscal Responsibility**

   - Governments should avoid excessive deficits and unsustainable borrowing, focusing on efficient resource allocation.

3. **Exchange Rate Stability**

   - Policies to stabilize the domestic currency, such as maintaining foreign exchange reserves, can prevent hyperinflation driven by currency depreciation.

4. **Strengthening Institutions**

   - Independent central banks and transparent governance systems are critical for preventing mismanagement of monetary and fiscal policies.

FOUR

MONEY, BANKING, AND MONETARY POLICY

4.1 Role of Money and Banking

Money and banking form the backbone of any modern economy. Money serves as a medium of exchange, a store of value, and a unit of account, facilitating economic transactions. Banking institutions, in turn, act as intermediaries that manage the supply of money, promote savings, extend credit, and drive investment. Together, they ensure the smooth functioning of economic activities and promote financial stability.

Functions of Money

Money performs several essential functions that underpin economic interactions, enabling trade, investment, and economic growth. These functions can be broadly categorized into **primary**, **secondary**, and **contingent** roles.

Primary Functions

1. **Medium of Exchange**

   - Money facilitates the exchange of goods and services, eliminating the inefficiencies of the barter system. In barter, the "double coincidence of wants" is required—both parties must desire what the other offers.

Money resolves this by acting as an intermediary.

- Example: A farmer can sell wheat for money and use that money to buy clothing without directly trading wheat for clothing.

2. Unit of Account

- Money provides a standard measure of value, enabling the consistent valuation of goods and services. This simplifies price comparisons and economic calculations.
- Example: Instead of comparing a car's value in terms of multiple goods (e.g., 10 cows or 20 barrels of oil), its price can be expressed in monetary terms, such as ₹10 lakhs.

Secondary Functions

1. Store of Value

- Money preserves purchasing power over time, allowing individuals and businesses to save wealth for future use. While inflation can erode its value, money remains more reliable than perishable or non-standardized commodities.
- Example: Saving ₹10,000 today ensures its future use for investments or emergencies, unlike saving crops that may spoil.

2. Standard of Deferred Payment

- Money facilitates credit transactions by acting as a medium for future payments. Borrowers and lenders can agree on terms in monetary units, ensuring consistency.
- Example: A business may take a loan of ₹1 crore today and repay it over five years in fixed monetary installments.

Contingent Functions

1. Measure of Economic Performance

- Money enables the aggregation of economic data, such as GDP, income levels, and inflation rates, facilitating policy-making and economic analysis.

2. **Promoting Liquidity**

- Money provides liquidity, allowing individuals and businesses to convert assets into cash quickly to meet immediate needs.

3. **Facilitating Specialization and Division of Labor**

- By simplifying exchange, money encourages specialization in production, improving productivity and economic efficiency.

Key Characteristics of Money

For money to perform these functions effectively, it must possess certain characteristics:

- **Durability**: Resistant to wear and tear over time.
- **Divisibility**: Easily divided into smaller units for transactions.
- **Portability**: Convenient to carry and use.
- **Uniformity**: Standardized in appearance and value.
- **Acceptability**: Widely recognized and accepted as a medium of exchange.
- **Limited Supply**: Scarcity ensures its value is preserved.

Evolution of Money

1. **Commodity Money**: Early forms of money included commodities like gold, silver, and salt, which had intrinsic value.
2. **Fiat Money**: Modern currencies, such as the rupee or dollar, derive value from government decree and public trust rather than intrinsic worth.
3. **Digital Money**: Advances in technology have introduced digital currencies, such as cryptocurrencies and central bank digital currencies (CBDCs), revolutionizing financial systems.

Significance of Money in the Economy

1. **Facilitates Trade**: By enabling seamless exchanges, money supports both local and global trade, promoting economic integration.
2. **Drives Economic Growth**: Access to money stimulates consumption, production, and investment, driving GDP growth.
3. **Supports Monetary Policy**: Central banks manage the money supply to stabilize prices, control inflation, and foster growth.

4.1 Role of Money and Banking

Structure of Modern Banking Systems

The **modern banking system** is an intricate network of institutions that facilitate the mobilization of funds, credit creation, financial stability, and economic growth. It comprises a multi-tiered framework designed to address the diverse financial needs of individuals, businesses, and governments. The structure is broadly categorized into **central banks**, **commercial banks**, and **specialized financial institutions**, each serving distinct roles while operating interdependently.

Components of the Modern Banking System

1. Central Banks

The **central bank** is the apex institution in any modern banking system, responsible for regulating and overseeing monetary and financial stability.

Functions of a Central Bank:

1. **Monetary Policy Implementation:**

   - Controls money supply and interest rates to manage inflation, unemployment, and economic growth.
   - Example: The Reserve Bank of India (RBI) adjusts repo rates to influence liquidity and inflation.

2. **Currency Issuance:**

   - Issues and manages the national currency. In most countries, this is the sole authority for currency creation.

3. **Regulation of Commercial Banks:**

   - Supervises and regulates commercial banks to ensure the health and stability of the financial system.

4. **Lender of Last Resort:**

- Provides emergency liquidity to banks facing financial distress to prevent systemic crises.

5. **Foreign Exchange Management**:

- Manages foreign exchange reserves and regulates currency exchange to stabilize the economy.

Examples: Federal Reserve (USA), European Central Bank (ECB), Reserve Bank of India (RBI).

2. Commercial Banks

Commercial banks form the backbone of the banking system, directly interacting with the public to provide essential financial services.

Functions of Commercial Banks:

1. **Deposit Mobilization**:

- Accept savings, fixed, and current account deposits from individuals and businesses.
- Example: A savings account with a 4% annual interest rate.

2. **Credit Creation**:

- Provide loans to individuals, businesses, and governments for consumption and investment purposes.
- Types of Loans: Personal loans, business loans, mortgages, and working capital loans.

3. **Payment and Settlement Services**:

- Facilitate domestic and international transactions through checks, demand drafts, credit/debit cards, and digital payment systems.

4. **Wealth Management and Advisory**:

- ○ Offer financial products like mutual funds, insurance, and retirement plans.

Types of Commercial Banks:

- **Public Sector Banks**: Owned by the government (e.g., State Bank of India).
- **Private Sector Banks**: Privately owned (e.g., ICICI Bank, HDFC Bank).
- **Foreign Banks**: Operate in a host country but headquartered abroad (e.g., Citibank).

3. Cooperative Banks

Cooperative banks are community-based financial institutions designed to serve their members. They focus on rural and agricultural development while offering services similar to commercial banks.

Features of Cooperative Banks:

- Owned and operated by members under cooperative principles.
- Primarily target small-scale borrowers, farmers, and rural communities.
- Regulated by the central bank and cooperative-specific regulatory bodies.

4. Development Banks

Development banks focus on financing long-term infrastructure, industrial, and agricultural projects that are vital for national development. They fill gaps left by commercial banks, which often prioritize short-term loans.

Examples:

- Industrial Development Bank of India (IDBI).
- National Bank for Agriculture and Rural Development (NABARD).

Key Functions:

1. Provide long-term loans for infrastructure and industrial projects.
2. Support agricultural development and rural innovation.

5. Non-Banking Financial Companies (NBFCs)

NBFCs operate alongside banks to provide financial services, particularly to underserved sectors and regions. They do not hold banking licenses but are regulated by the central bank.
Services Offered:

1. Loans and advances (e.g., microfinance).
2. Leasing, hire purchase, and asset management.
3. Insurance and investment services.

Examples: Bajaj Finance, Muthoot Finance.

6. Regional Rural Banks (RRBs)

RRBs are government-supported banks designed to serve rural areas, especially farmers, small entrepreneurs, and artisans.
Functions:

1. Provide affordable credit to rural communities.
2. Promote financial inclusion in underdeveloped regions.

Example: Prathama Bank in Uttar Pradesh, India.
7. International and Multilateral Development Banks
These institutions provide financial and technical assistance to countries for economic development.
Examples:

- World Bank
- Asian Development Bank (ADB)

Functions:

1. Fund large-scale infrastructure projects.

2. Provide concessional loans to developing nations.

Interconnections and Functions in Modern Banking

1. **Facilitating Liquidity**:

   ◦ Commercial banks rely on central banks for liquidity during crises, ensuring uninterrupted functioning.

2. **Promoting Financial Inclusion**:

   ◦ Cooperative banks, NBFCs, and RRBs ensure that marginalized populations have access to banking services.

3. **Economic Stability**:

   ◦ The central bank's regulatory role and monetary policies stabilize inflation, unemployment, and GDP growth.

4. **Encouraging Investment**:

   ◦ Development banks and commercial banks channel savings into productive investments, fueling economic growth.

Challenges in Modern Banking

1. **Regulatory Compliance**:

   ◦ Increasing regulations to prevent crises can strain banks' profitability.

2. **Technological Adaptation**:

   ◦ Rapid digitization demands investment in cybersecurity and tech infrastructure.

3. **Financial Inclusion**:

- Reaching remote or underserved populations remains a significant challenge.

4. **Global Interdependence**:

- Globalization has increased susceptibility to external shocks, such as economic crises or geopolitical tensions.

4.2 Key Tools of Monetary Policy

Repo Rate and Reverse Repo Rate

Central banks use a variety of monetary policy tools to regulate the economy, control inflation, and promote economic growth. Among the most prominent tools are the **Repo Rate** and the **Reverse Repo Rate**, which play a critical role in managing liquidity and influencing interest rates in the economy. These tools are part of the central bank's short-term operations in the financial markets, directly impacting borrowing, lending, and the overall money supply.

Repo Rate

Definition

The **Repo Rate** (Repurchase Rate) is the interest rate at which the central bank lends money to commercial banks against the collateral of government securities. It is a tool used to inject liquidity into the banking system, especially when banks face short-term liquidity shortages.

Mechanism

- In a **repo transaction**, commercial banks sell government securities to the central bank with an agreement to repurchase them at a predetermined price after a specific period, along with interest at the repo rate.
- By borrowing at the repo rate, banks can meet their immediate liquidity requirements.

Impact on the Economy

1. **Controlling Inflation:**

   - When inflation is high, the central bank increases the repo rate, making borrowing costlier for banks. Higher borrowing costs for banks are passed on to consumers and businesses in the form of higher interest rates, reducing demand and inflationary pressure.

2. **Boosting Growth**:

   ○ During economic slowdowns, the central bank reduces the repo rate, making borrowing cheaper for banks. This encourages lending and investment, stimulating economic growth.

Example

- **Repo Rate Increase**: If the central bank raises the repo rate from 6% to 6.5%, borrowing becomes more expensive for banks. This discourages excessive borrowing and spending, curbing inflation.
- **Repo Rate Decrease**: A reduction in the repo rate from 6% to 5.5% lowers the cost of funds for banks, encouraging them to lend more to businesses and individuals.

Current Application

Central banks, such as the Reserve Bank of India (RBI), frequently adjust the repo rate based on prevailing economic conditions. For instance, the RBI reduced the repo rate multiple times during the COVID-19 pandemic to support economic recovery.

Reverse Repo Rate

Definition

The **Reverse Repo Rate** is the interest rate at which the central bank borrows money from commercial banks by accepting surplus funds in exchange for government securities. It is used to absorb excess liquidity from the banking system.

Mechanism

- In a **reverse repo transaction**, banks park their surplus funds with the central bank and earn interest at the reverse repo rate.
- This provides banks with a risk-free investment option while allowing the central bank to manage liquidity in the economy.

Impact on the Economy

1. **Mopping Up Excess Liquidity**:

    ◦ When there is excess money in the system, the central bank increases the reverse repo rate to encourage banks to park their surplus funds, reducing liquidity and inflationary pressures.

2. **Encouraging Lending**:

    ◦ A lower reverse repo rate discourages banks from parking funds with the central bank, prompting them to lend more to businesses and consumers.

Example

- **Reverse Repo Rate Increase**: If the reverse repo rate is increased from 4% to 4.5%, banks find it more attractive to deposit their surplus funds with the central bank, reducing money supply in the market.
- **Reverse Repo Rate Decrease**: A reduction in the reverse repo rate makes lending to the central bank less lucrative, encouraging banks to lend to businesses and individuals instead.

Current Application

The reverse repo rate is often adjusted alongside the repo rate to fine-tune liquidity management. For instance, during periods of high inflation, the central bank might raise the reverse repo rate to absorb surplus funds from the economy.

Aspect	Repo Rate	Reverse Repo Rate
Purpose	Inject liquidity into the banking system.	Absorb excess liquidity from the banking system.
Central Bank's Role	Lender to commercial banks.	Borrower from commercial banks.
Impact on Liquidity	Increases liquidity in the economy.	Decreases liquidity in the economy.
Interest Payment	Banks pay interest to the central bank.	Central bank pays interest to the banks.

Repo Rate vs. Reverse Repo Rate

Policy Implications
1. Balancing Inflation and Growth
Central banks adjust the repo and reverse repo rates to strike a balance between curbing inflation and promoting economic growth. For example:

- **High Inflation**: Raise repo and reverse repo rates to control money supply and reduce demand.
- **Economic Slowdown**: Lower rates to inject liquidity and encourage lending.

2. Financial Market Stability
The repo and reverse repo rates influence interbank lending rates, affecting overall market interest rates. Stability in these rates ensures smooth functioning of financial markets.
3. Supporting Monetary Transmission
Changes in repo and reverse repo rates directly impact borrowing costs for businesses and households, ensuring effective transmission of monetary policy objectives.
Real-World Examples

1. **India (2020–2022)**:

   - During the COVID-19 pandemic, the RBI reduced the repo rate to a historic low of 4% to boost liquidity and support economic recovery. Simultaneously, it reduced the reverse repo rate to 3.35% to discourage banks from parking funds with the RBI and encourage lending.

2. **United States (2022)**:

   - The Federal Reserve raised its equivalent of the repo rate to combat soaring inflation, making borrowing costlier and reducing money supply.

4.2 Key Tools of Monetary Policy

CRR, SLR, and Bank Rate

Central banks use various monetary policy instruments to regulate liquidity, control inflation, and ensure financial stability. Among these tools, the **Cash Reserve Ratio (CRR), Statutory Liquidity Ratio (SLR),** and **Bank Rate** are essential components of liquidity and credit management. These tools influence the flow of money in the economy, shaping borrowing, lending, and overall economic activity.

Cash Reserve Ratio (CRR)

Definition

The **Cash Reserve Ratio** (CRR) is the percentage of a commercial bank's total deposits that it is required to maintain as reserves with the central bank. This reserve must be held in cash and cannot be used for lending or investment.

Purpose

- **Liquidity Control**: CRR helps regulate the money supply in the economy by controlling the funds available for lending.
- **Inflation Management**: By adjusting CRR, the central bank can influence liquidity to curb inflation or stimulate growth.

Mechanism

1. **Increase in CRR:**

   ◦ Reduces the funds available for banks to lend, tightening liquidity and controlling inflation.

2. **Decrease in CRR:**

   ◦ Increases the funds available for lending, boosting liquidity and promoting growth.

Example

- If a bank has deposits of ₹1,000 crore and the CRR is set at 5%, the bank must maintain ₹50 crore with the central bank.

Impact on the Economy

- A higher CRR reduces liquidity, slowing down credit growth and curbing inflation.
- A lower CRR boosts liquidity, encouraging borrowing and investment.

Statutory Liquidity Ratio (SLR)

Definition

The **Statutory Liquidity Ratio** (SLR) is the percentage of a commercial bank's net demand and time liabilities (NDTL) that must be maintained in the form of liquid assets, such as government securities, gold, or cash, before offering credit.

Purpose

- **Stability and Liquidity**: Ensures that banks maintain sufficient reserves to meet withdrawal demands.
- **Support for Government Borrowing**: SLR mandates investment in government securities, aiding in public financing.

Mechanism

1. **Increase in SLR**:

   ○ Reduces the funds available for lending, controlling liquidity and inflation.

2. **Decrease in SLR**:

   ○ Increases the funds available for lending, stimulating economic growth.

Example

- If a bank has NDTL of ₹500 crore and the SLR is set at 18%, the bank must maintain ₹90 crore in approved liquid assets.

Impact on the Economy

- A higher SLR tightens liquidity, slowing credit growth.
- A lower SLR encourages banks to lend more, boosting investment and consumption.

Bank Rate
Definition
The **Bank Rate** is the interest rate at which the central bank lends money to commercial banks without any collateral. Unlike the repo rate, bank rate loans are extended for longer durations and primarily influence long-term interest rates in the economy.
Purpose

- **Monetary Policy Adjustment**: Used to influence credit availability and regulate money supply.
- **Signaling Device**: Changes in the bank rate signal the central bank's stance on monetary policy.

Mechanism

1. **Increase in Bank Rate**:

   ◦ Makes borrowing costlier for banks, leading to higher lending rates for consumers and businesses, thereby curbing demand and inflation.

2. **Decrease in Bank Rate**:

   ◦ Reduces borrowing costs for banks, encouraging credit expansion and stimulating economic growth.

Example

- If the bank rate is raised from 6% to 6.5%, commercial banks may increase their lending rates, making loans more expensive for borrowers.

Impact on the Economy

- A higher bank rate discourages borrowing and reduces liquidity, slowing inflation.
- A lower bank rate encourages borrowing, boosting investment and consumption.

Aspect	CRR	SLR	Bank Rate
Definition	Percentage of deposits kept as reserves with the central bank.	Percentage of NDTL held in liquid assets.	Long-term interest rate for central bank loans.
Purpose	Liquidity regulation and inflation control.	Ensuring financial stability and supporting government borrowing.	Influencing credit availability and long-term rates.
Type of Reserve	Held in cash only.	Held in liquid assets (e.g., securities, gold).	No reserve; applies to borrowing.
Effect on Liquidity	Directly reduces cash available for lending.	Reduces investable funds indirectly.	Impacts credit costs and availability.

Comparison of CRR, SLR, and Bank Rate

Policy Implications

1. **Inflation Control:**

   - **CRR and SLR:** Raising these ratios tightens liquidity, helping control inflation.
   - **Bank Rate:** Increasing the bank rate reduces borrowing and spending, slowing inflation.

2. **Economic Growth:**

   - **CRR and SLR:** Lowering these ratios increases funds for lending, boosting investment and consumption.
   - **Bank Rate:** Reducing the bank rate makes credit cheaper, encouraging borrowing and economic activity.

3. **Financial Stability**:

   ○ **CRR and SLR** ensure that banks maintain adequate reserves to meet withdrawal demands and avoid liquidity crises.

Real-World Examples

1. **India (2020)**:

   ○ During the COVID-19 pandemic, the Reserve Bank of India reduced the CRR from 4% to 3% and the repo rate to 4%, injecting liquidity into the economy to support recovery.

2. **United States (2008–2009)**:

   ○ The Federal Reserve reduced interest rates and reserve requirements to combat the financial crisis, encouraging banks to lend and stabilize the economy.

Open Market Operations (OMO)

Open Market Operations (OMO) refer to the buying and selling of government securities in the open market by the central bank to regulate the money supply and liquidity in the economy. As a dynamic monetary policy tool, OMOs are essential for maintaining economic stability, controlling inflation, and promoting growth. They directly impact the liquidity available in the banking system, influencing interest rates and credit flow.

Definition and Objectives

OMOs are actions undertaken by the central bank to achieve the following objectives:

1. **Liquidity Management**: Adjusting the supply of money in the banking system to match economic needs.
2. **Interest Rate Regulation**: Influencing short-term interest rates to ensure financial stability.

3. **Inflation Control**: Reducing or increasing liquidity to curb inflation or deflationary pressures.
4. **Promoting Economic Growth**: Stimulating borrowing and investment during economic slowdowns.

Types of Open Market Operations
1. Expansionary OMO

- The central bank **purchases government securities** from commercial banks or the public to inject liquidity into the economy.
- **Purpose**: To address liquidity shortages, stimulate borrowing, and promote growth.
- **Example**: During an economic recession, the central bank buys securities to increase the money supply and reduce interest rates.

2. Contractionary OMO

- The central bank **sells government securities** to absorb excess liquidity from the banking system.
- **Purpose**: To curb inflation and prevent overheating of the economy.
- **Example**: During periods of high inflation, selling securities reduces money supply, making borrowing costlier and cooling demand.

Mechanism of Open Market Operations

1. **Purchasing Securities (Expansionary OMO)**:

   - The central bank buys government securities from banks or the public.
   - In return, it credits money to the banks' accounts, increasing their reserves.
   - Higher reserves enable banks to lend more, boosting credit flow and reducing interest rates.

2. **Selling Securities (Contractionary OMO)**:

   - The central bank sells government securities to banks or the public.

- Payments for these securities reduce the banks' reserves, tightening liquidity.
- Lower reserves constrain lending capacity, increasing interest rates and controlling demand.

Impact on the Economy

1. Money Supply Regulation

OMO directly affects the money available in the economy, influencing inflation and consumption.

- **Buying securities** increases the money supply, encouraging spending.
- **Selling securities** reduces the money supply, discouraging excessive demand.

2. Influence on Interest Rates

OMO affects short-term interest rates by altering liquidity in the banking system:

- Higher liquidity from securities purchases lowers interest rates, stimulating borrowing.
- Reduced liquidity from securities sales raises interest rates, discouraging borrowing.

3. Credit Availability

By adjusting bank reserves, OMOs impact the amount of credit banks can offer to businesses and consumers.

4. Currency Stability

OMO indirectly affects exchange rates by influencing capital flows and investor sentiment. A well-regulated money supply ensures currency stability.

Advantages of Open Market Operations

1. **Flexibility**: OMOs can be implemented quickly to respond to changing economic conditions.
2. **Market-Based Approach**: They operate through financial markets, allowing the central bank to influence liquidity efficiently without imposing direct controls.

3. **Dual Function**: OMOs help manage both inflation and deflation, making them versatile tools for economic stabilization.

Challenges of Open Market Operations

1. **Market Dependency**: The effectiveness of OMOs depends on the depth and liquidity of financial markets.
2. **Lag in Impact**: Changes in liquidity and interest rates may take time to affect the broader economy.
3. **Coordination with Fiscal Policy**: Conflict between monetary and fiscal policies can reduce the effectiveness of OMOs.
4. **Limited Scope in Underdeveloped Markets**: In economies with underdeveloped financial markets, OMOs may have limited reach.

Real-World Examples
1. United States (2008–2009 Financial Crisis)

- The Federal Reserve undertook large-scale asset purchases (often called **Quantitative Easing**) as part of its open market operations to inject liquidity and stabilize the financial system.
- Result: Increased money supply, reduced interest rates, and economic recovery.

2. India (2020 COVID-19 Pandemic)

- The Reserve Bank of India (RBI) conducted OMOs to inject liquidity into the economy. By purchasing government bonds, the RBI ensured that banks had sufficient funds to support businesses and consumers during the pandemic.

3. European Central Bank (2021)

- The ECB used OMOs under its **Pandemic Emergency Purchase Programme (PEPP)** to maintain liquidity and support economic activity in Eurozone countries affected by COVID-19.

Aspect	OMO	Repo Rate	CRR/SLR
Purpose	Liquidity regulation via securities trade.	Short-term liquidity adjustments via borrowing costs.	Reserve requirement adjustments for liquidity control.
Scope	Impacts overall liquidity in the banking system.	Targets bank borrowing rates.	Focuses on reserve maintenance.
Flexibility	High, as it is market-driven.	Moderate, requires rate adjustment.	Lower, requires statutory changes.

Comparison with Other Monetary Policy Tools

Aspect	OMO	Repo Rate	CRR/SLR
Purpose	Liquidity regulation via securities trade.	Short-term liquidity adjustments via borrowing costs.	Reserve requirement adjustments for liquidity control.
Scope	Impacts overall liquidity in the banking system.	Targets bank borrowing rates.	Focuses on reserve maintenance.
Flexibility	High, as it is market-driven.	Moderate, requires rate adjustment.	Lower, requires statutory changes.

4.3 Money Supply

Components: M1, M2, M3, M4

Money supply refers to the total amount of money available in an economy at a given time. It is a critical economic metric, as it influences inflation, interest rates, and overall economic activity. Central banks monitor and manage the money supply to maintain economic stability. The money supply is typically classified into various measures, commonly known as **M1, M2, M3**, and **M4**, each reflecting different levels of liquidity.

Definition of Money Supply

The money supply encompasses all forms of money in an economy, including cash, demand deposits, and near-money assets. It is categorized to provide insights into different types of money based on their liquidity, from the most liquid forms to less liquid forms.

Components of Money Supply

1. M1: Narrow Money

M1 represents the most liquid and immediately accessible components of the money supply. It is also referred to as **transaction money**, as it is used for daily transactions.

Components:

1. **Currency in Circulation:**

   - Notes and coins held by the public (excluding those with banks and the central bank).

2. **Demand Deposits with Banks:**

   - Funds held in checking/current accounts, available on demand without notice.

3. **Other Deposits with the Central Bank:**

   - Deposits by the public or institutions, such as balances with the Reserve Bank of India (RBI).

Example:

If a household holds ₹10,000 in cash and ₹50,000 in a checking account, the total contribution to M1 is ₹60,000.

Economic Significance:

M1 provides a snapshot of money available for immediate spending, directly influencing consumption and short-term liquidity.

2. M2: M1 + Savings Deposits

M2 expands on M1 by including near-money components that are slightly less liquid but still accessible relatively quickly.

Components:

1. **All Components of M1.**
2. **Savings Deposits with Post Offices**:

   ○ Deposits held in post office savings accounts, which are liquid but require notice for withdrawal.

Example:

If a household holds ₹5,000 in a post office savings account in addition to ₹60,000 in M1, the total M2 is ₹65,000.

Economic Significance:

M2 reflects the money readily available for short-term needs and savings, providing insights into consumer savings behavior.

3. M3: Broad Money

M3 is also known as **broad money** and includes components that provide a more comprehensive picture of the money supply, capturing longer-term deposits and economic liquidity.

Components:

1. **All Components of M1.**
2. **Time Deposits with Banks**:

   ○ Fixed deposits and recurring deposits held in commercial banks that require a fixed tenure for withdrawal.

Example:

If a household has ₹1,00,000 in fixed deposits in addition to ₹60,000 in M1, the total M3 is   ₹1,60,000.

Economic Significance:

M3 serves as a broader measure of money supply, influencing credit availability, long-term investment, and monetary policy decisions.

4. M4: M3 + Post Office Time Deposits

M4 is the most inclusive measure of money supply, accounting for money held in post office time deposits in addition to M3.

Components:

1. **All Components of M3.**
2. **Total Deposits with Post Offices (Excluding National Savings Certificates):**

   ○ Includes term deposits in post offices that are not immediately liquid.

Example:

If a household holds   ₹20,000 in post office term deposits in addition to ₹1,60,000 in M3, the total M4 is   ₹1,80,000.

Economic Significance:

M4 provides the most comprehensive view of money supply, capturing all monetary resources in the economy, including those held outside traditional banking systems.

Measure	Liquidity	Components	Purpose
M1	Most liquid	Currency + demand deposits + other central bank deposits	Daily transactions and liquidity.
M2	Slightly less liquid	M1 + savings deposits in post offices	Short-term liquidity and savings.
M3	Broad money	M1 + time deposits in banks	Overall economic liquidity.
M4	Least liquid	M3 + post office time deposits	Comprehensive money supply measure.

Comparison of M1, M2, M3, and M4

Economic Implications of Money Supply Components

1. **M1 and M2:**

- Reflect consumer spending patterns and short-term liquidity.
- Useful for understanding inflationary pressures and immediate economic conditions.

2. **M3 and M4**:

- Indicate overall credit availability and long-term investment trends.
- Essential for assessing monetary policy effectiveness and economic growth potential.

Policy Use of Money Supply Data
Central banks and policymakers use money supply data to:

1. **Control Inflation**:

- Tightening money supply (e.g., increasing CRR or SLR) reduces liquidity, curbing inflation.

2. **Stimulate Growth**:

- Increasing money supply (e.g., lowering repo rates) enhances liquidity, encouraging spending and investment.

3. **Monitor Economic Stability**:

- Tracking M1 through M4 helps identify potential economic imbalances or liquidity crises.

4.4 Inflation Targeting and Monetary Transmission

Role of the Monetary Policy Committee (MPC)

Inflation targeting is a monetary policy framework in which a central bank sets a specific inflation rate as its primary goal and uses various monetary tools to achieve it. Effective inflation targeting relies on clear communication, data-driven decision-making, and robust policy implementation, often overseen by a dedicated body like the **Monetary Policy Committee (MPC)**. The MPC plays a central role in formulating and executing monetary policy to achieve price stability and support economic growth.

Monetary Policy Committee (MPC): Overview

The **Monetary Policy Committee (MPC)** is a panel established by a central bank to decide on key policy rates, such as the repo rate, that influence inflation, liquidity, and overall economic activity. Its primary objective is to maintain inflation within a predefined target range, contributing to monetary stability and sustainable growth.

Key Features of the MPC:

1. **Composition**:

   - Typically comprises members from the central bank and external experts in economics or finance.
   - In India, the **MPC of the Reserve Bank of India (RBI)** has six members—three from the RBI (including the Governor) and three external members appointed by the government.

2. **Mandate**:

   - Formulate monetary policy to achieve inflation targets set by the government in consultation with the central bank.
   - Example: India's inflation target is **4% (+/- 2%)**, with the MPC tasked with keeping inflation within this range.

3. **Decision-Making Process**:

- The MPC meets periodically to review economic conditions and decide on policy changes.
- Decisions are made by majority vote, with the central bank governor having a casting vote in case of a tie.

Role of the MPC in Inflation Targeting
1. Setting the Inflation Target
The MPC ensures that inflation remains within the prescribed target range. It analyzes macroeconomic indicators such as CPI, WPI, GDP growth, and global factors to assess inflationary trends and make informed decisions.

2. Adjusting Policy Rates
The MPC uses policy rates, primarily the **repo rate**, to influence inflation:

- **To Control Inflation (Hawkish Stance):**

  - Increases the repo rate to make borrowing more expensive, reducing demand and cooling inflation.
  - Example: The MPC raised interest rates in 2022 to address global inflationary pressures driven by supply chain disruptions.

- **To Stimulate Growth (Dovish Stance):**

  - Reduces the repo rate to make borrowing cheaper, encouraging spending and investment to boost economic activity.

3. Monitoring Monetary Transmission
The MPC ensures that changes in policy rates are transmitted effectively to the broader economy through the banking system. This involves analyzing how banks adjust their lending and deposit rates in response to repo rate changes.

4. Communicating Policy Decisions
Transparency is a cornerstone of inflation targeting. The MPC issues policy statements explaining the rationale behind its decisions, fostering public and investor confidence in the central bank's objectives.

5. Balancing Growth and Inflation
The MPC aims to strike a balance between price stability and economic growth. While its primary mandate is inflation targeting, it also considers

factors like employment, investment, and external stability.

Monetary Transmission Mechanism

Monetary transmission refers to the process through which changes in the central bank's policy rates impact the economy. The MPC's decisions influence the following key channels:

1. Interest Rate Channel

Changes in the repo rate affect borrowing and lending rates in the banking system:

- **Higher Repo Rate**: Increases lending rates, discouraging borrowing and reducing consumption and investment.
- **Lower Repo Rate**: Reduces lending rates, encouraging borrowing and stimulating demand.

2. Credit Channel

Policy changes influence the availability of credit:

- Tight monetary policy reduces liquidity, limiting banks' ability to lend.
- Easy monetary policy enhances liquidity, encouraging credit flow.

3. Exchange Rate Channel

Changes in policy rates impact capital flows and exchange rates:

- **Higher Repo Rate**: Attracts foreign capital, appreciating the domestic currency and reducing import costs.
- **Lower Repo Rate**: May lead to capital outflows, depreciating the currency and increasing inflationary pressures through higher import costs.

4. Expectations Channel

The MPC shapes public expectations about future inflation and interest rates through clear communication, influencing consumer and business decisions.

5. Asset Price Channel

Monetary policy impacts financial markets:

- Lower rates boost asset prices (e.g., stocks, real estate), increasing wealth and stimulating spending.
- Higher rates may depress asset prices, curbing spending.

Challenges in MPC-Driven Inflation Targeting

1. **Transmission Delays**:

   - The impact of monetary policy decisions on the real economy is not immediate, leading to time lags in achieving objectives.

2. **External Shocks**:

   - Factors such as global commodity prices or geopolitical tensions can disrupt inflation targets, limiting the MPC's effectiveness.

3. **Structural Constraints**:

   - In developing economies like India, informal markets and limited financial penetration can hinder monetary transmission.

4. **Dual Mandates**:

   - Balancing inflation control with growth objectives can create conflicting pressures on the MPC.

5. **Public Perception**:

   - Misinformed expectations or lack of confidence in the central bank's actions can undermine the effectiveness of inflation targeting.

Real-World Examples
India

- **Formation of the MPC**: The RBI's MPC was established in 2016 to formalize inflation targeting as the primary goal of monetary policy.
- **COVID-19 Pandemic Response (2020–2021)**:

   - The MPC reduced the repo rate to a historic low of 4% to stimulate economic activity during the pandemic-induced slowdown.
   - Despite inflationary pressures, the MPC maintained an accommodative stance to support recovery.

United States

- The Federal Reserve, while not governed by an MPC, uses a similar inflation-targeting framework to achieve its dual mandate of price stability and maximum employment.

Lessons and Future Directions

1. **Data-Driven Decisions:**

   - The MPC must rely on robust data analytics to anticipate inflation trends and formulate timely policies.

2. **Enhancing Monetary Transmission:**

   - Improving financial inclusion and banking infrastructure can strengthen the link between policy decisions and economic outcomes.

3. **Global Coordination:**

   - Collaboration with international monetary bodies can help address global shocks affecting inflation.

4.4 Inflation Targeting and Monetary Transmission

Challenges in Monetary Transmission

Monetary transmission is the process through which changes in central bank policies, such as adjustments to the repo rate, impact the broader economy, including borrowing costs, investment, consumption, and inflation. While theoretically straightforward, in practice, monetary transmission is influenced by a host of factors, often creating delays, inefficiencies, or distortions in achieving the intended policy objectives.

Key Challenges in Monetary Transmission

1. Time Lags

One of the most significant challenges in monetary transmission is the delay between policy implementation and its impact on the economy. These lags occur at various stages:

- **Recognition Lag**: The time taken to identify economic conditions requiring intervention.
- **Implementation Lag**: The time needed to announce and implement policy changes.
- **Impact Lag**: The time before policy changes affect consumption, investment, and inflation.

Example:

An increase in the repo rate may take months to influence consumer behavior and inflation, as businesses and households gradually adjust their financial plans.

2. Imperfect Pass-Through

The effectiveness of monetary policy depends on how well changes in policy rates, such as the repo rate, are transmitted to market interest rates, lending rates, and deposit rates. However, this pass-through is often incomplete due to:

- **Sticky Lending Rates**: Banks may delay or partially pass on changes in policy rates to borrowers, influenced by factors like competition and existing contracts.

- **Mismatched Expectations**: Financial institutions may not adjust rates fully, anticipating future rate reversals or uncertainty.

Example:

In India, despite reductions in the repo rate during 2020, many banks delayed lowering their lending rates due to concerns over profitability and rising non-performing assets (NPAs).

3. Structural Issues in the Banking System

Structural inefficiencies in the banking sector can obstruct monetary transmission:

- **High Non-Performing Assets (NPAs)**: Banks with significant NPAs may hesitate to extend credit, even when liquidity is ample.
- **Capital Adequacy**: Under-capitalized banks may prioritize rebuilding reserves over expanding credit.
- **Liquidity Mismatches**: Poor liquidity management can prevent banks from adjusting their lending practices in response to policy changes.

4. Financial Market Fragmentation

In economies with fragmented financial markets, monetary transmission may be inconsistent across sectors or regions:

- **Rural vs. Urban Disparities**: Rural areas with limited banking infrastructure often experience weaker transmission.
- **Sectoral Inequities**: Certain industries may respond more quickly to policy changes than others, leading to uneven economic impacts.

5. Limited Financial Inclusion

In developing economies, a large portion of the population may lack access to formal financial systems, limiting the reach of monetary policy:

- Informal credit markets dominate in rural and semi-urban areas, where interest rates are often unaffected by central bank policies.
- Small and medium enterprises (SMEs) may rely on non-banking financial companies (NBFCs) or informal lenders, reducing the effectiveness of central bank interventions.

Example:

In India, despite significant efforts to promote financial inclusion, informal credit channels still play a substantial role in rural financing, weakening monetary transmission.

6. Global Factors

External economic conditions can dilute the impact of domestic monetary policy:

- **Exchange Rate Volatility**: Changes in global capital flows or currency markets can offset the effects of policy rate adjustments.
- **Commodity Price Shocks**: External factors like oil price volatility may exert inflationary pressures independent of domestic monetary policy.

Example:

Even if a central bank reduces rates to stimulate domestic growth, rising global oil prices may negate its efforts by increasing inflation.

7. Behavioral and Psychological Barriers

The expectations and behavior of consumers, businesses, and financial institutions play a significant role in monetary transmission:

- **Consumer Hesitancy**: During economic uncertainty, consumers may choose to save rather than spend, even if borrowing becomes cheaper.
- **Business Caution**: Businesses may delay investment decisions due to pessimistic market outlooks, regardless of lower interest rates.

Example:

During the COVID-19 pandemic, lower interest rates failed to boost demand significantly as uncertainty about the future restrained spending.

8. Policy Credibility and Communication

The credibility of the central bank and its ability to communicate effectively influence the success of monetary transmission:

- **Policy Uncertainty**: Frequent or unpredictable policy changes can reduce confidence in the central bank, weakening its influence on market behavior.
- **Lack of Transparency**: Poor communication about policy objectives or decision-making processes may create confusion, limiting the effectiveness of monetary tools.

Addressing Challenges in Monetary Transmission

To improve monetary transmission, central banks and policymakers can adopt the following measures:

1. Strengthening Banking Infrastructure

- Enhancing the capitalization of banks to ensure they can lend effectively.
- Addressing NPAs through stricter credit monitoring and resolution mechanisms.

2. Promoting Financial Inclusion

- Expanding access to formal financial systems in underserved regions to ensure wider policy impact.
- Encouraging digital banking and fintech solutions to bridge the gap between rural and urban areas.

3. Ensuring Effective Policy Communication

- Central banks should clearly articulate policy objectives, decisions, and expected outcomes to build trust and manage expectations.
- Publishing detailed monetary policy reports can improve transparency and accountability.

4. Integrating with Global Policies

- Coordinating with international monetary authorities to address global factors affecting monetary transmission.
- Building foreign exchange reserves to mitigate external shocks.

5. Developing Bond and Credit Markets

- Strengthening financial markets to improve the pass-through of monetary policy changes to various sectors.
- Encouraging corporate bond issuance to reduce reliance on bank credit.

Real-World Examples
India

- **Repo Rate Reductions (2020)**:
  Despite significant reductions in the repo rate by the RBI during the COVID-19 pandemic, monetary transmission was slow due to high NPAs and banks' cautious lending practices.

United States

- **Global Financial Crisis (2008)**:
  The Federal Reserve's aggressive monetary easing faced transmission delays as financial institutions, burdened with toxic assets, hesitated to extend credit.

FIVE

FISCAL POLICY AND PUBLIC FINANCE

5.1 Understanding Fiscal Policy

Objectives and Components

Fiscal policy refers to the use of government spending, taxation, and borrowing to influence a nation's economic activity. It is a critical tool for achieving macroeconomic stability, promoting growth, and addressing income inequalities. Fiscal policy plays a vital role in managing economic cycles and ensuring sustainable public finance.

Objectives of Fiscal Policy

Fiscal policy is designed to achieve several key objectives, which can vary based on a country's economic priorities and developmental goals:

1. Economic Stability

Fiscal policy helps mitigate economic fluctuations and maintain stability by influencing demand and supply in the economy.

- **Example**: During a recession, increased government spending can stimulate demand, while reduced spending can curb inflation during a boom.

2. Promotion of Economic Growth

Governments use fiscal measures to create an environment conducive to investment and growth, ensuring sustained development over time.

- **Example**: Investments in infrastructure and education enhance productivity and long-term economic growth.

3. Redistribution of Income and Wealth

Fiscal policy reduces income inequalities by taxing higher-income groups and reallocating resources through subsidies, social programs, and welfare schemes.

- **Example**: Progressive taxation systems ensure that wealthier individuals contribute more to government revenue.

4. Employment Generation

Public spending on infrastructure projects and social programs generates employment opportunities, particularly during economic downturns.

- **Example**: Rural employment programs like India's **MGNREGA** create jobs in underdeveloped areas.

5. Controlling Inflation

By adjusting taxation and public expenditure, fiscal policy helps regulate aggregate demand to control inflationary pressures.

- **Example**: Reducing public expenditure can decrease excess demand, thereby controlling inflation.

6. Encouraging Investment

Tax incentives and subsidies are often used to promote private sector investment and industrial growth.

- **Example**: Corporate tax cuts can attract foreign direct investment (FDI) and spur business expansion.

7. Addressing Balance of Payments (BoP) Issues

Fiscal measures like export incentives and import restrictions can help correct BoP deficits.

- **Example**: Providing subsidies to exporters increases the competitiveness of domestic goods in international markets.

Components of Fiscal Policy
The effectiveness of fiscal policy lies in its strategic deployment of three main components:
1. Government Expenditure
Government spending is a powerful fiscal tool for stimulating or slowing down economic activity. It includes capital and revenue expenditure:

1. **Capital Expenditure**:

   - Long-term investments in infrastructure, education, and healthcare that boost productive capacity.
   - **Example**: Building highways, railways, and power plants.

2. **Revenue Expenditure**:

   - Day-to-day operational costs like salaries, subsidies, and interest payments.
   - **Example**: Providing subsidies for fertilizers or food grains.

Role in Fiscal Policy:

- Increased spending during recessions stimulates demand.
- Reduced spending during booms controls inflation.

2. Taxation
Taxes are a primary source of government revenue and a key instrument in fiscal policy. They are used to influence consumer behavior, redistribute income, and stabilize the economy.

1. **Direct Taxes**:

   - Levied on income and wealth, such as personal income tax and corporate tax.
   - **Example**: A progressive income tax system ensures that high earners contribute more.

2. **Indirect Taxes**:

   ◦ Applied to goods and services, such as Goods and Services Tax (GST) or customs duties.
   ◦ **Example**: High taxes on luxury goods discourage non-essential consumption.

Role in Fiscal Policy:

- Lowering taxes boosts disposable income and demand.
- Increasing taxes curbs inflation and raises revenue.

3. Public Borrowing

When government revenue from taxes is insufficient to meet expenditures, public borrowing fills the gap. This can be through issuing government bonds, external loans, or borrowing from financial institutions.

1. **Domestic Borrowing**:

   ◦ Borrowing from the domestic market through bonds or treasury bills.
   ◦ **Example**: The government may issue bonds to fund infrastructure projects.

2. **External Borrowing**:

   ◦ Loans from international organizations or foreign governments.
   ◦ **Example**: Loans from the World Bank for specific development projects.

Role in Fiscal Policy:

- Borrowing finances fiscal deficits, enabling counter-cyclical spending during recessions.
- Excessive borrowing, however, can lead to debt crises and reduce fiscal flexibility.

Types of Fiscal Policy
1. Expansionary Fiscal Policy

- **Definition**: Involves increased government spending, tax reductions, or both to stimulate economic activity.
- **Objective**: Combat unemployment and spur growth.
- **Example**: Stimulus packages during the 2008 global financial crisis.

2. Contractionary Fiscal Policy

- **Definition**: Reduces government spending or increases taxes to control inflation and reduce deficits.
- **Objective**: Stabilize overheating economies.
- **Example**: Austerity measures adopted by Greece during the Eurozone crisis.

Challenges in Implementing Fiscal Policy

1. **Time Lags**:

   - Fiscal measures often take time to implement and show results, which may delay their impact on the economy.

2. **Political Influence**:

   - Fiscal decisions may prioritize political objectives over economic efficiency.

3. **Public Debt**:

   - Persistent fiscal deficits can lead to unsustainable levels of public debt.

4. **Structural Constraints**:

   - Limited fiscal space in developing economies due to low revenue generation and high expenditure requirements.

Real-World Examples
India

- **COVID-19 Stimulus (2020)**:

  - The Indian government announced a ₹20 lakh crore fiscal stimulus package, including direct cash transfers, infrastructure spending, and tax relief, to support economic recovery.

- **GST Implementation**:

  - Simplified the taxation system, enhancing compliance and revenue collection.

United States

- **American Rescue Plan (2021)**:

  - A $1.9 trillion fiscal package to stimulate economic recovery post-COVID-19 through direct payments, unemployment benefits, and vaccination programs.

European Union

- **Austerity Measures**:

  - Post-2008 financial crisis, many EU nations adopted contractionary fiscal policies to reduce deficits, leading to mixed economic outcomes.

5.2 Taxation Systems

Direct vs. Indirect Taxes

Taxation systems are fundamental to any economy, enabling governments to generate revenue for public expenditure, infrastructure development, and social welfare. Taxes can be broadly categorized into **direct taxes** and **indirect taxes**, each with distinct mechanisms, impacts, and implications for individuals, businesses, and the broader economy.

Definition and Key Features

Direct Taxes

Direct taxes are levied directly on individuals or entities based on their income, wealth, or profits. These taxes are non-transferable, meaning the burden of the tax is borne by the individual or entity on whom it is imposed.

Examples:

- Income Tax
- Corporate Tax
- Wealth Tax
- Capital Gains Tax
- Estate Tax

Key Features:

1. **Progressive Nature**: Most direct taxes, such as income tax, are progressive, meaning higher income earners pay a higher percentage of their income as tax.
2. **Non-Transferability**: The tax liability cannot be shifted to another party.

Indirect Taxes

Indirect taxes are levied on goods and services at the point of production, distribution, or consumption. Unlike direct taxes, the burden of indirect taxes can be passed on to consumers in the form of higher prices.

Examples:

- Goods and Services Tax (GST)
- Value-Added Tax (VAT)

- Customs Duty
- Excise Duty
- Sales Tax

Key Features:

1. **Regressive Nature**: Indirect taxes are considered regressive because they impose the same rate on all consumers, regardless of income, disproportionately affecting lower-income groups.
2. **Transferability**: The tax burden is transferred to end consumers through price mechanisms.

Aspect	Direct Taxes	Indirect Taxes
Definition	Levied directly on income or wealth.	Levied on goods and services.
Examples	Income tax, corporate tax, wealth tax.	GST, customs duty, excise duty.
Nature	Progressive (based on income levels).	Regressive (same rate for all consumers).
Burden	Cannot be transferred.	Can be passed on to consumers.
Complexity	Requires detailed records and compliance.	Simpler to collect through transactions.
Impact on Consumers	Affects only those liable to pay the tax.	Affects all consumers who purchase goods/services.
Revenue Stability	Subject to fluctuations based on income/profits.	More stable as consumption remains relatively constant.

Comparison Between Direct and Indirect Taxes

Examples of Direct Taxes

1. Income Tax

Income tax is levied on the income of individuals and businesses.

- **Progressive Structure**: Higher income slabs are taxed at higher rates.
- **Example**:

  - Income up to ₹2,50,000: Exempt
  - Income between ₹2,50,001 and ₹5,00,000: Taxed at 5%

2. Corporate Tax

Corporate tax is imposed on the profits of companies.

- **Example**: In India, domestic companies pay a corporate tax of around 25%, with lower rates for small enterprises.

3. Wealth Tax (Abolished in India)

Previously levied on the net wealth of individuals or entities exceeding a specified threshold.

Examples of Indirect Taxes

1. Goods and Services Tax (GST)

GST is a comprehensive tax on the supply of goods and services, subsuming multiple indirect taxes like VAT, excise duty, and service tax.

- **Example**: GST rates in India range from 0% (essential goods) to 28% (luxury items).

2. Customs Duty

Levied on imported and exported goods to regulate trade and protect domestic industries.

- **Example**: Import duty on electronic goods to encourage local manufacturing.

3. Excise Duty (Now Subsumed Under GST)

Previously levied on the production of goods within a country.

Economic Impacts of Direct Taxes

Advantages

1. **Equity**: Progressive taxation ensures that higher-income individuals contribute more.
2. **Revenue Generation**: Direct taxes provide a significant and predictable revenue stream.
3. **Economic Redistribution**: Supports wealth redistribution by taxing higher-income groups and funding social welfare.

Disadvantages

1. **Complex Compliance**: Filing returns and maintaining records can be burdensome.
2. **Risk of Evasion**: High rates may encourage tax evasion.
3. **Economic Disincentives**: High taxes on income or profits may discourage productivity and investment.

Economic Impacts of Indirect Taxes
Advantages

1. **Ease of Collection**: Collected at the point of sale or production, simplifying administration.
2. **Broader Base**: Covers a larger segment of the population, including those not paying direct taxes.
3. **Encourages Savings**: Taxes consumption rather than income, potentially incentivizing saving and investment.

Disadvantages

1. **Regressiveness**: Affects low-income groups disproportionately, as they spend a larger share of their income on consumption.
2. **Inflationary**: Can increase the cost of goods and services, reducing purchasing power.
3. **Economic Burden**: Excessive indirect taxes may discourage consumption, impacting growth.

Balancing Direct and Indirect Taxes
Governments strive to strike a balance between direct and indirect taxes to achieve economic equity, efficiency, and revenue stability.

- **Optimal Taxation Policy**: A mix of progressive direct taxes and broad-based indirect taxes ensures fair distribution of tax burdens while maintaining robust revenue.
- **Example**:

  - In India, GST complements income tax as part of an integrated tax system.
  - Corporate tax reforms, coupled with rationalization of GST rates, aim to balance growth and equity.

Real-World Examples of Taxation Systems
India

- **Direct Taxes**: Income tax, corporate tax, and securities transaction tax (STT).
- **Indirect Taxes**: GST is the primary indirect tax, covering multiple goods and services with varying rates.

United States

- **Direct Taxes**: Federal income tax and state income taxes.
- **Indirect Taxes**: Sales tax varies by state, and excise duties apply to specific goods like alcohol and tobacco.

European Union

- **Direct Taxes**: Income and corporate taxes are levied by member states.
- **Indirect Taxes**: Value-Added Tax (VAT) is a harmonized system across EU countries.

Progressive, Regressive, and Proportional Taxation

Tax systems are designed to achieve various economic and social objectives, such as revenue generation, equitable wealth distribution, and economic stability. The way a tax system affects different income groups is broadly categorized into **progressive**, **regressive**, and **proportional taxation**, each with distinct impacts on individuals, businesses, and the broader economy.

Progressive Taxation

Definition

A **progressive tax** system imposes a higher tax rate on higher income levels. As income increases, the percentage of income paid as tax also rises. This system is based on the principle of **ability to pay**, ensuring that individuals with higher incomes contribute more to government revenue.

Features

1. **Higher Rates for Higher Incomes**: Tax brackets define income ranges with increasing tax rates.
2. **Income Redistribution**: Ensures wealth redistribution by taxing the wealthy more heavily.

Examples

- **Income Tax**:

  - In India:

    - Income up to ₹2,50,000: Exempt
    - Income between ₹2,50,001 and ₹5,00,000: 5%
    - Income above ₹15,00,000: 30%

  - Higher income earners pay a larger proportion of their earnings as tax.

- **Estate Tax**: Levied on large inheritances, typically exempting smaller estates.

Economic Impacts

1. **Advantages**:

   - **Equity**: Reduces income inequality by taxing the rich more.
   - **Social Welfare**: Generates revenue for public services benefiting lower-income groups.

2. **Disadvantages**:

   - **Economic Disincentives**: High tax rates may discourage productivity and investment.
   - **Tax Evasion**: Wealthy individuals may exploit loopholes to avoid high taxes.

Regressive Taxation

Definition

A **regressive tax** system imposes a higher relative burden on lower-income individuals. Although the tax amount may be the same, it represents a larger proportion of income for low earners compared to high earners.

Features

1. **Uniform Rate**: The tax rate is the same for all individuals, regardless of income level.
2. **Greater Impact on Low-Income Groups**: A fixed tax or consumption tax disproportionately affects those with limited earnings.

Examples

- **Indirect Taxes**:

  - **Goods and Services Tax (GST)**: Applied uniformly on goods, low-income consumers spend a larger share of their income on taxed goods.
  - **Excise Duty**: Taxes on fuel or alcohol impact all consumers equally but represent a larger burden for lower-income individuals.

- **Flat Fees**: A fixed property tax or vehicle registration fee is regressive in nature.

Economic Impacts

1. **Advantages**:

   - **Simplicity**: Easy to administer and understand.
   - **Incentive to Earn More**: Low tax rates on higher incomes may encourage productivity.

2. **Disadvantages**:

   - **Inequity**: Worsens income inequality by imposing a heavier relative burden on the poor.

- ◦ **Reduced Spending Power**: Limits disposable income for lower-income groups, reducing consumption.

Proportional Taxation

Definition

A **proportional tax**, also known as a **flat tax**, imposes the same tax rate on all income levels. Regardless of how much an individual earns, the percentage of income paid as tax remains constant.

Features

1. **Flat Rate**: All taxpayers contribute the same proportion of their income.
2. **Neutral Impact on Income Levels**: The tax does not differentiate between high and low earners.

Examples

- **Corporate Tax**: Some countries impose a flat corporate tax rate for all companies, regardless of size or revenue.
- **Income Tax**: In certain countries, personal income is taxed at a uniform rate (e.g., 10% flat tax).

Economic Impacts

1. **Advantages**:

   - ◦ **Simplicity**: Reduces complexity in tax administration.
   - ◦ **Encourages Growth**: Does not penalize higher earnings, potentially promoting productivity and investment.

2. **Disadvantages**:

   - **Limited Equity**: Does not address income inequality.
   - **Lower Revenue Potential**: Compared to progressive systems, it generates less revenue from higher-income groups.

Aspect	Progressive Tax	Regressive Tax	Proportional Tax
Definition	Higher rates on higher incomes.	Higher relative burden on lower incomes.	Same rate for all income levels.
Equity	Promotes income redistribution.	Worsens income inequality.	Neutral impact on income levels.
Examples	Income tax, estate tax.	GST, excise duty.	Flat income or corporate tax.
Impact on Low Earners	Lower tax burden.	Higher relative burden.	Equal percentage of income.
Revenue Generation	High, due to higher rates for the wealthy.	Moderate, depends on consumption levels.	Moderate, uniform rates apply to all.
Administrative Complexity	Relatively high.	Simple to administer.	Simple and straightforward.

Comparison of Tax Systems

Real-World Applications
Progressive Taxation

- **United States**:

  ○ Federal income tax rates increase with income, reaching as high as 37% for the highest earners.

- **India**: The progressive tax system applies to personal income tax and corporate profits, supporting social welfare programs.

Regressive Taxation

- **Value-Added Tax (VAT) in Europe**: A uniform tax on goods and services impacts lower-income consumers more significantly.
- **Fuel Taxes in India**: Uniform excise duties on petrol and diesel represent a higher burden for low-income groups.

Proportional Taxation

- **Russia**: Implements a flat income tax rate of 13%, irrespective of income level.
- **Corporate Taxes in UAE**: A flat corporate tax is applied uniformly to businesses.

Choosing the Right System

Governments often use a combination of these systems to balance equity, simplicity, and revenue generation:

1. **Progressive Taxes** are ideal for reducing inequality and funding public services.
2. **Regressive Taxes** are useful for generating stable revenue through consumption.
3. **Proportional Taxes** simplify administration and encourage economic growth.

5.3 Fiscal Deficits

Fiscal Deficit, Revenue Deficit, and Primary Deficit

Fiscal deficits are critical indicators of a government's financial health, reflecting its ability to manage revenues and expenditures. These deficits provide insight into the sustainability of fiscal policies, the need for borrowing, and the overall economic stability. The three primary measures of fiscal imbalances are **Fiscal Deficit**, **Revenue Deficit**, and **Primary Deficit**, each highlighting different aspects of government finances.

Fiscal Deficit

Definition

The **Fiscal Deficit** is the shortfall between the government's total expenditures (including capital and revenue expenditures) and its total revenues (excluding borrowings). It represents the amount the government needs to borrow to meet its spending obligations.

Fiscal Deficit=Total Expenditure–(Revenue Receipts + Non-Revenue Receipts)

Key Features

1. **Reflects Borrowing Needs**: Indicates the extent to which the government relies on borrowings to finance its budgetary needs.
2. **Influences Economic Policies**: A high fiscal deficit often prompts tighter monetary policies to curb inflationary pressures.

Implications of Fiscal Deficit

1. **Positive Impact** (If used prudently):

   - Can stimulate economic growth by financing infrastructure, healthcare, and education.
   - Example: Government investment in highways boosts employment and GDP.

2. **Negative Impact** (If excessive):

   ◦ Increases public debt, leading to higher interest obligations.
   ◦ Crowds out private investment by raising interest rates.

Example

If a government's total expenditure is ₹50 lakh crore and total revenue is ₹40 lakh crore, the fiscal deficit is:

Fiscal Deficit= ₹50 lakh crore– ₹40 lakh crore= ₹10 lakh crore

Revenue Deficit

Definition

The **Revenue Deficit** is the shortfall between the government's revenue expenditures and its revenue receipts. It highlights the inability of the government to meet its day-to-day expenses (such as salaries, subsidies, and pensions) through its regular income (like taxes and dividends).

Formula

Revenue Deficit=Revenue Expenditure–Revenue Receipts

Key Features

1. **Focus on Current Expenditures**: Reflects how well the government manages routine operational costs without resorting to borrowing.
2. **Indicator of Structural Imbalances**: A persistent revenue deficit indicates inefficiencies in tax collection or excessive recurrent expenditures.

Implications of Revenue Deficit

1. **Fiscal Health**: A high revenue deficit reduces funds available for development projects, as borrowings are diverted to cover routine expenses.
2. **Long-Term Risk**: Reliance on borrowed funds for operational costs can lead to unsustainable debt levels.

Example

If the revenue expenditure is ₹25 lakh crore and revenue receipts are ₹20 lakh crore, the revenue deficit is:

Revenue Deficit= ₹25 lakh crore– ₹20 lakh crore= ₹5 lakh crore

Primary Deficit

Definition

The **Primary Deficit** is the fiscal deficit minus interest payments on previous borrowings. It measures the current fiscal imbalance, excluding the burden of past debts.

Formula

Formula

Primary Deficit=Fiscal Deficit–Interest Payments

Key Features

1. **Focus on Current Policies**: Highlights whether the government's current spending is sustainable without the influence of existing debt obligations.
2. **Indicator of Debt Management**: A low or zero primary deficit suggests that debt servicing does not overly burden the fiscal policy.

Implications of Primary Deficit

1. **Positive Impact**: A shrinking primary deficit indicates effective fiscal management and reduced reliance on borrowing for current needs.
2. **Negative Impact**: A widening primary deficit suggests fiscal slippage, leading to increased debt accumulation.

Example

If the fiscal deficit is ₹10 lakh crore and interest payments are ₹3 lakh crore, the primary deficit is:

Primary Deficit= ₹10 lakh crore– ₹3 lakh crore= ₹7 lakh crore

Aspect	Fiscal Deficit	Revenue Deficit	Primary Deficit
Definition	Total expenditure exceeding total revenue (excluding borrowings).	Revenue expenditure exceeding revenue receipts.	Fiscal deficit minus interest payments.
Focus	Overall fiscal health and borrowing needs.	Day-to-day operational financial imbalance.	Fiscal gap excluding past debt obligations.
Formula	Total Expenditure - Total Revenue	Revenue Expenditure - Revenue Receipts	Fiscal Deficit - Interest Payments
Implication	Indicates borrowing requirement.	Highlights inefficiency in managing current expenses.	Reflects sustainability of current policies.
Example	₹50 lakh crore - ₹40 lakh crore = ₹10 lakh crore.	₹25 lakh crore - ₹20 lakh crore = ₹5 lakh crore.	₹10 lakh crore - ₹3 lakh crore = ₹7 lakh crore.

Comparison of Deficits

Economic Implications
1. Fiscal Deficit

- **Positive**: Supports growth if borrowed funds are invested in productive assets.
- **Negative**: Excessive fiscal deficits can lead to inflation, crowding out private investment, and higher public debt.

2. Revenue Deficit

- Reduces funds available for capital expenditure, impacting long-term economic growth.
- Indicates the need for structural reforms in taxation or expenditure management.

3. Primary Deficit

- A low or negative primary deficit is a sign of fiscal discipline.
- A high primary deficit may signal the need for immediate corrective measures to prevent debt escalation.

Real-World Examples
India

- **Fiscal Deficit**: The government of India's fiscal deficit for FY 2023–24 was budgeted at **5.9% of GDP**, reflecting a balance between growth stimulation and fiscal prudence.
- **Revenue Deficit**: Persistent revenue deficits highlight the need for reforms in tax collection and subsidy rationalization.
- **Primary Deficit**: In years of high borrowing, the primary deficit often widens, necessitating tighter fiscal policies.

United States

- **Fiscal Deficit**: The U.S. often runs large fiscal deficits, particularly during economic downturns, such as the 2020 COVID-19 pandemic, when massive stimulus packages were financed through borrowing.

5.4 Budgeting Practices

Capital Budgeting

Capital budgeting is a critical financial process that involves planning, evaluating, and selecting long-term investment projects to maximize a government's or organization's economic value. It plays a central role in public and private sector budgeting practices, guiding decisions on infrastructure, equipment, and other capital-intensive projects. For governments, capital budgeting ensures efficient allocation of resources to meet developmental goals and enhance public services.

Definition of Capital Budgeting

Capital budgeting refers to the systematic process of evaluating potential long-term investments and expenditures that require substantial initial outlays and are expected to yield benefits over multiple years. It focuses on the acquisition and maintenance of fixed assets, such as buildings, roads, machinery, and other infrastructural projects.

Objectives of Capital Budgeting

1. **Efficient Resource Allocation**: Ensures that funds are directed toward projects with the highest economic and social returns.
2. **Long-Term Planning**: Aligns capital investments with strategic objectives and developmental priorities.
3. **Economic Growth**: Promotes productivity and public welfare through investments in infrastructure and technology.
4. **Debt Management**: Helps manage public debt by prioritizing investments based on feasibility and expected returns.

Key Components of Capital Budgeting

1. **Capital Expenditure**:

   - Involves spending on long-term assets that provide benefits beyond the current fiscal year.
   - Example: Construction of highways, railways, hospitals, or renewable energy plants.

2. **Capital Receipts**:

   - Funds generated to finance capital expenditures, including loans, grants, and proceeds from asset sales.
   - Example: Issuance of government bonds to fund a metro rail project.

3. **Evaluation of Investment Proposals**:

   - Analyzing the feasibility and economic impact of potential projects.

Steps in the Capital Budgeting Process

1. **Identification of Projects**:

   - Governments identify critical infrastructure needs, such as transportation, education, or healthcare facilities.
   - Example: A city government may prioritize building a new airport to support economic growth.

2. **Project Appraisal**:

   - Evaluating the costs, benefits, risks, and feasibility of each proposed project.
   - Common appraisal methods include cost-benefit analysis and economic impact studies.

3. **Budgeting and Approval**:

   - Allocating funds to selected projects based on priority, feasibility, and available resources.
   - Example: Approval of ₹10,000 crore for building national highways.

4. **Implementation and Monitoring**:

   - Ensuring that projects are executed within budget and on schedule. Regular monitoring ensures accountability and efficiency.

5. **Post-Implementation Evaluation**:

- ○ Assessing the performance and impact of completed projects to guide future investment decisions.

Techniques Used in Capital Budgeting

Governments and organizations employ various techniques to evaluate the viability of capital projects:

1. **Net Present Value (NPV)**

   - ○ Measures the present value of cash inflows minus the initial investment cost.
   - ○ A positive NPV indicates that the project will generate more value than it costs.

Formula:

$$NPV = \sum \frac{C_t}{(1+r)^t} - C_0$$

Where:

- C_t: Cash inflows in year t.

- r: Discount rate.

- C_0: Initial investment cost.

1. **Internal Rate of Return (IRR)**

- The discount rate at which the NPV of a project becomes zero.
- Higher IRR values indicate more profitable projects.

2. Benefit-Cost Ratio (BCR)

- Compares the total benefits of a project to its costs.
- A BCR greater than 1 indicates that benefits outweigh costs.

1. Payback Period

- The time it takes to recover the initial investment.
- Shorter payback periods are preferred for reducing risk.

2. Cost-Benefit Analysis

- Quantifies the economic, social, and environmental impacts of a project to assess its overall feasibility.

Importance of Capital Budgeting in Public Finance

1. Economic Development:

- Capital investments in infrastructure and public services drive economic growth and improve living standards.
- Example: Building highways reduces transportation costs and boosts trade.

2. Resource Optimization:

- Ensures that limited resources are allocated efficiently to maximize public welfare.

3. Debt Sustainability:

- By prioritizing high-return projects, governments can manage public debt effectively and avoid fiscal crises.

4. **Transparency and Accountability**:

   ○ A structured budgeting process promotes transparency in public spending and ensures accountability for resource utilization.

Challenges in Capital Budgeting

1. **Budget Constraints**:

   ○ Limited fiscal resources may force governments to delay or scale down critical projects.

2. **Risk and Uncertainty**:

   ○ Infrastructure projects are exposed to risks such as cost overruns, delays, and unforeseen economic changes.

3. **Political Influence**:

   ○ Decisions may be influenced by political considerations rather than economic feasibility.

4. **Inefficiency in Implementation**:

   ○ Delays and corruption in project execution can undermine the effectiveness of capital budgeting.

Real-World Examples
India

- **Budget Allocation for Infrastructure (2023)**:
  The Government of India allocated ₹10 lakh crore for capital expenditure in the Union Budget 2023-24, focusing on highways, railways, and renewable energy.
- **National Infrastructure Pipeline (NIP)**:
  A ₹111 lakh crore initiative to improve infrastructure across sectors by 2025, emphasizing capital budgeting.

United States

- **Infrastructure Investment and Jobs Act (2021)**:
A $1.2 trillion plan focusing on roads, bridges, public transit, and broadband to modernize U.S. infrastructure.

European Union

- **European Green Deal**:
Massive investments in renewable energy and sustainable projects to combat climate change, funded through structured capital budgeting.

5.4 Budgeting Practices

Grants-in-Aid

Grants-in-aid are financial transfers from one level of government to another or from a central authority to local or regional entities, typically aimed at funding specific projects, programs, or addressing fiscal imbalances. These grants play a crucial role in ensuring equitable resource distribution and addressing regional disparities in public services.

Definition and Purpose of Grants-in-Aid

Grants-in-aid refer to **non-repayable funds** provided by a higher authority (e.g., the central government) to lower levels of government or specific institutions for designated purposes. Unlike loans, grants do not create debt obligations but often come with conditions or guidelines for their utilization.

Purpose:

1. **Promote Fiscal Equity**: Address imbalances in revenue generation and expenditure responsibilities across different regions or levels of government.
2. **Support Developmental Programs**: Fund essential services such as education, healthcare, and infrastructure in resource-constrained areas.
3. **Encourage Policy Implementation**: Incentivize regional governments or institutions to adopt and implement national policies or reforms.
4. **Disaster Relief**: Provide immediate funds to manage natural disasters or emergencies.

Types of Grants-in-Aid

Grants-in-aid are typically classified based on their purpose and the degree of autonomy given to recipients:

1. Conditional Grants

These grants come with specific terms and conditions that the recipient must fulfill to utilize the funds.

- **Example**: A grant for constructing schools that requires the recipient government to match a portion of the funds or maintain certain educational standards.

2. Unconditional Grants

These grants provide recipients with flexibility to use the funds as needed, without predefined restrictions.

- **Example**: General-purpose grants given to states for enhancing public services.

3. Specific-Purpose Grants

Provided to finance specific programs or projects, such as rural electrification or urban development.

- **Example**: Grants for building highways under a national infrastructure initiative.

4. Matching Grants

Recipients are required to contribute a specified amount of funds to receive the grant.

- **Example**: A central grant of ₹10 crore for rural healthcare requiring state governments to contribute ₹5 crore.

Mechanism of Grants-in-Aid

1. **Identification of Need**:

   - Grants are allocated based on factors such as regional income disparities, developmental priorities, or emergency requirements.

2. **Allocation Formula**:

   - Central governments often use formulas incorporating criteria like population, income levels, and fiscal capacity to determine grant amounts.

3. **Monitoring and Evaluation:**

   - Conditional and specific-purpose grants are monitored to ensure compliance with guidelines and effective utilization of funds.

4. **Disbursement:**

   - Funds are released in installments, contingent on meeting specified milestones or submission of progress reports.

Advantages of Grants-in-Aid

1. **Promotes Regional Equity:**

   - Reduces fiscal disparities by channeling resources to underdeveloped regions or communities.
   - **Example:** Grants to tribal areas for education and healthcare.

2. **Supports Public Welfare:**

   - Enables the delivery of essential services, such as drinking water, sanitation, and health infrastructure.

3. **Encourages Policy Alignment:**

   - Incentivizes regional governments to align with national priorities, such as environmental sustainability or digital governance.

4. **Emergency Relief:**

   - Provides immediate financial support for disaster recovery, pandemics, or other emergencies.

Challenges in Grants-in-Aid

1. **Inefficiency in Utilization:**

- Mismanagement, delays, or corruption can hinder effective use of grant funds.

2. **Overdependence**:

- Regional governments may rely excessively on grants, neglecting their own revenue generation efforts.

3. **Conditionality Conflicts**:

- Stringent conditions attached to grants may limit the autonomy of local governments or institutions.

4. **Inequitable Distribution**:

- Allocation mechanisms may favor politically influential regions, exacerbating inequalities.

5. **Monitoring Challenges**:

- Ensuring accountability and compliance with grant conditions can be resource-intensive.

Real-World Examples
India

1. **Finance Commission Grants**:

- Allocated by the central government to states based on recommendations of the Finance Commission, addressing fiscal needs and promoting equity.
- **Example**: Disaster relief grants for states affected by floods or droughts.

2. **Centrally Sponsored Schemes (CSS)**:

- Specific-purpose grants to implement flagship programs like the Mahatma Gandhi National Rural Employment Guarantee Scheme

(MGNREGS) and the Pradhan Mantri Awas Yojana (PMAY).

3. **Grant for Aspirational Districts**:

   ○ Funds allocated to backward districts to improve socio-economic indicators.

United States

1. **Federal Grants**:

   ○ Education, healthcare, and infrastructure projects receive grants from the federal government to support state-level initiatives.
   ○ **Example**: Medicaid funding for state healthcare programs.

2. **Disaster Relief Grants**:

   ○ Grants from FEMA (Federal Emergency Management Agency) to states hit by hurricanes, wildfires, or floods.

Reforms for Effective Grants-in-Aid

1. **Improved Allocation Criteria**:

   ○ Develop transparent and objective mechanisms to ensure equitable distribution.

2. **Capacity Building**:

   ○ Strengthen administrative capacity at the regional level for efficient grant management.

3. **Enhanced Monitoring Systems**:

   ○ Leverage technology to track fund utilization and outcomes.

4. **Encourage Self-Reliance**:

○ Complement grants with programs to enhance local revenue-generating capacities.

SIX

GLOBAL TRADE AND BALANCE OF PAYMENTS

6.1 Trade Basics

Understanding Tariffs, Quotas, and Trade Agreements

Global trade facilitates the exchange of goods, services, and capital across international borders, fostering economic growth, specialization, and cultural exchange. However, trade policies, instruments, and agreements significantly influence the flow of goods and services. **Tariffs**, **quotas**, and **trade agreements** are key tools used by countries to manage and regulate international trade, each with distinct purposes, impacts, and implications.

Tariffs

Definition

A **tariff** is a tax imposed by a government on imported or exported goods. Tariffs are used to generate revenue, protect domestic industries, or influence trade balances.

Types of Tariffs

1. **Ad Valorem Tariff:**

- A percentage of the value of the imported goods.
- Example: A 10% tariff on imported cars worth ₹10 lakhs would be ₹1 lakh.

2. **Specific Tariff**:

- A fixed amount charged per unit of the imported goods.
- Example: ₹500 tariff per imported smartphone.

3. **Compound Tariff**:

- A combination of ad valorem and specific tariffs.
- Example: 5% of the value plus ₹200 per unit.

Purpose and Impact

1. **Revenue Generation**: Provides income for governments, especially in developing economies.
2. **Protecting Domestic Industries**: Shields local industries from foreign competition by making imports more expensive.
3. **Trade Balances**: Reduces reliance on imports, promoting local production.

Challenges:

- May lead to retaliation from trading partners, escalating trade wars.
- Increases costs for consumers and businesses dependent on imports.

Quotas

Definition

A **quota** is a quantitative restriction on the amount or value of a specific good that can be imported or exported during a specified period.

Types of Quotas

1. **Import Quotas**: Limit the volume or value of goods that can be imported.

- Example: Allowing only 1 million tons of steel imports per year.

2. **Export Quotas**: Restrict the volume of goods exported to maintain domestic supply or stabilize prices.

   - Example: A country limiting rice exports to ensure sufficient domestic availability.

3. **Tariff Rate Quotas**: A combination of tariffs and quotas where lower tariffs apply to imports within the quota limit, and higher tariffs apply to imports exceeding the limit.

Purpose and Impact

1. **Domestic Protection**: Ensures that domestic industries are not overwhelmed by foreign competition.
2. **Market Stabilization**: Helps stabilize prices of goods by controlling supply.
3. **Trade Negotiations**: Used as a bargaining tool in international trade agreements.

Challenges:

- May result in higher prices for consumers.
- Can create inefficiencies by limiting competition.

Trade Agreements

Definition

A **trade agreement** is a formal accord between two or more countries to reduce trade barriers, enhance economic cooperation, and promote the flow of goods, services, and investments.

Types of Trade Agreements

1. **Bilateral Agreements**:

   - Between two countries to promote trade and reduce barriers.

- Example: India-Sri Lanka Free Trade Agreement (ISFTA).

2. **Multilateral Agreements**:

   - Involving multiple countries, often under international organizations.
   - Example: The World Trade Organization (WTO) agreements.

3. **Regional Trade Agreements (RTAs)**:

   - Among countries within a specific region to promote economic integration.
   - Example: European Union (EU), North American Free Trade Agreement (NAFTA), now replaced by USMCA.

Purpose and Impact

1. **Reduce Trade Barriers**: Eliminates tariffs, quotas, and other restrictions to promote free trade.
2. **Enhance Cooperation**: Strengthens economic and political ties between member countries.
3. **Economic Growth**: Expands market access, boosts exports, and attracts foreign investments.

Challenges:

- Disputes over unfair practices, such as subsidies or dumping.
- Potential loss of sovereignty in trade policy decisions.
- Trade agreements may benefit certain sectors while disadvantaging others

Aspect	Tariffs	Quotas	Trade Agreements
Definition	Taxes on imports or exports.	Limits on the quantity of trade.	Formal pacts to reduce trade barriers.
Purpose	Revenue generation, protection.	Market control, domestic protection.	Promoting free trade and cooperation.
Impact on Trade	Increases cost of imports.	Limits volume of trade.	Encourages trade by reducing barriers.
Flexibility	Can be adjusted dynamically.	Fixed for specific periods.	Long-term commitment.
Challenges	Retaliation, higher consumer costs.	Price hikes, inefficiencies.	Complex negotiations, uneven benefits.

Comparison: Tariffs, Quotas, and Trade Agreements

Real-World Examples
India

1. **Tariffs**:

   - India imposes tariffs on imported electronics to promote domestic manufacturing under the "Make in India" initiative.

2. **Quotas**:

   - Quotas on sugar exports to ensure sufficient domestic availability during peak demand periods.

3. **Trade Agreements**:

   - Comprehensive Economic Partnership Agreement (CEPA) with Japan to enhance bilateral trade.

United States

1. **Tariffs**:

- Tariffs on steel and aluminum imports during the 2018 trade war with China.

2. **Quotas**:

   - Import quotas on dairy products under agricultural policies.

3. **Trade Agreements**:

   - United States-Mexico-Canada Agreement (USMCA) replaced NAFTA to modernize trade relationships.

European Union

- The EU eliminates internal tariffs and quotas among member states, creating a seamless single market while negotiating multilateral trade agreements globally.

6.2 Balance of Payments (BoP)

Current Account and Capital Account

The **Balance of Payments (BoP)** is a comprehensive record of a country's economic transactions with the rest of the world over a specific period. It reflects the inflow and outflow of money for trade, investment, and financial transfers, ensuring that a nation's international financial position is accurately represented. The BoP is divided into two primary components: the **Current Account** and the **Capital Account**, each detailing specific types of transactions.

Balance of Payments: Overview

The BoP tracks two key aspects:

1. **Surplus or Deficit**: Indicates whether a country earns more from foreign transactions than it spends or vice versa.
2. **Net Zero Balance**: In theory, the BoP always balances, as inflows (credits) equal outflows (debits) when all components are considered.

Current Account

Definition

The **Current Account** records the flow of goods, services, income, and transfers between a country and the rest of the world. It reflects a country's short-term economic activities.

Components of the Current Account

1. **Trade in Goods (Merchandise Trade)**:

   - Exports and imports of physical goods such as machinery, food, and raw materials.
   - A **trade surplus** occurs when exports exceed imports, while a **trade deficit** occurs when imports surpass exports.

2. **Trade in Services**:

   - Transactions involving services such as tourism, IT services, banking, and consulting.

- Example: India earns significant revenue from IT service exports to the US.

3. **Income Receipts and Payments**:

   - Earnings from investments abroad (e.g., dividends, interest, wages) and payments to foreign investors.
   - Example: Remittances sent by expatriates to their home country.

4. **Current Transfers**:

   - One-way transfers of money or goods, including remittances, foreign aid, and grants.
   - Example: Financial assistance received by a developing country from international organizations.

Formula

Current Account Balance=(Exports of Goods and Services+Income Receipts+Current Transfers)–(Imports of Goods and Services+Income Payments)

Capital Account

Definition

The **Capital Account** records financial transactions that involve the transfer of ownership of assets between a country and the rest of the world. It reflects long-term investments and financial flows.

Components of the Capital Account

1. **Foreign Direct Investment (FDI)**:

   - Investments made by foreign entities in domestic businesses, such as acquiring equity stakes or establishing operations.
   - Example: A Japanese company investing in manufacturing plants in India.

2. **Portfolio Investments**:

   - Investments in stocks, bonds, and other financial assets, typically for short-term gains.

- ◦ Example: Foreign investors purchasing shares in a domestic stock market.

3. **Loans and Borrowings**:

    - ◦ Financial inflows and outflows related to international borrowing or lending by governments, businesses, and financial institutions.
    - ◦ Example: A country borrowing funds from the International Monetary Fund (IMF).

4. **Foreign Exchange Reserves**:

    - ◦ Changes in the central bank's foreign currency holdings to manage currency stability.

Formula

Capital Account Balance=Capital Inflows–Capital Outflows

Aspect	Current Account	Capital Account
Definition	Tracks trade in goods, services, and transfers.	Tracks investments, loans, and asset ownership changes.
Nature	Focuses on short-term economic activities.	Focuses on long-term financial transactions.
Components	Exports, imports, income, and transfers.	FDI, portfolio investments, and loans.
Impact on Economy	Reflects production, consumption, and trade.	Reflects investment and financial stability.
Examples	Export of software services, remittances.	Foreign investments, international loans.

Comparison: Current Account vs. Capital Account

Economic Implications of BoP Components
Current Account Surplus or Deficit

1. **Surplus**:

    - ◦ Indicates strong export performance and robust income from abroad.

- Example: China often runs a current account surplus due to high merchandise exports.

2. **Deficit:**

   - Reflects reliance on foreign goods, services, or income.
   - Can signal economic imbalances if persistent or excessive.

Capital Account Surplus or Deficit

1. **Surplus:**

   - Suggests high foreign investments or borrowing, which can drive economic growth.
   - Example: India attracts significant FDI in technology and infrastructure.

2. **Deficit:**

   - Reflects outflow of investments or repayment of loans, potentially straining foreign reserves.

Real-World Examples
India

1. **Current Account:**

   - India often has a **current account deficit** due to high imports of crude oil and gold, despite strong service exports and remittances.

2. **Capital Account:**

   - Capital inflows, including FDI in sectors like technology and telecommunications, help offset the current account deficit.

United States

1. **Current Account:**

- The US typically runs a current account deficit due to high imports of consumer goods and reliance on foreign energy sources.

2. **Capital Account:**

- Surpluses in the capital account result from foreign investments in US assets, including treasury bonds and equities.

China

1. **Current Account:**

- Persistent surpluses driven by strong exports, particularly in manufacturing.

2. **Capital Account:**

- Capital controls restrict significant outflows, maintaining stability in foreign exchange reserves.

Challenges in Managing BoP

1. **Sustainability of Deficits:**

- Persistent current account deficits can lead to excessive borrowing and currency depreciation.

2. **Capital Flow Volatility:**

- Sudden capital outflows can destabilize financial markets and foreign exchange reserves.

3. **Global Imbalances:**

- Trade imbalances between major economies (e.g., US-China trade deficit) can lead to geopolitical tensions.

4. **Dependence on Remittances:**

- Over-reliance on income transfers may signal structural weaknesses in domestic production.

6.3 Exchange Rate Mechanisms

Fixed vs. Floating Exchange Rates

The **exchange rate** is the price of one currency in terms of another and plays a pivotal role in international trade, investment, and monetary stability. Exchange rate mechanisms determine how a country manages the value of its currency relative to others. Two primary exchange rate systems are **fixed exchange rates** and **floating exchange rates**, each with distinct characteristics, advantages, and challenges.

Fixed Exchange Rate System

Definition

In a **fixed exchange rate system**, the value of a country's currency is pegged or tied to another currency (usually a stable and widely used currency like the US Dollar) or a basket of currencies. The central bank intervenes in the foreign exchange market to maintain the currency at the fixed rate.

How It Works

1. The central bank maintains reserves of foreign currencies to buy or sell its own currency as needed.
2. The exchange rate is kept constant, regardless of market demand or supply.

Examples

- **Hong Kong Dollar (HKD)**: Pegged to the US Dollar.
- **Bretton Woods System**: Post-World War II, currencies were pegged to the US Dollar, which was convertible to gold.

Advantages of Fixed Exchange Rates

1. **Stability**:

- Provides certainty in international trade and investment by eliminating exchange rate fluctuations.

2. **Inflation Control**:

- Pegging to a stable currency can help control domestic inflation.

3. **Encourages Foreign Investment**:

- Stability in exchange rates reduces risk for foreign investors.

4. **Discipline in Economic Policy**:

- Governments are forced to maintain prudent fiscal and monetary policies to support the peg.

Challenges of Fixed Exchange Rates

1. **High Reserve Requirements**:

- Central banks must maintain large reserves of foreign currency to defend the peg.

2. **Lack of Flexibility**:

- Cannot adjust to economic shocks, such as trade imbalances or external crises.

3. **Risk of Speculative Attacks**:

- Speculators may challenge the central bank's ability to maintain the peg, causing financial instability.

4. **Economic Misalignment**:

- A fixed rate may not reflect the true value of the currency, leading to competitiveness issues.

Floating Exchange Rate System

Definition

In a **floating exchange rate system**, the value of a country's currency is determined by market forces, such as demand and supply in the foreign exchange market. There is no direct intervention by the central bank to fix the exchange rate.

How It Works

1. **Appreciation**: If demand for a currency increases, its value rises (e.g., due to higher exports or foreign investments).
2. **Depreciation**: If demand decreases, the currency's value falls.

Examples

- **US Dollar (USD)**: Floats freely in international markets.
- **Euro (EUR)**: Managed by the European Central Bank with minimal intervention.

Advantages of Floating Exchange Rates

1. **Automatic Adjustment**:

   - The exchange rate adjusts automatically to economic conditions, correcting trade imbalances over time.

2. **Monetary Policy Independence**:

   - Central banks can focus on domestic objectives, such as controlling inflation or stimulating growth.

3. **No Reserve Requirement**:

   - No need for large foreign currency reserves to maintain a peg.

4. **Market-Driven**:

- Reflects the true value of the currency based on market demand and supply.

Challenges of Floating Exchange Rates

1. **Volatility:**

   - Exchange rates can fluctuate widely, creating uncertainty for traders and investors.

2. **Inflation Risk:**

   - Depreciation of the currency can lead to imported inflation.

3. **Speculative Attacks:**

   - While less vulnerable than fixed systems, excessive speculation can destabilize markets.

4. **Impact on Trade:**

   - Currency fluctuations can affect export competitiveness and import costs.

Aspect	Fixed Exchange Rate	Floating Exchange Rate
Determination	Set by the central bank or government.	Determined by market demand and supply.
Stability	Provides stability in trade and investment.	Subject to market fluctuations.
Flexibility	Inflexible, cannot adjust to shocks.	Flexible, adjusts to economic conditions.
Reserve Requirements	Requires large foreign currency reserves.	No need for reserves.
Policy Independence	Limits monetary policy autonomy.	Allows independent monetary policies.
Examples	Hong Kong Dollar, Bretton Woods.	US Dollar, Euro, Japanese Yen.

Comparison: Fixed vs. Floating Exchange Rates

Real-World Examples
Fixed Exchange Rate

- **China**:

  - The Chinese Yuan was historically pegged to the US Dollar to stabilize trade. In recent years, it has shifted to a managed float system.

- **Gulf Cooperation Council (GCC)**:

  - Countries like Saudi Arabia peg their currencies to the US Dollar to stabilize oil revenues.

Floating Exchange Rate

- **United States**:

  - The US Dollar operates on a freely floating exchange rate, influenced by global trade and investment flows.

- **Eurozone**:

  - The Euro is largely market-determined, with occasional interventions by the European Central Bank.

Hybrid Systems: Managed Float
Some countries adopt a hybrid system known as a **managed float**, where the exchange rate is primarily market-driven, but the central bank intervenes occasionally to stabilize the currency.

- **Example**: India's exchange rate is managed by the Reserve Bank of India (RBI) to reduce excessive volatility while allowing market forces to play a role.

Economic Implications

1. **Fixed Exchange Rate**:

- Suitable for economies with limited foreign exchange fluctuations and stable trade flows.

2. **Floating Exchange Rate**:

- Ideal for large, open economies with diverse trade and investment networks.

3. **Global Competitiveness**:

- A floating system allows countries to remain competitive by adjusting currency values, whereas a fixed system can create artificial price disparities.

6.3 Exchange Rate Mechanisms

Devaluation vs. Depreciation

Both **devaluation** and **depreciation** refer to a decline in the value of a country's currency relative to foreign currencies. However, the two terms differ significantly in their causes, implementation, and economic implications. Understanding these concepts is essential for grasping how exchange rates impact international trade, investment, and economic policy.

Devaluation

Definition

Devaluation occurs when a government or central bank **deliberately reduces the value of its currency** in a fixed exchange rate system. The government sets a new, lower value for the currency relative to a foreign currency or a basket of currencies.

How It Happens

- Devaluation is a **policy decision** taken to address specific economic goals, such as improving export competitiveness or correcting trade imbalances.
- It is often announced as part of broader economic reforms.

Example

- **India (1966):**

  ○ The Indian Rupee was devalued by 57% against the US Dollar, reducing the exchange rate from ₹4.76/USD to ₹7.50/USD, to address a severe balance of payments crisis.

Depreciation

Definition

Depreciation refers to a **natural decline in the value of a currency** due to market forces in a floating exchange rate system. Unlike devaluation, it is not caused by government intervention.

How It Happens

- Depreciation occurs when demand for a currency decreases or its supply increases in the foreign exchange market.
- Factors influencing depreciation include trade deficits, inflation, political instability, or lower interest rates compared to other countries.

Example

- **Indian Rupee (2022)**:

  - The Rupee depreciated from ₹74/USD to over ₹80/USD due to factors such as rising crude oil prices and global economic uncertainty.

Aspect	Devaluation	Depreciation
Definition	Deliberate reduction in currency value by the government.	Natural decline in currency value due to market forces.
System	Occurs in a fixed exchange rate system.	Occurs in a floating exchange rate system.
Cause	Policy decision by the central bank or government.	Driven by market factors such as supply and demand.
Control	Controlled and intentional.	Uncontrolled and market-driven.
Purpose	Improve trade competitiveness, correct trade imbalances.	Reflects economic conditions or investor sentiment.
Example	India's devaluation in 1966.	Rupee depreciation in 2022.

Comparison: Devaluation vs. Depreciation

Impacts of Devaluation and Depreciation
1. On Exports and Imports

- **Devaluation**:

  - Makes exports cheaper and more competitive in global markets.
  - Imports become costlier, discouraging excessive reliance on foreign goods.
  - Example: Devaluation of the Chinese Yuan has historically boosted China's export-driven economy.

- **Depreciation**:

  - Similar effects as devaluation but often accompanied by market volatility, impacting export-import dynamics unpredictably.

2. On Inflation

- Both devaluation and depreciation can lead to **imported inflation**, as the cost of foreign goods and services rises.
- Example: Depreciation of the Indian Rupee increases the cost of imported crude oil, contributing to domestic fuel price hikes.

3. On Foreign Debt

- A decline in currency value increases the burden of foreign debt, as repayments in foreign currency become more expensive.
- Example: Developing countries with significant dollar-denominated debt often face fiscal pressure during currency depreciation.

4. On Investor Confidence

- **Devaluation**:

  - May erode investor confidence if perceived as a sign of economic weakness or poor policy management.
  - Example: The 1997 Asian Financial Crisis saw mass devaluations that spooked investors.

- **Depreciation**:

  - Sharp or prolonged depreciation can trigger capital outflows and reduce foreign direct investment (FDI).

Advantages of Devaluation and Depreciation
Devaluation

1. **Boosts Exports**: Makes domestic goods more attractive to foreign buyers.

2. **Improves Trade Balance**: Reduces trade deficits by curbing imports and encouraging exports.
3. **Stimulates Domestic Production**: Higher import costs encourage consumption of locally produced goods.

Depreciation

1. **Natural Adjustment**: Reflects real economic conditions, aligning currency value with market fundamentals.
2. **Attracts Foreign Investment**: Depreciation may lower the cost of investing in domestic assets for foreign investors.
3. **Encourages Tourism**: A weaker currency makes the country a cheaper destination for foreign tourists.

Challenges of Devaluation and Depreciation
Devaluation

1. **Imported Inflation**: Costlier imports can increase inflation, reducing purchasing power.
2. **Erosion of Savings**: Currency devaluation may devalue foreign currency-denominated savings.
3. **Political Backlash**: Public discontent and loss of confidence in the government's economic policies.

Depreciation

1. **Market Volatility**: Currency depreciation can create uncertainty, affecting trade and investment decisions.
2. **Capital Outflows**: Depreciation may trigger panic among investors, leading to a flight of capital.
3. **Higher Debt Servicing Costs**: Developing economies with significant foreign debt may struggle to manage repayments.

Real-World Examples
Devaluation

- **India (1991)**:

- ○ The Indian Rupee was devalued as part of economic reforms during a severe balance of payments crisis. This action, combined with structural reforms, laid the foundation for economic liberalization.

Depreciation

- **Japanese Yen (2022):**

  - ○ The Yen depreciated significantly against the US Dollar due to diverging monetary policies, with Japan maintaining low interest rates while the US Federal Reserve raised rates.

6.4 Role of Foreign Exchange Reserves

Importance in Stabilizing Economies

Foreign exchange reserves are assets held by a country's central bank in foreign currencies, gold, and other international financial instruments. These reserves play a critical role in maintaining economic stability, supporting the national currency, and ensuring a buffer against external economic shocks. As global trade and financial integration expand, foreign exchange reserves have become indispensable for both developed and developing economies.

What Are Foreign Exchange Reserves?

Foreign exchange reserves consist of:

1. **Foreign Currencies**: Holdings of major global currencies like the US Dollar, Euro, Japanese Yen, and Pound Sterling.
2. **Gold**: Often considered a hedge against inflation and currency devaluation.
3. **Special Drawing Rights (SDRs)**: Allocated by the International Monetary Fund (IMF) as a supplementary international reserve asset.
4. **IMF Reserve Position**: The country's quota contributions to the IMF, which can be accessed during financial crises.

Importance in Stabilizing Economies

1. Exchange Rate Stability

Foreign exchange reserves enable central banks to intervene in the foreign exchange market to stabilize the national currency.

- **Intervention**: Reserves are used to buy or sell the domestic currency to counter excessive volatility or speculative attacks.
- **Example**: The Reserve Bank of India (RBI) uses its reserves to stabilize the Rupee during sharp depreciations.

2. Buffer Against External Shocks

Reserves act as a safeguard against external economic shocks, such as:

- **Global Financial Crises**: Reserves provide liquidity to manage sudden capital outflows.
- **Commodity Price Volatility**: Countries reliant on commodity exports can use reserves to mitigate revenue shortfalls during price drops.

3. Import Cover

Adequate reserves ensure that a country can meet its import obligations even during economic disruptions.

- **Example**: Import cover is measured by how many months' worth of imports can be financed by reserves. The IMF recommends a minimum of 3–6 months.

4. Debt Servicing

Countries with significant external debt rely on reserves to meet repayment obligations.

- **Importance**: Reserves reduce the risk of default and enhance creditworthiness, lowering borrowing costs.

5. Enhancing Investor Confidence

A robust reserve position signals economic stability, attracting foreign direct investment (FDI) and portfolio investment.

- **Example**: China's large reserves boost confidence in its ability to manage trade and financial imbalances.

6. Monetary Policy Support

Reserves provide flexibility in implementing monetary policies:

- **Inflation Control**: Reserves can be used to stabilize the currency, reducing imported inflation.
- **Liquidity Management**: Central banks can use reserves to inject or absorb liquidity in the domestic economy.

7. Trade Facilitation

Foreign exchange reserves ensure smooth international trade by providing the liquidity needed for cross-border transactions.

- **Example**: Exporters and importers rely on stable currency markets to minimize transaction risks.

Real-World Examples
India

- **Rising Reserves (2022)**:
India's foreign exchange reserves peaked at over $600 billion, providing a cushion against global uncertainties, such as rising crude oil prices and capital outflows.
- **Rupee Stabilization**:
The Reserve Bank of India frequently intervenes in currency markets to stabilize the Rupee during periods of high volatility.

China

- **Largest Reserves Globally**:
China holds over $3 trillion in reserves, giving it significant leverage in global trade and monetary policy.
- **Trade Buffer**:
The reserves enable China to manage its trade surplus and maintain stability during global trade tensions.

Brazil (1999)

- During the currency crisis, Brazil depleted its reserves to defend the Real against speculative attacks, eventually leading to a currency float.

Challenges in Managing Foreign Exchange Reserves

1. **Opportunity Costs**:

   - Holding large reserves involves costs, as these funds could be invested in infrastructure or development projects.

2. **Valuation Risks**:

- Reserves denominated in foreign currencies are subject to fluctuations in exchange rates.

3. **Inflationary Pressures**:

   - Excessive accumulation of reserves may lead to liquidity surpluses, fueling inflation.

4. **Geopolitical Risks**:

   - Sanctions or global tensions can restrict access to reserves held in foreign institutions.

Optimal Reserve Management

1. **Diversification**:

   - Reserves should be diversified across currencies, gold, and other assets to minimize risks.

2. **Adequate Import Cover**:

   - Maintaining sufficient reserves to cover at least 3–6 months of imports ensures economic stability.

3. **Strategic Interventions**:

   - Central banks should intervene selectively to prevent overuse of reserves while maintaining market confidence.

4. **Global Coordination**:

   - Collaboration with international organizations like the IMF can enhance reserve management and mitigate crises.

SEVEN

INTERNATIONAL INSTITUTIONS AND FINANCE

7.1 Bretton Woods System

Evolution and Impact

The **Bretton Woods System** was a landmark framework established in 1944 to govern international monetary relations after World War II. Designed to ensure global economic stability and prevent the financial turmoil of the interwar period, the system introduced mechanisms for exchange rate stability and economic cooperation. Its evolution and impact profoundly shaped the post-war global economy, leaving a legacy that continues to influence international finance.

Evolution of the Bretton Woods System
Background

1. **Pre-War Financial Instability:**

   - The interwar period (1918–1939) was marked by economic disruptions, hyperinflation, and competitive devaluations that destabilized global trade.
   - The **Great Depression (1929–1939)** exacerbated these issues, leading to protectionist policies like the **Smoot-Hawley Tariff Act** in the US,

which further crippled global trade.

2. **Need for a Stable Monetary Framework**:

   - Policymakers recognized the necessity of a system to promote stable exchange rates, prevent economic conflicts, and encourage global cooperation.

Bretton Woods Conference (1944)

- Delegates from **44 Allied nations** convened at the Mount Washington Hotel in Bretton Woods, New Hampshire, to design a post-war international monetary system.
- Key architects included **John Maynard Keynes** (UK) and **Harry Dexter White** (US).

Objectives:

1. Establish a framework for stable exchange rates.
2. Promote international trade and economic growth.
3. Create institutions to manage global monetary issues.

Key Features of the Bretton Woods System

1. **Fixed Exchange Rates**:

   - Member countries pegged their currencies to the US Dollar, which was convertible to gold at a fixed rate of **$35 per ounce**.
   - The US Dollar became the central reserve currency, anchoring the system.

2. **Role of Gold**:

   - Gold served as the ultimate standard, ensuring confidence in the system.

3. **Adjustable Peg Mechanism**:

- Exchange rates could be adjusted if a country faced persistent economic imbalances, subject to approval by the International Monetary Fund (IMF).

4. **Creation of International Institutions**:

- **International Monetary Fund (IMF)**: Established to provide short-term financial assistance and oversee exchange rate policies.
- **International Bank for Reconstruction and Development (IBRD)** (later part of the World Bank Group): Focused on post-war reconstruction and development financing.

5. **Capital Controls**:

- Restrictions on capital flows were implemented to prevent speculative attacks on currencies.

Impact of the Bretton Woods System
Positive Impacts

1. **Global Economic Stability**:

- The fixed exchange rate system reduced volatility in international trade and investment.
- Encouraged a period of unprecedented global economic growth and reconstruction, particularly in Europe and Japan.

2. **Promotion of Trade and Investment**:

- Stable exchange rates facilitated cross-border trade and foreign direct investment, driving economic globalization.

3. **Foundation of International Institutions**:

- The IMF and World Bank became pillars of global financial governance, supporting economic stability and development.

4. **US Dollar Dominance**:

- The system cemented the US Dollar's role as the world's primary reserve currency, giving the US significant influence over global finance.

5. **Post-War Reconstruction**:

   - The system enabled war-torn economies to rebuild through financial assistance and policy coordination.

Challenges and Shortcomings

1. **Dependence on the US Dollar**:

   - The system's reliance on the US Dollar as the global reserve currency made it vulnerable to US economic policies.
   - As the US printed more dollars to finance domestic programs and the Vietnam War, the dollar's credibility weakened.

2. **Imbalances in Gold Reserves**:

   - By the 1960s, the US gold reserves were insufficient to back the growing volume of dollars in circulation, leading to doubts about dollar convertibility.

3. **Limited Flexibility**:

   - Fixed exchange rates restricted countries' ability to adjust to changing economic conditions.

4. **Speculative Pressures**:

   - Persistent trade deficits and capital imbalances created pressures on fixed exchange rates, destabilizing the system.

Collapse of the Bretton Woods System

1. **US Dollar Crisis**:

- By the late 1960s, the US faced mounting trade deficits, inflation, and dwindling gold reserves.
- Countries like France began demanding gold in exchange for dollars, depleting US gold reserves.

2. **Nixon Shock (1971)**:

- US President **Richard Nixon** announced the suspension of dollar convertibility into gold, effectively ending the gold standard.

3. **Transition to Floating Rates**:

- In 1973, the system formally collapsed, and most major currencies shifted to a **floating exchange rate regime**, where market forces determined currency values.

Legacy of the Bretton Woods System

1. **Enduring Institutions**:

- The IMF and World Bank continue to play pivotal roles in global economic governance, addressing financial crises and promoting development.

2. **Dollar as a Global Reserve Currency**:

- Despite the system's collapse, the US Dollar remains the dominant currency in global trade and finance.

3. **Lessons for Monetary Policy**:

- Highlighted the need for flexibility in exchange rate systems to adapt to changing economic conditions.

4. **Economic Integration**:

- Set the stage for subsequent agreements, such as the General Agreement on Tariffs and Trade (GATT), which evolved into the **World**

Trade Organization (WTO).

Real-World Examples of Impact

1. **European Reconstruction**:

   - The Marshall Plan, supported by the Bretton Woods framework, enabled Europe to recover rapidly from World War II.

2. **Japan's Growth**:

   - Stable exchange rates under Bretton Woods facilitated Japan's export-led economic boom in the 1950s and 1960s.

3. **Globalization Foundations**:

   - The system laid the groundwork for increased trade liberalization and economic interdependence.

7.2 World Trade Organization (WTO)

Functions and Relevance

The **World Trade Organization (WTO)** is a global institution that oversees the rules of international trade, aiming to promote free and fair trade among nations. Established in 1995 as a successor to the General Agreement on Tariffs and Trade (GATT), the WTO plays a pivotal role in regulating trade policies, resolving disputes, and fostering economic cooperation. Its functions and relevance have been instrumental in shaping the modern global trade environment.

Functions of the WTO

1. Administering Trade Agreements

The WTO is responsible for implementing and monitoring a wide range of trade agreements negotiated by its members. These agreements cover various aspects of trade, such as goods, services, and intellectual property.

- **Example**: The Agreement on Agriculture (AoA) promotes fair trade in agricultural products by reducing subsidies and barriers.

2. Forum for Trade Negotiations

The WTO provides a platform for member countries to negotiate trade agreements and resolve trade issues.

- **Example**: The **Doha Development Round**, initiated in 2001, aims to address trade barriers and enhance market access for developing nations.

3. Dispute Settlement Mechanism (DSM)

The WTO offers a structured process for resolving trade disputes between member countries.

- **Steps in Dispute Settlement**:

1. Consultation.
2. Panel formation and investigation.
3. Appellate review (if required).

4. Implementation of rulings.

- **Example**: The WTO resolved the dispute between the US and the EU over subsidies provided to Boeing and Airbus.

4. Monitoring Trade Policies

Through its **Trade Policy Review Mechanism (TPRM)**, the WTO regularly reviews the trade policies and practices of its member nations. This ensures transparency and compliance with international trade rules.

- **Example**: WTO reviews India's trade policies to assess compliance with its trade commitments.

5. Capacity Building and Technical Assistance

The WTO provides training and support to developing and least-developed countries (LDCs) to help them build trade-related capacities and integrate into the global trading system.

- **Example**: Technical assistance programs for African nations to enhance export competitiveness.

6. Promoting Global Trade Liberalization

The WTO advocates for reducing trade barriers such as tariffs, quotas, and subsidies to ensure smoother and more inclusive trade flows.

- **Example**: WTO agreements have reduced average global tariffs significantly since 1995.

7. Ensuring Trade as a Tool for Development

The WTO emphasizes the role of trade in fostering economic growth and reducing poverty, particularly in developing nations.

Relevance of the WTO

1. Ensuring Predictability and Stability in Trade

The WTO's rules-based system provides predictability, reducing the uncertainty and risks associated with international trade.

- **Impact**: Businesses and investors are more confident about entering global markets.

2. Addressing Protectionism

The WTO works to curb protectionist policies, ensuring that nations adhere to the principles of non-discrimination and fair competition.

- **Example**: The **Most-Favored Nation (MFN)** principle ensures that member countries treat each other equally in trade relations.

3. Dispute Resolution as a Neutral Arbiter

The WTO's dispute settlement mechanism ensures that trade conflicts are resolved impartially, preventing escalation into trade wars.

4. Supporting Developing Nations

By providing technical assistance and advocating for special and differential treatment (S&DT), the WTO helps developing countries enhance their trade capacities and benefit from global trade.

- **Example**: The Trade Facilitation Agreement (TFA) simplifies customs procedures, benefiting developing nations.

5. Promoting Sustainable Development

The WTO aligns its trade policies with sustainable development goals (SDGs), encouraging trade practices that balance economic growth, environmental protection, and social equity.

- **Example**: Negotiations on eliminating fisheries subsidies aim to prevent overfishing and protect marine ecosystems.

6. Facilitating Economic Recovery

During global crises such as the COVID-19 pandemic, the WTO has played a role in ensuring the smooth flow of essential goods, such as medical supplies and vaccines.

Challenges Facing the WTO

1. Trade Disputes and Ineffectiveness

- **Dispute Settlement Challenges**: The Appellate Body has been hampered by disagreements among major members, particularly the US.

2. Rise of Protectionism

- Increasing trade restrictions and unilateral measures by major economies challenge the WTO's principles of free trade.

3. Developing Country Concerns

- Many developing nations feel that WTO policies disproportionately favor developed countries, limiting their growth potential.

4. Inadequate Progress on Reforms

- The slow pace of negotiations, such as the Doha Round, raises concerns about the WTO's effectiveness in addressing modern trade issues like e-commerce and digital trade.

5. Climate and Sustainability Issues

- The WTO needs to integrate climate change considerations more effectively into its trade policies.

Real-World Examples of WTO's Impact
Global Trade Growth

- Since its inception in 1995, the WTO has contributed to a fourfold increase in world trade, fostering economic growth and poverty reduction.

Landmark Disputes

- **Boeing-Airbus Dispute**: WTO rulings helped mitigate trade tensions between the US and EU over aircraft subsidies.
- **US-China Tariff Wars**: The WTO provides a framework for addressing tariff-related disputes between these major economies.

Agricultural Reforms

- The WTO's Agreement on Agriculture (AoA) has encouraged reductions in trade-distorting subsidies and improved access to global agricultural markets.

7.3 International Monetary Fund (IMF)

Role in Stabilizing Economies

The **International Monetary Fund (IMF)** is a global financial institution established in 1944 at the Bretton Woods Conference to promote international monetary cooperation, ensure financial stability, and facilitate economic growth. With 190 member countries, the IMF plays a critical role in stabilizing economies during financial crises, addressing balance-of-payments challenges, and fostering sustainable development through financial assistance and policy guidance.

Role of the IMF in Stabilizing Economies

1. Providing Financial Assistance

The IMF offers financial support to countries facing severe economic crises, such as balance-of-payments deficits or currency instability. This assistance helps countries stabilize their economies and restore confidence in their financial systems.

- **Mechanisms of Financial Support:**

  - **Stand-By Arrangements (SBA):** Short-term financial support for addressing immediate economic crises.
  - **Extended Fund Facility (EFF):** Longer-term financial assistance to address structural imbalances.
  - **Rapid Financing Instrument (RFI):** Emergency financial support for countries facing unexpected shocks, such as natural disasters or pandemics.

- **Example:**

  - During the 2008 global financial crisis, the IMF provided over $250 billion in financial assistance to stabilize economies, including support for Greece, Ireland, and Portugal.

2. Addressing Balance-of-Payments Issues

The IMF assists countries in managing balance-of-payments deficits, ensuring they can meet international payment obligations without resorting to disruptive economic measures. This support prevents crises that could destabilize global trade and financial markets.

- **Example**:

  - In 1991, India faced a severe balance-of-payments crisis. The IMF provided a $2.2 billion loan, enabling India to stabilize its economy and implement economic reforms.

3. Exchange Rate Stability

The IMF monitors global exchange rate systems to prevent excessive volatility or misalignments that could disrupt international trade and investment. By offering policy recommendations and financial support, the IMF helps countries maintain stable exchange rates.

- **Example**:

  - The IMF assisted Argentina in 2018 with a $57 billion loan to stabilize its currency and address exchange rate fluctuations.

4. Technical Assistance and Capacity Development

The IMF provides technical assistance to strengthen the institutional and policy frameworks of member countries. This support is particularly crucial for developing and emerging economies.

- **Areas of Technical Assistance**:

  - **Public Finance Management**: Enhancing budgetary processes and fiscal transparency.
  - **Monetary Policy**: Developing frameworks for inflation targeting and central bank operations.
  - **Financial Sector Oversight**: Strengthening banking regulations and supervision.

- **Example**:

  - The IMF provided technical assistance to African nations to improve tax administration and public debt management.

5. Economic Surveillance and Policy Guidance

Through its **Article IV Consultations**, the IMF conducts regular assessments of member countries' economic policies and performance. This surveillance helps identify potential risks and recommend corrective actions to ensure economic stability.

- **Example**:

  - The IMF's surveillance reports often highlight risks like rising inflation, unsustainable debt levels, or structural weaknesses in member economies.

6. Crisis Prevention and Early Warning

The IMF plays a proactive role in preventing financial crises by monitoring global economic trends and providing early warnings of potential risks. Its research and analysis guide policymakers in adopting measures to mitigate vulnerabilities.

- **Example**:

  - The IMF's early warnings during the Asian Financial Crisis (1997) emphasized the risks of excessive short-term capital flows and weak financial regulations.

7. Supporting Global Economic Recovery

The IMF mobilizes resources to support global economic recovery during major crises, such as pandemics or financial meltdowns. Its coordinated efforts help stabilize economies, restore investor confidence, and promote inclusive growth.

- **Example**:

  - During the COVID-19 pandemic, the IMF deployed $650 billion in **Special Drawing Rights (SDRs)** to provide liquidity to member countries, particularly those with limited fiscal space.

Impact of the IMF on Global Economic Stability
Positive Contributions

1. **Economic Stabilization**:

   - Timely financial support and policy advice prevent deeper economic crises and restore stability.

2. **Global Coordination**:

   - The IMF facilitates international cooperation to address global challenges, such as climate change and financial inequality.

3. **Support for Developing Economies**:

   - Provides essential resources and expertise to low-income countries, enabling them to achieve sustainable development.

4. **Research and Data Analysis**:

   - The IMF produces authoritative economic forecasts and policy analyses, guiding decision-making at national and global levels.

Criticisms and Challenges

1. **Conditionality of Loans**:

   - IMF assistance often comes with stringent conditions, such as austerity measures, which can exacerbate economic hardships for vulnerable populations.
   - **Example**: Greece faced significant public backlash during its IMF-supported bailout for implementing austerity measures.

2. **Influence of Major Economies**:

   - The governance structure of the IMF is criticized for favoring wealthy nations, limiting the influence of developing countries.

3. **Overemphasis on Fiscal Austerity**:

- Critics argue that the IMF's focus on fiscal discipline can stifle economic recovery and social welfare spending.

4. **Limited Success in Crisis Prevention**:

   - Despite its surveillance role, the IMF has faced criticism for failing to predict or prevent major crises, such as the 2008 financial crisis.

Real-World Examples of IMF's Role
Asian Financial Crisis (1997)

- The IMF provided over $110 billion in financial assistance to countries like Thailand, Indonesia, and South Korea, stabilizing their economies through structural reforms and financial oversight.

Argentina (2018)

- To combat a severe economic crisis, the IMF approved a $57 billion loan—the largest in its history—supporting currency stabilization and fiscal adjustments.

India (1991)

- The IMF's assistance during India's balance-of-payments crisis facilitated economic liberalization, leading to sustained growth in subsequent decades.

COVID-19 Pandemic (2020-2021)

- The IMF's allocation of SDRs provided liquidity to member countries, helping them manage the economic fallout of the pandemic.

7.4 Special Drawing Rights (SDRs)

Concept and Applications

Special Drawing Rights (SDRs) are international reserve assets created by the **International Monetary Fund (IMF)** to supplement the official foreign exchange reserves of member countries. Introduced in 1969, SDRs serve as a potential claim on freely usable currencies of IMF member nations, enhancing global liquidity and supporting financial stability.

Concept of SDRs

Definition

An SDR is not a currency but an international reserve asset whose value is based on a basket of major global currencies. It acts as a unit of account for the IMF and a tool for stabilizing global financial systems.

Key Features of SDRs

1. **Basket of Currencies**:

   - The value of an SDR is determined by a weighted average of five major currencies:

     - **US Dollar (USD)**
     - **Euro (EUR)**
     - **Chinese Renminbi (CNY)**
     - **Japanese Yen (JPY)**
     - **British Pound (GBP)**

2. **Allocation**:

   - The IMF allocates SDRs to member countries based on their **IMF quotas**, reflecting the relative size of their economies in the global system.

3. **Value Determination**:

   - The SDR value is recalculated daily based on exchange rates of the basket currencies.

4. **Not a Currency**:

- ○ SDRs cannot be used for transactions in markets like traditional currencies but can be exchanged for freely usable currencies through the IMF or voluntary trading arrangements.

Applications of SDRs
1. Supplementing Foreign Exchange Reserves
SDRs serve as an additional reserve asset for countries, reducing reliance on foreign currencies like the US Dollar or Euro.

- **Example**: During economic crises, countries can use SDRs to meet balance-of-payments obligations or stabilize their currencies.

2. Supporting Global Liquidity
The IMF allocates SDRs during global financial crises to enhance liquidity and enable countries to address immediate economic challenges.

- **Example**: In 2021, the IMF allocated $650 billion in SDRs to member countries to help mitigate the economic impact of the COVID-19 pandemic.

3. Facilitating International Trade and Payments
SDRs can be exchanged for freely usable currencies, supporting international trade and payments, especially for countries with limited foreign exchange reserves.

4. As a Unit of Account
The IMF and other international organizations use SDRs as a standard unit of account to price and settle transactions, ensuring consistency and neutrality.

- **Example**: SDRs are used to price IMF loans and determine interest rates for borrowing arrangements.

5. Reducing Dependency on Single Currencies
By diversifying reserve assets, SDRs help reduce global dependence on dominant currencies like the US Dollar, promoting monetary stability.
Advantages of SDRs

1. **Enhancing Global Liquidity**:

   - SDR allocations provide countries with immediate access to reserve assets, boosting confidence in their ability to meet external obligations.

2. **Supporting Economic Stability**:

   - SDRs offer a lifeline to countries facing currency crises or balance-of-payments challenges.

3. **Promoting Multilateralism**:

   - SDRs represent a collective global asset, encouraging international cooperation in addressing economic challenges.

4. **Flexibility in Use**:

   - Countries can voluntarily trade SDRs for other currencies, tailoring their use to specific economic needs.

Challenges of SDRs

1. **Limited Use in Practice**:

   - Despite their potential, SDRs are not widely used as a medium of exchange or store of value outside the IMF framework.

2. **Dependence on Major Economies**:

   - The value of SDRs depends on the stability of the basket currencies, primarily from developed economies, leaving it vulnerable to global currency fluctuations.

3. **Unequal Distribution**:

   - SDR allocations are based on IMF quotas, which disproportionately favor advanced economies, limiting their impact on low-income countries.

4. **Lack of Market Integration:**

- ○ SDRs are not fully integrated into global financial markets, restricting their broader application.

Real-World Applications and Examples
COVID-19 Pandemic Response (2021)

- The IMF allocated $650 billion in SDRs to member countries to bolster reserves and support economic recovery.
- **Impact:**

  - ○ Low-income countries received approximately $21 billion, enabling them to address immediate fiscal challenges.

Eurozone Debt Crisis (2010)

- SDRs were used to stabilize economies like Greece and Portugal by providing additional reserve liquidity.

Developing Economies

- Countries like Zimbabwe and Bangladesh have used
- SDRs to strengthen reserves and finance critical imports during economic difficulties.

Aspect	SDRs	Traditional Reserve Assets
Nature	International reserve asset issued by the IMF.	Currency reserves like USD, EUR, or gold.
Value Determination	Based on a basket of five major currencies.	Market value of the specific currency or gold.
Liquidity	Freely exchangeable among IMF members.	Usable directly in global trade and finance.
Allocation	Allocated by the IMF based on quotas.	Accumulated through trade, investment, or borrowing.

SDRs vs. Traditional Reserve Assets

Future of SDRs

1. **Greater Integration into Financial Systems**:

   ○ Expanding the role of SDRs in international transactions and reserve management can enhance their relevance.

2. **Reforming IMF Quotas**:

   ○ Adjusting quota allocations to better reflect the economic contributions of emerging markets can address concerns about inequality.

3. **Climate Financing**:

   ○ SDRs could be used to support global efforts in financing climate change mitigation and adaptation projects.

4. **Reducing Global Currency Dependence**:

   ○ Promoting SDRs as an alternative to dominant currencies like the US Dollar could mitigate global financial risks.

EIGHT

DEMAND, SUPPLY, AND MARKET FORCES

8.1 Law of Demand and Supply

The **Law of Demand and Supply** is the cornerstone of economic theory, offering a foundational understanding of how prices and quantities of goods are determined in a market. These concepts underpin the dynamics of economic activity, serving as the basis for decision-making by consumers, producers, and policymakers.

8.1.1 Understanding the Law of Demand

The **Law of Demand** states that, all else being equal, as the price of a good decreases, the quantity demanded increases, and vice versa. This inverse relationship between price and quantity demanded is rooted in consumer behavior. For instance, when the price of a product like sugar falls, consumers are more likely to buy it in larger quantities because it becomes relatively more affordable. Conversely, if the price rises, consumers might reduce their consumption or switch to substitutes.

Principles Behind Demand

1. **Substitution Effect**: When the price of a good increases, consumers tend to substitute it with cheaper alternatives. For example, a rise in the price of butter may lead to increased demand for margarine.
2. **Income Effect**: A price change affects the real purchasing power of a consumer's income. For instance, if the price of rice decreases, consumers feel wealthier as their money buys more.

The relationship between price and demand can be illustrated using a **demand curve**, typically downward sloping from left to right.

Mathematical Representation

The demand function can be expressed as:

$$Q_d = f(P, Y, T, Ps, Pc)$$

Where:

- Q_d = Quantity demanded
- P = Price of the good
- Y = Consumer income
- T = Consumer tastes and preferences
- Ps = Price of substitutes
- Pc = Price of complementary goods

8.1.2 Determinants of Demand

Demand for a good does not depend solely on its price. Several other factors play a critical role:

Consumer Income (Y)

Higher disposable income usually increases demand for normal goods like cars or electronics, while it might reduce demand for inferior goods such as second-hand clothing.

Prices of Related Goods

- **Substitutes**: Goods that can replace each other, like tea and coffee. A price increase in one often raises demand for the other.
- **Complements**: Goods consumed together, such as petrol and cars. A price decrease in one often boosts demand for the other.

Tastes and Preferences

Cultural, social, or psychological changes can shift demand. For example, increased awareness of health benefits can raise demand for organic products.

Future Expectations

Expectations about future prices or income levels can influence present demand. If consumers expect prices to rise, they may buy more now, boosting current demand.

8.1.3 Elasticity of Demand

Price elasticity of demand (PED) measures the responsiveness of quantity demanded to changes in price. It is calculated as:

$$PED = \frac{\%\Delta Q_d}{\%\Delta P}$$

Where:

- $\%\Delta Q_d$ = Percentage change in quantity demanded
- $\%\Delta P$ = Percentage change in price

Types of Elasticity

1. **Elastic Demand** (PED>1): Quantity demanded changes significantly with a small price change, common in luxury goods like electronics.
2. **Inelastic Demand** (PED<1): Quantity demanded changes little with a price change, typical for necessities like medicines.
3. **Unitary Elastic Demand** (PED=1): Quantity demanded changes proportionally to price.

8.1.4 Understanding the Law of Supply

The **Law of Supply** posits a direct relationship between price and quantity supplied. As the price of a good rises, producers are incentivized to increase supply because of the potential for higher profits. Conversely, lower prices discourage production.

Principles Behind Supply

1. **Profit Motive**: Higher prices provide greater profit margins, motivating producers to allocate more resources to the production of that good.
2. **Costs of Production**: A rise in input costs can constrain supply even if prices rise, highlighting the importance of efficiency and innovation in production processes.

The supply curve is generally upward sloping, reflecting this positive relationship between price and quantity supplied.

Mathematical Representation

The supply function can be expressed as:

$$Q_s = f(P, C, T, N)$$

Where:

- Q_s = Quantity supplied

- P = Price of the good

- C = Cost of production

- T = Technology

- N = Number of suppliers

8.1.5 Determinants of Supply

Several factors influence supply beyond just the price:

Cost of Inputs

Higher costs of raw materials or labor reduce supply, as producing becomes more expensive. For example, a rise in the price of steel may decrease the supply of automobiles.

Technological Advancements

Innovations can lower production costs and increase efficiency, enhancing supply. Automation in manufacturing, for instance, has significantly boosted production in industries like electronics.

Government Policies

Taxes, subsidies, and regulations can impact supply. For instance, subsidies on fertilizers can increase agricultural output.

8.1.6 Market Equilibrium

Market equilibrium occurs when the quantity demanded equals the quantity supplied at a particular price, leading to no shortages or surpluses. This price is called the **equilibrium price**, and the corresponding quantity is the **equilibrium quantity**.

Graphical Representation

The equilibrium point is where the demand and supply curves intersect. Any deviation from this point leads to market imbalances:

- **Surplus**: When supply exceeds demand, leading to downward pressure on prices.
- **Shortage**: When demand exceeds supply, causing upward pressure on prices.

Mathematical Approach

Equilibrium can be calculated by equating the demand and supply functions:

Qd=Qs

8.1.7 Challenges in Real-World Applications

The theoretical simplicity of the Law of Demand and Supply often meets challenges in real-world scenarios:

- **Market Imperfections**: Monopolies, price controls, and asymmetric information can disrupt equilibrium.
- **External Shocks**: Natural disasters, geopolitical tensions, or pandemics can lead to sudden shifts in demand and supply.
- **Behavioral Factors**: Consumer behavior is not always rational and can be influenced by emotions, trends, or misinformation.

8.1.8 Practical Applications

The principles of demand and supply are applied across various domains:

- **Pricing Strategies**: Businesses use demand elasticity to set optimal prices for products and services.
- **Policy Formulation**: Governments analyze demand-supply dynamics to implement effective economic policies, such as taxation or subsidies.
- **Market Analysis**: Investors and economists assess market conditions by studying supply-demand trends, helping predict price movements and economic health.

8.2 Utility Theory

The concept of **Utility Theory** is foundational in economics, offering insights into consumer behavior and decision-making. It explains how individuals derive satisfaction or benefit from consuming goods and services, enabling economists to predict consumption patterns. At its core, utility reflects the value or satisfaction a consumer perceives from consuming a particular good or service.

8.2.1 Marginal Utility

Understanding Marginal Utility

Marginal Utility refers to the additional satisfaction or utility a consumer gains from consuming one more unit of a good or service. It is a fundamental concept in understanding how consumers make choices, especially when faced with resource constraints like limited income or time.

For example, consider a person eating slices of pizza. The first slice may provide immense satisfaction, but as they consume more, the additional satisfaction derived from each subsequent slice diminishes. This diminishing satisfaction illustrates the principle of **diminishing marginal utility**, a cornerstone of utility theory.

Principles of Marginal Utility

Total Utility vs. Marginal Utility

- **Total Utility (TU)**: The overall satisfaction a consumer derives from consuming a specific quantity of goods.

Marginal Utility (MU): The change in total utility when an additional unit of a good is consumed. It can be mathematically represented as:

$$MU = \frac{\Delta TU}{\Delta Q}$$

Where:

ΔTU = Change in total utility

ΔQ = Change in quantity consumed

Diminishing Marginal Utility

The **Law of Diminishing Marginal Utility** states that as a consumer consumes more units of a good, the marginal utility of each additional unit decreases. While the first unit of a product may provide high satisfaction, subsequent units yield progressively lower satisfaction.

For example:

- The first glass of water on a hot day might provide immense relief (high utility).
- The second glass is still satisfying but less so.
- By the fourth or fifth glass, the utility may approach zero or even turn negative if it becomes excessive.

Utility Maximization

Consumers aim to maximize their total utility given their budget constraints. This behavior is guided by the principle of **equimarginal utility**, which states that consumers allocate their resources such that the **marginal utility per unit of currency spent** on all goods is equal.

Mathematical Expression

Let Mu_x and MU_y represent the marginal utilities of goods X and Y, and P_x and P_y represent their prices, respectively. Utility maximization occurs when:

$$\frac{MU_x}{P_x} = \frac{MU_y}{P_y}$$

This equation ensures the consumer derives the maximum possible satisfaction from their budget.

Applications of Marginal Utility

Pricing and Demand

The concept of marginal utility helps explain consumer demand and price elasticity. Goods with high marginal utility at low consumption levels tend to command higher prices, while those with low marginal utility might be priced lower. For instance:

- Essential items like water or food typically have high utility but low marginal utility with increasing consumption.
- Luxury items like jewelry may have consistently high utility, affecting their pricing strategies.

Public Policy

Policymakers often use utility theory to design tax systems or subsidies. For instance, progressive taxation is based on the idea that the marginal utility of income decreases as income rises, making it equitable to tax higher-income individuals more heavily.

Behavioral Economics

Marginal utility also explains irrational behaviors, such as overconsumption or addiction, where consumers prioritize immediate satisfaction over long-term utility.

Challenges and Limitations

While utility theory provides a robust framework, it is not without limitations:

1. **Subjectivity**: Utility is inherently subjective and varies from person to person, making it difficult to measure precisely.
2. **Non-Quantifiable Preferences**: Some utilities, like emotional satisfaction, are challenging to quantify.
3. **Assumption of Rationality**: Utility theory assumes consumers are rational decision-makers, which may not hold true in real-world scenarios influenced by emotions or biases.
4. **Impact of External Factors**: External influences like advertising, social norms, or peer pressure can alter perceived utility, complicating predictions.

Real-World Example

To understand marginal utility, consider a consumer purchasing coffee. The first cup provides a significant energy boost and satisfaction. However, as they consume additional cups, the boost diminishes, and by the third or fourth cup, the satisfaction may turn into discomfort. Businesses like coffee shops leverage this concept by offering promotions like "buy one, get one free," encouraging consumers to purchase more while maximizing their utility.

Utility Theory and Economic Efficiency

Marginal utility plays a crucial role in ensuring **allocative efficiency**, where resources are distributed in a manner that maximizes total societal satisfaction. Firms produce goods up to the point where the **marginal cost of production equals the marginal utility to consumers**, achieving equilibrium in resource allocation.

8.2.2 Diminishing Marginal Utility

The **Law of Diminishing Marginal Utility** is a fundamental principle in economics, explaining how the satisfaction derived from consuming additional units of a good or service decreases over time. This concept helps to understand consumer behavior, decision-making, and resource allocation, forming the basis for various economic theories and policies.

Understanding Diminishing Marginal Utility

The **Law of Diminishing Marginal Utility** states that as an individual consumes more units of a good or service within a given time period, the additional utility or satisfaction gained from each successive unit decreases. While the total utility might still increase with more consumption, the rate at which it increases slows down, eventually reaching a point where it could even decline.

For example, consider a person eating chocolate. The first piece provides immense pleasure, the second piece still brings joy but slightly less than the first, and by the fifth or sixth piece, the person might feel satiated or even uncomfortable.

Principles of the Law

1. **Utility as a Measure of Satisfaction**: Utility refers to the benefit or satisfaction derived from consuming goods. Marginal utility specifically measures the additional satisfaction obtained from one more unit of consumption.
2. **Diminishing Gains**: As consumption increases, the utility derived from each additional unit diminishes because the consumer's need for the product is increasingly satisfied.

This principle assumes that other factors, such as consumer preferences, availability of substitutes, and the time of consumption, remain constant.

Mathematical Representation

The marginal utility can be represented as the change in total utility divided by the change in the quantity consumed:

$$MU = \frac{\Delta TU}{\Delta Q}$$

Where:

- MU = Marginal Utility

- ΔTU = Change in Total Utility

- ΔQ = Change in Quantity Consumed

The **Law of Diminishing Marginal Utility** implies that MUMUMU decreases as QQQ increases.

Graphical Representation

In a graph, the **total utility curve** initially rises at a decreasing rate, eventually reaching a maximum point where any additional consumption may lead to negative utility (disutility). The **marginal utility curve** slopes downward, reflecting the decline in additional satisfaction with each unit consumed.

Real-Life Examples

1. **Food Consumption**: A person eating slices of pizza derives maximum satisfaction from the first slice, less from the second, and so on. Eventually, additional slices may lead to discomfort or waste.
2. **Clothing Purchases**: Buying a first winter coat offers essential warmth and satisfaction. A second coat might provide variety, but its utility is less compared to the first.
3. **Leisure Activities**: Watching the first episode of a favorite TV series can be thrilling, but binge-watching the entire season in one sitting may lead to fatigue.

Economic Implications

Consumer Behavior

The diminishing marginal utility influences how consumers allocate their resources. Individuals prioritize goods or services that offer the highest initial satisfaction and gradually diversify their consumption as utility diminishes.

Pricing and Demand

The principle explains why prices decline as the quantity consumed increases. Businesses often offer bulk discounts because the additional satisfaction consumers derive from extra units is low. For example, supermarkets sell larger packs of goods at reduced per-unit prices to encourage higher purchases.

Taxation Policies

Governments apply this concept to justify progressive taxation. Since the utility of income decreases as wealth increases, higher-income individuals are taxed at a higher rate without significantly impacting their overall satisfaction.

Limitations and Exceptions

Although widely accepted, the **Law of Diminishing Marginal Utility** has limitations and exceptions:

1. **Non-Uniform Goods**: Some goods, such as collectibles or luxury items, may provide increasing satisfaction with each additional unit due to factors like rarity or prestige.
2. **Changing Preferences**: Consumer tastes and preferences can fluctuate, altering the perceived utility of subsequent units.
3. **Time Sensitivity**: The law applies only when consumption occurs within a short time. For example, the enjoyment of consuming chocolates might reset if there is a significant gap between consumption events.

Applications in Economics

Optimal Consumption

Consumers aim to maximize their total utility by distributing their spending so that the marginal utility per unit of currency is equal across all goods.

This behavior is governed by the **Law of Equi-Marginal Utility**:

$$\frac{MU_A}{P_A} = \frac{MU_B}{P_B}$$

Where A and B are two goods, and P_A and P_B are their respective prices

Public Goods Allocation

Governments use the concept to distribute public goods and services efficiently. For instance, public healthcare funding prioritizes areas where the utility derived from additional resources is highest.

Behavioral Insights

The diminishing marginal utility also finds relevance in behavioral economics, explaining phenomena like overconsumption and addictive behavior. While the marginal utility decreases, individuals may irrationally continue consumption due to emotional or psychological factors, often leading to negative consequences.

8.3 Market Equilibrium

Market Equilibrium is a state in which the quantity of goods or services demanded by consumers equals the quantity supplied by producers, resulting in a stable market price. This balance ensures that resources are efficiently allocated, avoiding surpluses and shortages. Understanding market equilibrium is crucial for analyzing how prices are determined in a competitive market and how external factors can disrupt this balance.

8.3.1 Concept of Market Equilibrium

Market equilibrium occurs at the intersection of the **demand curve** and the **supply curve** on a graph. At this point, the market-clearing price ensures that the intentions of both buyers and sellers align, leading to an optimal allocation of resources.

For example, in a fruit market, if apples are priced too high, consumers may reduce their purchases, leading to a surplus. If priced too low, there may be a shortage as demand exceeds supply. The equilibrium price balances these forces.

Mathematical Representation

The equilibrium condition is defined as:

$$Q_d = Q_s$$

Where:

- Q_d: Quantity demanded

- Q_s: Quantity supplied

By substituting the demand and supply functions:

$$a - bP = c + dP$$

Where:

- a, b: Constants in the demand function

- c, d: Constants in the supply function

- P: Equilibrium price

Solving for P gives the equilibrium price, and substituting P into either function gives the equilibrium quantity.

8.3.2 Impact of Changes in Demand and Supply

In real-world markets, demand and supply are dynamic, influenced by various factors such as consumer preferences, technological advancements, and economic policies. Changes in these factors can shift the demand or supply curves, leading to a new equilibrium.

8.3.2.1 Impact of Changes in Demand

When demand increases or decreases while supply remains constant, the equilibrium price and quantity are affected.

Increase in Demand

An increase in demand shifts the demand curve to the right. This results in:

- A higher equilibrium price.
- A higher equilibrium quantity.

Example: During a heatwave, the demand for air conditioners increases, driving up both their price and quantity sold.

Decrease in Demand

A decrease in demand shifts the demand curve to the left. This results in:

- A lower equilibrium price.
- A lower equilibrium quantity.

Example: A new health trend reducing sugar consumption may lower the demand for sugary beverages, leading to reduced prices and sales.

8.3.2.2 Impact of Changes in Supply

When supply increases or decreases while demand remains constant, the equilibrium price and quantity change accordingly.

Increase in Supply

An increase in supply shifts the supply curve to the right. This results in:

- A lower equilibrium price.
- A higher equilibrium quantity.

Example: Technological improvements in agriculture may increase the supply of wheat, lowering its price while increasing the quantity available.

Decrease in Supply

A decrease in supply shifts the supply curve to the left. This results in:

- A higher equilibrium price.
- A lower equilibrium quantity.

Example: A natural disaster destroying crops can reduce the supply of vegetables, increasing their price while reducing their availability.

8.3.2.3 Simultaneous Changes in Demand and Supply

When both demand and supply change simultaneously, the impact on equilibrium price and quantity depends on the relative magnitude and direction of the changes.

Case 1: Increase in Both Demand and Supply

- **Outcome:** The equilibrium quantity increases, but the effect on price depends on the relative magnitude of the shifts. If demand increases more, prices rise; if supply increases more, prices fall.

Case 2: Decrease in Both Demand and Supply

- **Outcome:** The equilibrium quantity decreases, but the price impact depends on the relative shifts. If demand decreases more, prices fall; if supply decreases more, prices rise.

Case 3: Opposing Shifts

- **Increase in Demand and Decrease in Supply:** Both factors push the price upward, but the quantity effect depends on the magnitude of the shifts.
- **Decrease in Demand and Increase in Supply:** Both factors push the price downward, with the quantity determined by the stronger shift.

8.3.3 Real-World Applications of Market Equilibrium

The concept of market equilibrium is applied across various industries and economic policies to understand and predict market behavior.

Pricing Strategies

Businesses use equilibrium analysis to set prices that maximize profits while meeting consumer demand. For instance, seasonal pricing of products like fruits adjusts to shifts in demand and supply.

Government Policies

Policymakers monitor market equilibrium to address shortages or surpluses. For example:

- **Price Floors:** Set above equilibrium price to protect producers, e.g., minimum wage laws.
- **Price Ceilings:** Set below equilibrium price to protect consumers, e.g., rent control policies.

Market Forecasting

Economists use equilibrium models to predict market trends, such as the impact of rising fuel prices on transportation costs and consumer spending.

Challenges in Achieving Equilibrium

1. **Market Imperfections**: Factors like monopolies, lack of information, or barriers to entry can prevent markets from reaching equilibrium.
2. **External Shocks**: Events like natural disasters, geopolitical tensions, or pandemics can disrupt supply chains, causing sudden imbalances.
3. **Behavioral Factors**: Consumer preferences and irrational behavior can create deviations from theoretical predictions.

NINE

MARKET STRUCTURES AND COMPETITION

Market structures define the characteristics and behaviors of industries and markets, shaping how goods and services are produced, priced, and distributed. The classification of markets into distinct structures provides a framework for understanding the dynamics of competition, consumer choice, and economic efficiency. **Market structures** primarily differ based on the number of producers, the nature of the product, entry barriers, and the degree of market power held by firms.

9.1 Types of Market Structures

Market structures are broadly categorized into four types: **Perfect Competition**, **Monopoly**, **Monopolistic Competition**, and **Oligopoly**. Each structure has unique characteristics and implications for businesses and consumers. This section delves into **Perfect Competition**, the most idealized and theoretical market structure.

9.1.1 Perfect Competition

Perfect Competition is a market structure characterized by many buyers and sellers trading homogeneous products, with no individual entity having the power to influence prices. While rarely found in its pure form in the real world, it serves as a benchmark for assessing other market structures.

Key Characteristics of Perfect Competition

1. **Large Number of Buyers and Sellers**
   In a perfectly competitive market, no single buyer or seller can dictate the market price. Instead, prices are determined collectively through the interaction of demand and supply.
2. **Homogeneous Products**
   All firms sell identical products, meaning consumers perceive no difference between the goods offered by various sellers. For example, agricultural products like wheat or rice often approximate this condition.
3. **Free Entry and Exit**
   There are no significant barriers to entry or exit, allowing firms to freely join or leave the market based on profitability.
4. **Perfect Information**
   Buyers and sellers have complete knowledge about market conditions, including prices, quality, and availability of goods.
5. **Price Takers**
   Firms in a perfectly competitive market are **price takers**, meaning they accept the prevailing market price and cannot influence it.
6. **No Government Intervention**
   Markets operate without significant interference from government regulations, taxes, or subsidies.

Theoretical Foundation of Perfect Competition

Perfect competition is grounded in the principle of **Pareto Efficiency**, where resources are allocated in the most efficient manner possible. Under this structure, markets reach equilibrium where:

P=MC

Here:

- P: Price of the product
- MC: Marginal cost of production

At equilibrium, the price reflects both the cost of production and the value consumers place on the good, ensuring optimal distribution of resources.

Firm Behavior in Perfect Competition
Short-Run Equilibrium

In the short run, firms may earn abnormal profits, normal profits, or incur losses based on market conditions. Profit maximization occurs when:

MR=MC

Where:

- MR: Marginal revenue (equal to price in perfect competition)
- MC: Marginal cost

If P>ATC (Average Total Cost), the firm earns a profit. If P<ATC, the firm incurs a loss but may continue operating if P>AVC(Average Variable Cost).

Long-Run Equilibrium

In the long run, entry and exit of firms drive the market toward normal profits:

- **Entry**: When firms earn abnormal profits, new firms enter the market, increasing supply and driving prices down.
- **Exit**: When firms incur losses, some exit the market, reducing supply and increasing prices.

At long-run equilibrium:

P=MC=ATC

Firms produce at the minimum point of their average cost curve, ensuring productive and allocative efficiency.

Graphical Representation

1. **Short-Run Profits and Losses**

   In the short run, the firm's marginal cost curve above the average variable cost represents the supply curve. The intersection of market demand and supply determines the price, which each firm takes as given.

2. **Long-Run Adjustment**

   Over time, adjustments in firm entry and exit shift the supply curve, stabilizing prices and eliminating abnormal profits or losses.

Applications of Perfect Competition

While perfect competition rarely exists in its pure form, its principles provide valuable insights for understanding market behavior:

Agricultural Markets

Markets for commodities like wheat, corn, and rice often approximate perfect competition, as many producers supply similar products, and prices are largely determined by global demand and supply.

Stock Markets

Stock exchanges exhibit features of perfect competition, with numerous buyers and sellers trading standardized securities based on transparent information.

Policy Benchmarking

Perfect competition serves as a benchmark for assessing market efficiency and the welfare effects of policies like subsidies or tariffs.

Challenges and Limitations

While idealized, perfect competition is challenging to achieve due to the following factors:

1. **Product Differentiation**

   Real-world markets often involve differentiated products, making goods less than perfectly homogeneous.

2. **Barriers to Entry**

   Economic, legal, or technological barriers can restrict the free entry and exit of firms.

3. **Imperfect Information**

   Asymmetric information, where one party has more knowledge than another, disrupts the assumption of perfect knowledge.

4. **Economies of Scale**

   Large-scale production can give firms cost advantages, leading to market power and deviation from perfect competition.

9.1.2 Monopoly

A **Monopoly** represents the opposite end of the market structure spectrum from perfect competition. It is a market structure characterized by a single seller dominating the entire market for a good or service, with no close substitutes available. The monopolist wields significant market power, enabling them to influence prices and control supply. Understanding the dynamics of monopoly is crucial to examining the implications of market power on pricing, efficiency, and consumer welfare.

Key Characteristics of Monopoly

1. **Single Seller**
   In a monopoly, a single firm supplies the entire market. This firm faces no competition, and its decisions directly affect market outcomes.
2. **No Close Substitutes**
   The monopolist's product is unique, and consumers have no viable alternatives. For example, patented drugs or local utilities like water supply often operate as monopolies.
3. **High Barriers to Entry**
   Entry into a monopolistic market is restricted due to legal, technological, or economic barriers, preventing potential competitors from challenging the monopolist.
4. **Price Maker**
   Unlike firms in perfect competition, a monopolist is a **price maker**. It has the power to set prices by controlling the quantity supplied, constrained only by consumer demand.
5. **Market Power**
   The monopolist enjoys significant market power, allowing it to earn abnormal profits in both the short and long run.

Sources of Monopoly Power

Monopoly power arises from various factors that create and sustain barriers to entry:

1. **Legal Barriers**
   Governments may grant exclusive rights through patents, copyrights,

or franchises. For instance, pharmaceutical companies often hold monopolies on patented drugs.

2. **Natural Monopolies**

Some industries, such as utilities, operate more efficiently as monopolies due to high fixed costs and economies of scale. It is more practical for a single provider to serve the entire market.

3. **Ownership of Key Resources**

Exclusive control over critical resources, such as rare minerals or proprietary technology, can create monopolies. For example, De Beers historically controlled the diamond market.

4. **Strategic Barriers**

Monopolists may engage in practices like predatory pricing, exclusive contracts, or lobbying to block new entrants.

Monopoly Pricing and Output Decisions

A monopolist determines its price and output by analyzing demand and cost structures. Unlike in perfect competition, the monopolist faces a downward-sloping demand curve, meaning it must lower prices to sell more units.

A monopolist determines its price and output by analyzing demand and cost structures. Unlike in perfect competition, the monopolist faces a downward-sloping demand curve, meaning it must lower prices to sell more units.

Profit Maximization

The monopolist maximizes profit by producing at a quantity where:

MR=MC

Where:

- MR: Marginal Revenue
- MC: Marginal Cost

Price Determination

The monopolist sets the price based on the demand curve at the profit-maximizing quantity. This price is typically higher, and the quantity produced is lower than in a competitive market.

Graphical Representation of Monopoly

1. **Demand and Marginal Revenue Curves**
   The monopolist's demand curve is downward-sloping, and the marginal revenue curve lies below it due to the need to lower prices for additional sales.
2. **Profit Maximization**
   The intersection of the MR and MC curves determines the profit-maximizing quantity. The price is set at the corresponding point on the demand curve, leading to economic profits.
3. **Consumer Surplus and Deadweight Loss**
   Monopolies create **deadweight loss** by producing less and charging higher prices than in a competitive market, reducing consumer and producer surplus.

Implications of Monopoly
Advantages

1. **Economies of Scale**
   Monopolies, particularly natural monopolies, can achieve lower average costs due to large-scale production, benefiting consumers in certain industries like utilities.
2. **Innovation and Research**
   The potential for sustained abnormal profits incentivizes monopolists to invest in research and development. For example, pharmaceutical companies often use monopoly profits to fund new drug development.
3. **Stability**
   Monopolistic markets are less prone to disruptive competition, leading to price stability.

Disadvantages

1. **Higher Prices**
   Monopolies restrict output and charge higher prices, leading to reduced consumer welfare.
2. **Inefficiency**
   Monopolies may lack incentives to minimize costs or improve quality due to the absence of competition, resulting in **allocative inefficiency** (resources are not optimally distributed) and **productive inefficiency** (firms do not produce at the lowest possible cost).

3. **Consumer Exploitation**
   Consumers are forced to pay higher prices due to the monopolist's pricing power, reducing disposable income and limiting access to essential goods or services.
4. **Barriers to Innovation**
   In some cases, monopolies may stifle innovation by suppressing competitors or failing to innovate once market dominance is established.

Real-World Examples of Monopolies

1. **Utility Companies**
   Electric, gas, and water utilities often operate as natural monopolies to avoid the inefficiency of duplicating infrastructure.
2. **Technology Giants**
   Companies like Microsoft (historically for operating systems) or Google (for online search) have faced monopoly allegations due to their market dominance.
3. **Pharmaceuticals**
   Firms with patents on specific drugs hold temporary monopolies, allowing them to charge premium prices.

Regulation of Monopolies

Governments often regulate monopolies to protect consumer welfare and ensure fair competition:

1. **Price Controls**
   Governments may impose price caps to prevent monopolists from charging excessively high prices, particularly in essential services.
2. **Antitrust Laws**
   Legislation like the Sherman Act in the U.S. or the Competition Act in India aims to curb monopolistic practices, promote competition, and prevent abuse of market power.
3. **Public Ownership**
   In some cases, governments take ownership of monopolistic industries, such as public transportation or healthcare, to ensure equitable access.
4. **Subsidies and Incentives**
   Governments may provide subsidies to encourage competition or offset high costs in monopolistic industries.

Feature	Monopoly	Perfect Competition
Number of Sellers	One	Many
Product Differentiation	Unique	Homogeneous
Price Control	Significant	None (Price Taker)
Entry Barriers	High	None
Efficiency	Often Inefficient	Productive and Allocative Efficiency

Comparison with Perfect Competition

9.1.3 Oligopoly

An **Oligopoly** is a market structure characterized by a small number of firms dominating an industry. These firms hold significant market power, but their decisions are interdependent due to the presence of a few competitors. Oligopolies are common in industries where barriers to entry are high, leading to limited competition and distinctive market dynamics.

Key Characteristics of Oligopoly

1. **Few Dominant Firms**

   Oligopolies are marked by a small number of firms, each holding a substantial share of the market. Examples include the automobile, telecommunications, and airline industries.

2. **Interdependence**

   Firms in an oligopoly are highly interdependent. Decisions by one firm, such as pricing or output changes, significantly affect competitors, often triggering strategic responses.

3. **Barriers to Entry**

   High barriers, such as large capital requirements, economies of scale, or strong brand loyalty, prevent new entrants from competing effectively.

4. **Differentiated or Homogeneous Products**

   Oligopolistic markets can have either:

   - **Differentiated products**, such as cars or smartphones, where branding and features matter.

◦ **Homogeneous products**, such as steel or cement, where price competition is prevalent.

5. **Non-Price Competition**
Due to the risk of price wars, oligopolies often compete through non-price strategies like advertising, product differentiation, and customer service enhancements.
6. **Market Power**
Firms have significant control over prices but are constrained by mutual dependence and the possibility of regulatory scrutiny.

Theoretical Models of Oligopoly
Several models explain the behavior of firms in an oligopoly, focusing on pricing, output, and strategic interactions.

Cournot Model

The **Cournot Model** assumes that firms decide their output levels simultaneously, considering their competitors' output as fixed. The equilibrium is reached when each firm's output maximizes its profit, given the output of the other firms.

For two firms ($Firm_1$ and $Firm_2$) producing a homogeneous product:

$$Q = Q_1 + Q_2$$

$$P = a - bQ$$

Where:

- Q: Total market quantity

- Q_1, Q_2: Quantities produced by $Firm_1$ and $Firm_2$

- P: Price

- a, b: Demand curve parameters

Each firm maximizes its profit:

$$\pi_1 = (P - C_1)Q_1 \quad \text{and} \quad \pi_2 = (P - C_2)Q_2$$

The Nash equilibrium occurs where neither firm can improve its profit by unilaterally changing its output.

Bertrand Model

The **Bertrand Model** assumes firms compete by setting prices rather than output. In this model, firms produce identical products, and the firm offering the lowest price captures the entire market.

Key Insights

- If firms have identical costs, the equilibrium price equals marginal cost, similar to perfect competition.
- When products are differentiated, firms can maintain some pricing power.

Kinked Demand Curve Model

The **Kinked Demand Curve Model** explains price stability in oligopolies. Firms face:

- **Elastic demand** for price increases: Consumers switch to competitors if a firm raises prices.
- **Inelastic demand** for price decreases: Competitors match price cuts, negating the firm's advantage.

This leads to a kinked demand curve, where firms are reluctant to change prices significantly.

Game Theory in Oligopoly

Game theory provides a framework for analyzing strategic interactions in oligopolistic markets.

Prisoner's Dilemma

The classic prisoner's dilemma illustrates the conflict between cooperation and self-interest. In an oligopoly, firms benefit from collusion (cooperating to fix prices), but each firm has an incentive to cheat by undercutting prices.

Nash Equilibrium

In an oligopoly, the Nash equilibrium represents a stable outcome where no firm can improve its position unilaterally, given the strategies of competitors.

Collusion and Cartels

Firms in an oligopoly may collude to maximize joint profits by fixing prices, limiting output, or dividing the market. Such collusion can be:

1. **Formal (Cartels)**: Organizations like OPEC explicitly coordinate actions, often legally sanctioned in certain contexts.
2. **Tacit Collusion**: Firms implicitly agree to avoid price wars without explicit communication.

Challenges with Collusion

1. **Incentive to Cheat**: Individual firms may secretly undercut prices to gain market share.
2. **Regulatory Scrutiny**: Antitrust laws in many countries prohibit collusion to protect consumer welfare.

Examples of Oligopolies

1. **Automobile Industry**
   Companies like Toyota, Ford, and Volkswagen dominate the global automobile market, competing through innovation, branding, and product differentiation.
2. **Telecommunications**
   In many countries, a handful of firms control mobile and internet services, engaging in price wars and offering bundled services.
3. **Airlines**
   Airlines operate in an oligopolistic market, competing on routes, service quality, and loyalty programs while often facing regulatory oversight.

Economic Implications of Oligopoly
Advantages

1. **Innovation**: Large firms have resources to invest in research and development, driving technological progress.

2. **Economies of Scale**: Oligopolies often benefit from lower costs due to large-scale operations.
3. **Price Stability**: Firms in an oligopoly may maintain stable prices, benefiting consumers and reducing uncertainty.

Disadvantages

1. **Higher Prices**: Reduced competition can lead to higher prices and limited choices for consumers.
2. **Inefficiency**: Firms may produce below optimal output levels to maintain high prices, leading to allocative inefficiency.
3. **Barriers to Entry**: New entrants face significant challenges, stifling innovation and competition.

9.2 Monopolistic Competition

Monopolistic Competition is a market structure that combines elements of both perfect competition and monopoly. It is characterized by many sellers offering products that are similar but differentiated. Firms in monopolistic competition have some degree of market power due to product differentiation, but they also face competition from other firms offering substitutes.

9.2.1 Features of Monopolistic Competition

Monopolistic competition exhibits a unique blend of characteristics that distinguish it from other market structures:

1. Large Number of Sellers and Buyers

There are numerous sellers, each holding a relatively small share of the market. While no single firm dominates, each has some influence over its pricing due to product differentiation. Buyers, on the other hand, have diverse preferences, contributing to market dynamics.

2. Product Differentiation

Firms differentiate their products through branding, quality, features, or marketing strategies. While products may serve the same purpose, they are not perfect substitutes. For example:

- Toothpaste brands may differ in flavor, whitening properties, or packaging.
- Coffee shops may offer variations in taste, ambiance, or service.

This differentiation creates customer loyalty, giving firms limited pricing power.

3. Freedom of Entry and Exit

Entry barriers are relatively low, allowing new firms to enter the market when profits are high. Similarly, firms can exit easily if they are unable to compete. This dynamic ensures that abnormal profits are temporary in the long run.

4. Independent Decision-Making

Each firm makes independent decisions about pricing and production without collusion or strategic interdependence, unlike in an oligopoly.

5. Price and Non-Price Competition

While firms have some control over prices due to differentiation, they often rely heavily on non-price competition. This includes:

- Advertising and promotional campaigns.
- Enhancements in product quality and customer service.
- Loyalty programs or exclusive offers.

6. Demand Curve for Individual Firms

Firms in monopolistic competition face a **downward-sloping demand curve**, meaning they can sell more by reducing prices. However, the demand is more elastic compared to a monopoly because substitutes are available.

9.2.2 *Impacts of Monopolistic Competition*

Monopolistic competition has significant implications for businesses, consumers, and the economy as a whole.

1. Impact on Prices and Output

Short-Run Effects

In the short run, firms can earn abnormal profits or incur losses, depending on market conditions. Profit maximization occurs where

MR=MC

Where:

- MR: Marginal Revenue
- MC: Marginal Cost

Firms set prices above marginal cost, leveraging their market power from product differentiation.

Long-Run Effects

In the long run, the entry of new firms erodes abnormal profits due to increased competition. Eventually:

P=ATC

Where:

- P: Price

- ATC: Average Total Cost

Firms earn only normal profits, and prices settle at a level that covers production costs and includes a reasonable return.

2. Consumer Benefits

Consumers benefit from a wide variety of choices and innovations. Product differentiation ensures that firms cater to diverse preferences, enhancing customer satisfaction.

Example:

The smartphone industry demonstrates monopolistic competition. Consumers can choose from brands offering various features, designs, and price points, such as Apple, Samsung, or Xiaomi.

3. Economic Efficiency

Allocative Efficiency

Allocative efficiency occurs when the price of a product reflects its marginal cost, ensuring optimal resource allocation. In monopolistic competition, $P > MCP > MCP > MC$, leading to **allocative inefficiency**.

Productive Efficiency

Productive efficiency occurs when firms produce at the lowest point on the average cost curve. Monopolistic competition fails to achieve this, as firms operate with excess capacity to maintain differentiation.

4. Innovation and Advertising

Firms invest heavily in advertising and innovation to differentiate their products. While this drives progress and consumer choice, it also increases costs, which are often passed on to consumers.

Example:

The cosmetics industry thrives on branding and advertising, with companies like L'Oréal and Estée Lauder competing for market share through aggressive marketing and continuous product innovation.

5. Shortcomings of Monopolistic Competition

Higher Costs for Consumers

Firms incur significant costs on advertising and product differentiation, which may lead to higher prices for consumers compared to perfect competition.

Wasteful Competition

The focus on branding and marketing can result in wasteful expenditure without necessarily improving product quality or utility.

Inefficiency

The market operates below full capacity due to excess capacity and underutilized resources, leading to inefficiency.

6. Real-World Examples

1. **Restaurants** The restaurant industry exemplifies monopolistic competition, with numerous establishments offering differentiated menus, ambiance, and service quality to attract customers.
2. **Clothing and Apparel** Brands like Nike, Adidas, and Puma compete not just on functionality but also on design, branding, and cultural relevance.
3. **Consumer Electronics** The consumer electronics market, with brands offering slightly varied features in smartphones, laptops, and cameras, illustrates this market structure.

9.3 Pricing and Output Decisions

Pricing and output decisions are central to the operation of firms and vary significantly under different market structures. These decisions depend on factors such as the number of competitors, the nature of products, market power, and the elasticity of demand. Understanding how firms determine prices and output in various market conditions is critical for analyzing market behavior, consumer welfare, and economic efficiency.

9.3.1 Pricing and Output in Perfect Competition

In a **perfectly competitive market**, firms are price takers, meaning they cannot influence the market price. Prices are determined by the interaction of market demand and supply, and individual firms adjust their output to maximize profits.

Key Features

1. **Price Determination**
   The market price is set at the equilibrium point where the demand and supply curves intersect.
2. **Profit Maximization Rule**
   Firms maximize profit by producing at a level where:MR=MC

   MR=MC
   Since MR (Marginal Revenue) equals the market price (P) in perfect competition, the firm adjusts its output to equate marginal cost (MC) with the pricea

Short-Run Decisions

1. **Economic Profits**
   If P> ATC (Average Total Cost), the firm earns abnormal profits.
2. **Economic Losses**
   If AVC<P<ATC, the firm incurs losses but continues operating to cover variable costs.
3. **Shutdown Point**
   If P<AVC, the firm shuts down as it cannot cover even its variable costs.

Long-Run Adjustments

In the long run, entry and exit of firms ensure that only normal profits are earned

P=ATC=MC

9.3.2 Pricing and Output in Monopoly

A **monopoly** firm is a price maker with significant control over market prices due to the absence of competition. It determines both the price and output level by analyzing the demand curve and cost structure.

Key Features

1. **Profit Maximization Rule**

   The monopolist maximizes profit where:

MR=MC

1. The price is then determined from the demand curve corresponding to the profit-maximizing quantity.
2. **Price-Output Relationship**

   A monopolist's price is higher, and output is lower compared to a perfectly competitive market.

Implications

1. **Deadweight Loss**

   Monopolists produce less than the socially optimal quantity, leading to allocative inefficiency and a deadweight loss.
2. **Price Discrimination**

   Monopolists may engage in price discrimination by charging different prices to different consumers based on their willingness to pay.

9.3.3 Pricing and Output in Oligopoly

In an **oligopolistic market**, firms' pricing and output decisions are interdependent due to the presence of a few dominant competitors. The strategic behavior of firms is central to this market structure.

Key Features

1. **Interdependence**
Firms closely monitor competitors' pricing and output decisions and respond strategically.
2. **Profit Maximization**
Oligopolies aim to maximize joint profits, often leading to collusion or tacit agreements.

Pricing Models

1. **Kinked Demand Curve Model**

   - Prices are sticky because firms fear losing customers if they raise prices (elastic demand above the kink) and matching price cuts by competitors (inelastic demand below the kink).
   - The result is price stability, with firms focusing on non-price competition.

2. **Collusion and Cartels**

   - Firms may collude to fix prices and output, as seen in cartels like OPEC.
   - Collusion maximizes joint profits but risks regulatory action.

3. **Game Theory**

   - Pricing strategies in oligopolies often follow game-theoretic models, like the **Prisoner's Dilemma**, where firms balance cooperation and competition.

9.3.4 Pricing and Output in Monopolistic Competition

In a **monopolistic competition** market, firms have some control over prices due to product differentiation. However, the presence of many competitors limits their pricing power.

Key Features

1. **Profit Maximization Rule**
   Firms set prices and output where:

MR=MC
· **Short-Run Decisions**

- Firms may earn abnormal profits or incur losses depending on market demand and costs.
- Prices are set above marginal cost but below monopoly levels due to competition.

· **Long-Run Adjustments**

- Free entry and exit ensure only normal profits in the long run.
- Prices stabilize at a level where

P=ATC but P>MC indicating allocative inefficiency.
9.3.5 Real-World Applications
Perfect Competition

- Agricultural markets like wheat or rice, where firms cannot control prices.

Monopoly

- Utility companies like electricity providers, setting prices based on demand and cost conditions.

Oligopoly

- Automobile industry, where pricing strategies consider competitors' moves and market trends.

Monopolistic Competition

- Retail clothing brands, using pricing, advertising, and branding to attract customers.

TEN
ECONOMIC DEVELOPMENT AND INEQUALITY

Economic development is the process by which a nation improves the economic, social, and political well-being of its people. It involves not only increasing income and wealth but also enhancing the quality of life through better health, education, and equality. Measuring economic development is critical for assessing progress, identifying challenges, and shaping policies to reduce inequality and promote sustainable growth.

10.1 Measuring Economic Development

Measuring economic development is a complex task that requires capturing multiple dimensions of progress, including economic, social, and environmental factors. Traditional indicators like Gross Domestic Product (GDP) provide insights into economic growth but fail to address broader aspects of development. This has led to the adoption of more comprehensive measures like the **Human Development Index (HDI)**.

10.1.1 Human Development Index (HDI)

The **Human Development Index (HDI)**, developed by the United Nations Development Programme (UNDP), is a composite measure designed to assess the overall development of a country. It goes beyond economic metrics by incorporating dimensions that reflect the quality of life and human capabilities.

Key Components of HDI

HDI combines three critical dimensions of human development:

1. **Health**

   - Measured by **life expectancy at birth**, this dimension reflects a country's ability to ensure a long and healthy life for its citizens.
   - A higher life expectancy indicates better healthcare systems, nutrition, and living conditions.

2. **Education**

   - Captured through two indicators:

     - **Mean years of schooling**: Average number of years of education received by people aged 25 and older.
     - **Expected years of schooling**: The number of years a child entering school is expected to complete.

   - This dimension highlights access to knowledge and the quality of education systems.

3. **Standard of Living**

   - Measured by **Gross National Income (GNI) per capita**, adjusted for purchasing power parity (PPP).
   - This reflects the economic resources available to individuals and their capacity to lead a decent life.

Calculation of HDI

HDI is calculated as the geometric mean of the normalized indices for each dimension:

$$HDI = \sqrt[3]{I_{Health} \cdot I_{Education} \cdot I_{Income}}$$

Where:

- $I_{Health} = \dfrac{LE - LE_{min}}{LE_{max} - LE_{min}}$

- $I_{Education} = \dfrac{MYS + EYS}{2}$

- $I_{Income} = \dfrac{\ln(GNI) - \ln(GNI_{min})}{\ln(GNI_{max}) - \ln(GNI_{min})}$

Parameters:
LE: Life expectancy
MYS: Mean years of schooling
EYS: Expected years of schooling
GNI: Gross National Income

Each dimension is normalized to a scale of 0 to 1, ensuring comparability across countries.

HDI Classification

Based on HDI values, countries are classified into four categories:

- **Very High Human Development**: HDI > 0.8
- **High Human Development**: HDI between 0.7 and 0.8
- **Medium Human Development**: HDI between 0.55 and 0.7
- **Low Human Development**: HDI < 0.55

This classification helps policymakers and analysts identify disparities and prioritize development efforts.

Advantages of HDI

1. **Holistic Approach**

   - Unlike GDP, HDI considers health, education, and income, providing a broader view of development.

2. **Comparability**

- HDI allows cross-country comparisons, making it easier to assess relative progress and inequalities.

3. **Focus on Human Development**

- The emphasis on life expectancy and education underscores the importance of non-economic factors in improving well-being.

Limitations of HDI

1. **Exclusion of Inequality**

- HDI does not account for income or social inequality. For instance, two countries with the same HDI may have vastly different distributions of wealth.

2. **Simplistic Metrics**

- The three dimensions may oversimplify development, ignoring factors like environmental sustainability, political freedom, or cultural diversity.

3. **Static Indicators**

- HDI is calculated annually, making it less responsive to rapid changes or crises.

Enhanced HDI Metrics
To address the limitations of HDI, the UNDP introduced related indices:

1. **Inequality-Adjusted HDI (IHDI)**

- Adjusts HDI to reflect inequality in health, education, and income.
- The greater the inequality, the larger the gap between HDI and IHDI.

2. **Gender Development Index (GDI)**

- Compares HDI values for men and women to highlight gender disparities.

3. **Multidimensional Poverty Index (MPI)**

- Incorporates indicators like nutrition, child mortality, and access to basic services to measure poverty in a multidimensional framework.

Real-World Applications of HDI

1. **Policy Design**

- Governments use HDI to identify areas requiring investment, such as healthcare infrastructure or educational reform.

2. **Global Rankings**

- International organizations use HDI rankings to allocate aid, attract investment, and monitor development goals.

3. **Sustainable Development Goals (SDGs)**

- HDI aligns closely with SDGs, serving as a benchmark for tracking progress in reducing poverty, improving health, and ensuring quality education.

Criticism of HDI

While HDI provides valuable insights, it faces criticism for being overly simplified and not capturing the complexity of development:

- **Environmental Factors**: HDI overlooks ecological sustainability, a critical aspect of long-term development.
- **Cultural Differences**: Development priorities may vary by region, but HDI uses a one-size-fits-all approach.
- **Subjectivity in Weightage**: The equal weighting of dimensions may not reflect their relative importance in different contexts.

10.1.2 Poverty Line

The **Poverty Line** is a critical measure used to identify the minimum level of income required to meet the basic needs of individuals and households. It serves as a benchmark for classifying populations into those living above and below the poverty threshold. Understanding the concept of the poverty line is essential for assessing economic development, formulating policies, and addressing inequality.

Definition and Concept

The poverty line represents the income or consumption level necessary to maintain a minimum standard of living. This standard typically includes access to adequate food, clothing, shelter, and other basic necessities. Those falling below this line are considered impoverished, highlighting their inability to fulfill fundamental needs.

Determination of the Poverty Line

The poverty line is calculated using various methodologies, which may differ across countries and institutions. Common approaches include:

1. Income-Based Poverty Line

This approach defines poverty based on the minimum income required to purchase essential goods and services. For example:

- The World Bank's international poverty line is set at **$2.15 per day** (in 2017 PPP), identifying those living below this amount as being in extreme poverty.

2. Consumption-Based Poverty Line

This method assesses poverty by measuring household consumption. It considers the cost of a basket of goods and services that satisfies basic caloric and non-food requirements.

3. Caloric Intake Method

In this approach, the poverty line is determined by the minimum daily calorie intake required to sustain a healthy life, which is then translated into monetary terms. For example:

- In India, the **Tendulkar Committee** defined poverty based on a calorie requirement of 2,400 kcal per person in rural areas and 2,100 kcal in urban areas.

4. Relative Poverty Line

Unlike absolute measures, the relative poverty line considers income inequality. It defines poverty in relation to the median income of the population, identifying those earning less than a specific percentage (e.g., 50%) of the median as poor.

Global Standards and Comparisons

1. **World Bank Poverty Line**

   - The World Bank uses an international poverty line to facilitate comparisons across countries. In addition to the extreme poverty line of **$2.15/day**, it also defines thresholds for higher poverty levels, such as **$3.65/day** and **$6.85/day** for lower- and upper-middle-income countries.

2. **National Poverty Lines**

   - Many countries establish their own poverty lines based on local cost-of-living conditions. For instance, India's poverty line, as calculated by the **NITI Aayog**, reflects the consumption patterns and economic conditions of the country.

Applications of the Poverty Line

1. **Policy Formulation**

   - Governments use poverty line data to design and implement welfare programs like food subsidies, housing assistance, and healthcare for low-income populations.

2. **Monitoring and Evaluation**

   - Measuring poverty levels helps track progress in reducing poverty and achieving development goals like the **Sustainable Development Goals (SDGs).**

3. **Global Aid Allocation**

- International organizations, such as the United Nations and World Bank, use poverty line data to prioritize resource allocation and target interventions.

Limitations of the Poverty Line

Despite its utility, the poverty line has several limitations:

1. **Focus on Income and Consumption**

   - The poverty line often ignores non-monetary dimensions of poverty, such as access to education, healthcare, and social inclusion.

2. **Static Nature**

   - Fixed poverty lines may not adequately account for inflation, regional variations, or changes in consumption patterns over time.

3. **Arbitrary Thresholds**

   - Setting a universal poverty line can oversimplify the complex nature of poverty, as the cost of living varies significantly across regions and countries.

4. **Exclusion of Relative Poverty**

   - Absolute poverty lines fail to capture relative deprivation, where individuals may be excluded from societal participation despite being above the poverty threshold.

Poverty Line and Inequality

While the poverty line measures the prevalence of poverty, it does not directly address income inequality. A society with a low poverty rate can still have significant disparities in wealth distribution. Complementary measures like the **Gini coefficient** and **Palma ratio** are often used alongside the poverty line to assess inequality.

Poverty Line in India

India has adopted various methodologies over the years to define the poverty line. Key approaches include:

1. **Planning Commission Approach**

    ○ The initial poverty line was based on calorie intake requirements, adjusted for inflation.

2. **Tendulkar Committee Report (2009)**

    ○ This report shifted focus from calorie intake to consumption expenditure, incorporating health and education expenses.

3. **Rangarajan Committee Report (2014)**

    ○ This method revised poverty estimates by including basic necessities beyond food, such as education, health, and shelter.

Indian Poverty Line Example

- **Tendulkar Committee**: Defined the poverty line at ₹32/day in rural areas and ₹47/day in urban areas (2011–12).
- **Rangarajan Committee**: Revised it to ₹33/day in rural areas and ₹47/day in urban areas (2014).

Global Efforts to Address Poverty
1. Sustainable Development Goals (SDGs)
Goal 1 of the SDGs aims to **end poverty in all its forms everywhere** by 2030. Key targets include:

- Eradicating extreme poverty for people living on less than **$2.15/day**.
- Reducing the proportion of people living in poverty based on national definitions.

2. Poverty Alleviation Programs
Governments and international agencies implement various programs, such as:

- **Direct Cash Transfers**: Unconditional or conditional cash transfers to support low-income households.

- **Microfinance Initiatives**: Providing small loans to empower entrepreneurs in impoverished communities.
- **Food Security Schemes**: Ensuring access to affordable nutrition for vulnerable populations.

Criticisms and Challenges

1. **Underestimation of Poverty**

   - Official poverty lines often understate the extent of poverty due to narrow definitions and outdated benchmarks.

2. **Regional Disparities**

   - National poverty lines may not capture regional variations in cost of living, leading to misallocation of resources.

3. **Exclusion Errors**

   - Many genuinely poor individuals fail to qualify for poverty-alleviation programs due to inaccurate targeting.

10.2 Inequality and Distribution

Economic inequality refers to the unequal distribution of wealth, income, and opportunities among individuals or groups within a society. Understanding inequality is vital for designing policies that foster social justice and inclusive growth. Measuring inequality involves quantifying the disparities in resource allocation, and one of the most widely used tools for this purpose is the **Gini Coefficient**.

10.2.1 Gini Coefficient

The **Gini Coefficient** is a statistical measure used to represent income or wealth inequality within a population. Developed by the Italian statistician Corrado Gini in 1912, it provides a single number ranging from **0 to 1** (or sometimes expressed as a percentage, **0% to 100%**) to quantify inequality.

- **A Gini Coefficient of 0** indicates perfect equality, where everyone has the same income or wealth.
- **A Gini Coefficient of 1** signifies perfect inequality, where one individual or group controls all income or wealth.

Mathematical Representation
The Gini Coefficient is derived from the **Lorenz Curve**, which plots the cumulative percentage of income (or wealth) against the cumulative percentage of the population. The coefficient is calculated as:

$$G = \frac{A}{A + B}$$

Where:
A: Area between the line of perfect equality and the Lorenz Curve

B: Area under the Lorenz Curve

The more the Lorenz Curve deviates from the line of perfect equality, the higher the Gini Coefficient, indicating greater inequality.

Calculation of Gini Coefficient

For practical computation, the Gini Coefficient can also be expressed as:

$$G = 1 - \sum_{i=1}^{n} (L_i + L_{i-1}) \times W_i$$

Where:

- n: Number of population segments (e.g., income groups)

- L_i: Cumulative share of income for the i-th group

- W_i: Population share of the i-th group

This formula is widely used when data is grouped into income or wealth brackets

Interpretation of Gini Coefficient

- **Low Gini Coefficient (0–0.3)**: Indicates a relatively equal income distribution. Common in countries with strong redistributive policies.
- **Moderate Gini Coefficient (0.3–0.5)**: Reflects moderate inequality. This range is common in developing nations.
- **High Gini Coefficient (0.5–1.0)**: Signifies significant inequality, often seen in countries with limited redistribution or systemic disparities.

Examples

1. **Countries with Low Gini Coefficients**

   - **Sweden**: Strong welfare systems and progressive taxation result in low income inequality.
   - **Norway**: Gini Coefficient ~0.25.

2. **Countries with High Gini Coefficients**

   - **South Africa**: A legacy of apartheid and systemic inequality leads to a high Gini Coefficient (~0.63).
   - **Brazil**: Historically marked by wealth concentration in the top economic tiers.

Implications of the Gini Coefficient
Economic Insights

1. **Economic Growth and Stability**
   High inequality, as indicated by a high Gini Coefficient, can hinder economic growth by limiting access to education, healthcare, and credit for a significant portion of the population.
2. **Social Cohesion**
   Rising inequality can lead to social unrest, reduced trust in institutions, and increased crime rates.

Policy Applications

1. **Redistribution Strategies**
   Governments use Gini Coefficient data to design policies that promote equitable income distribution, such as progressive taxation, social welfare programs, and universal healthcare.
2. **Targeted Interventions**
   Identifying regions or demographic groups with high inequality enables tailored interventions, such as skill development programs or microfinance initiatives.
3. **Global Comparisons**
   The Gini Coefficient allows for cross-country comparisons of inequality, helping international organizations prioritize resource allocation and development efforts.

Advantages of the Gini Coefficient

1. **Simplicity**
   A single numerical value provides a clear and concise measure of inequality.

2. **Applicability**

The coefficient can be applied to various datasets, including income, wealth, or consumption.

3. **Versatility**

It facilitates comparisons across countries, regions, and time periods.

Limitations of the Gini Coefficient

1. **Loss of Specificity**

The Gini Coefficient does not indicate where inequality is concentrated (e.g., among the poorest or wealthiest segments).

2. **Static Nature**

It provides a snapshot at a single point in time, lacking insight into the dynamics of inequality over time.

3. **Exclusion of Non-Monetary Factors**

The Gini Coefficient focuses solely on income or wealth, ignoring other dimensions of inequality, such as access to education or healthcare.

4. **Impact of Population Composition**

Demographic changes, such as migration or age structure, can distort the interpretation of the Gini Coefficient.

Real-World Applications

1. **Welfare Programs in India**

India uses income and consumption data, often assessed through the Gini Coefficient, to identify areas requiring subsidies like the **Public Distribution System (PDS)** or schemes like **MGNREGA** (Mahatma Gandhi National Rural Employment Guarantee Act).

2. **OECD Inequality Reports**

The Organisation for Economic Co-operation and Development (OECD) uses the Gini Coefficient to compare inequality across member countries, guiding policy discussions on tax reforms and social welfare.

Complementary Measures of Inequality

While the Gini Coefficient is a valuable tool, it is often used alongside other indicators for a comprehensive analysis of inequality:

1. **Palma Ratio**
   Compares the income share of the top 10% of earners to the bottom 40%.

   - High Palma ratios indicate concentrated wealth among the elite.

2. **Theil Index**
   Decomposes inequality into within-group and between-group components for detailed analysis.

3. **Multidimensional Poverty Index (MPI)**
   Captures non-monetary aspects of inequality, such as education, health, and living standards.

10.2.2 Lorenz Curve

The **Lorenz Curve** is a graphical representation of income or wealth distribution within a population. Developed by economist Max Lorenz in 1905, it illustrates the degree of inequality in a society by showing the cumulative share of income or wealth earned by the cumulative percentage of the population. It is often used in conjunction with the **Gini Coefficient**, which quantifies the inequality depicted by the Lorenz Curve.

Understanding the Lorenz Curve

The Lorenz Curve compares the actual distribution of income or wealth to a hypothetical scenario of perfect equality.

- The **x-axis** represents the cumulative percentage of the population, ranked from poorest to richest.
- The **y-axis** represents the cumulative percentage of income or wealth.

The closer the Lorenz Curve is to the line of perfect equality (a 45-degree diagonal line), the more equitable the distribution. Conversely, the farther the Lorenz Curve lies from this line, the greater the inequality.

Components of the Lorenz Curve

1. **Line of Perfect Equality**

   - A straight diagonal line representing a scenario where every individual or household has an equal share of total income or wealth.

- Example: If 10% of the population earns 10% of the total income, 20% earns 20%, and so on.

2. **Lorenz Curve**

   - The actual curve showing the cumulative distribution of income or wealth.
   - It begins at the origin (0,0) and ends at (100,100), with the degree of curvature indicating inequality.

3. **Area Between Curves**

   - The area between the Lorenz Curve and the Line of Perfect Equality is used to calculate the **Gini Coefficient**.

How to Draw the Lorenz Curve

1. **Step 1: Collect Data**

   - Gather data on income or wealth distribution for the population. Divide the population into groups (e.g., deciles or quintiles).

2. **Step 2: Calculate Cumulative Percentages**

   - For each group, calculate the cumulative percentage of the population and the cumulative percentage of income or wealth.

3. **Step 3: Plot the Points**

   - Plot the cumulative population percentage on the x-axis and the cumulative income percentage on the y-axis.

4. **Step 4: Draw the Curve**

   - Connect the plotted points with a smooth line to form the Lorenz Curve.

Population Group	Cumulative % of Population	Cumulative % of Income
Lowest 20%	20%	5%
Next 20%	40%	15%
Middle 20%	60%	35%
Next 20%	80%	60%
Highest 20%	100%	100%

- **Lorenz Curve**: Connect the points (0,0), (20,5), (40,15), (60,35), (80,60), and (100,100).

- The closer the curve is to the diagonal, the more equitable the income distribution.

Lorenz Curve: Connect the points (0,0), (20,5), (40,15), (60,35), (80,60), and (100,100).

The closer the curve is to the diagonal, the more equitable the income distribution.

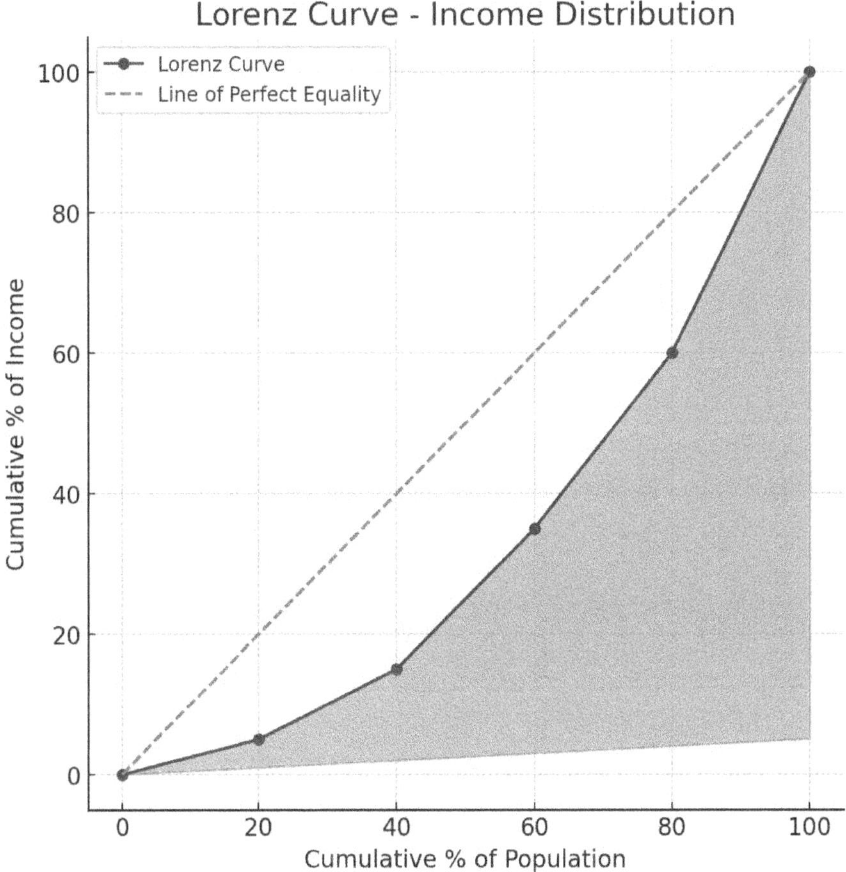

Lorenz Curve - Income Distribution

Interpreting the Lorenz Curve

1. **Equality vs. Inequality**

   - **Perfect Equality**: The Lorenz Curve coincides with the diagonal line, indicating everyone has an equal share.
   - **Extreme Inequality**: The Lorenz Curve hugs the axes, indicating all income is concentrated in the hands of a single individual or group.

2. **Relationship with the Gini Coefficient**

- The Gini Coefficient is calculated as the ratio of the area between the Lorenz Curve and the Line of Perfect Equality to the total area under the Line of Perfect Equality:

$$G = \frac{\text{Area between Lorenz Curve and Line of Perfect Equality}}{\text{Total area under Line of Perfect Equality}}$$

A larger area corresponds to a higher Gini Coefficient, signifying greater inequality.

Applications of the Lorenz Curve

1. **Policy Analysis**

   - Governments use the Lorenz Curve to assess the effectiveness of redistributive policies, such as taxation or social welfare programs.

2. **Comparative Studies**

   - Economists compare Lorenz Curves of different countries or regions to evaluate inequality levels.

3. **Corporate Responsibility**

   - Companies analyze the Lorenz Curve of wages within their organizations to promote equitable compensation practices.

Advantages of the Lorenz Curve

1. **Visual Representation**

   - The Lorenz Curve provides an intuitive and clear visualization of inequality.

2. **Versatility**

- It can be applied to various distributions, including income, wealth, or consumption.

3. Complementary to Other Measures

- It complements numerical measures like the Gini Coefficient by providing a graphical context.

Limitations of the Lorenz Curve

1. Static Snapshot

- The Lorenz Curve represents inequality at a single point in time and does not capture dynamic changes.

2. Ambiguity in Overlapping Curves

- Comparing two Lorenz Curves can be inconclusive if they intersect, as one curve may indicate less inequality in some population segments but more in others.

3. Ignores Other Dimensions of Inequality

- The Lorenz Curve focuses solely on economic measures, neglecting non-economic aspects like access to education, healthcare, or opportunities.

Real-World Examples

1. Global Inequality

- Countries with high inequality, such as South Africa or Brazil, have Lorenz Curves that deviate significantly from the diagonal.

2. Welfare Impact

- Countries with extensive social welfare systems, like Sweden or Denmark, show Lorenz Curves closer to the line of equality.

3. **Corporate Applications**

- ◦ Firms may use Lorenz Curves to analyze disparities in employee compensation or bonuses across departments.

• 244 •

10.3 Gender and Multidimensional Indices

Economic development cannot be fully understood or achieved without addressing disparities in gender equality and multidimensional well-being. Gender-focused indices provide crucial insights into the inequalities faced by women and men in various aspects of life, including health, education, and income. One such tool is the **Gender Development Index (GDI)**, which measures gender disparities in human development outcomes.

10.3.1 Gender Development Index (GDI)

The **Gender Development Index (GDI)**, introduced by the United Nations Development Programme (UNDP), is a gender-focused adaptation of the **Human Development Index (HDI)**. It measures the differences in achievement between men and women in the three key dimensions of human development: **health**, **education**, and **standard of living**.

The GDI reflects gender inequalities by comparing female and male HDI values, offering a clearer perspective on the disparities in access to resources and opportunities.

Key Components of GDI

The GDI utilizes the same dimensions as the HDI but calculates separate indices for men and women:

1. **Health Dimension**

   - Measured by **life expectancy at birth**, this reflects the ability of both men and women to lead long and healthy lives.
   - Adjustments account for biological differences in life expectancy.

2. **Education Dimension**

   - Captures gender differences in access to knowledge through:

     - **Mean years of schooling**: Average number of years of education received by people aged 25 and older.

- **Expected years of schooling**: Number of years a child entering school is expected to complete.

3. **Standard of Living Dimension**

   ○ Measured by **Gross National Income (GNI) per capita**, adjusted for purchasing power parity (PPP).

Calculation of GDI

The GDI is calculated as the ratio of the female HDI to the male HDI:

$$GDI = \frac{\text{HDI for females}}{\text{HDI for males}}$$

Interpreting GDI Values

- **GDI = 1**: Indicates perfect gender equality in human development outcomes.
- **GDI < 1**: Highlights gender disparities, with women experiencing lower levels of development than men.
- **GDI > 1**: Rare, but indicates instances where women have higher human development outcomes than men.

Global Trends in GDI
High GDI Countries
Countries with high GDI values, such as **Norway**, **Sweden**, and **Denmark**, exhibit minimal gender disparities due to strong social policies promoting gender equality in education, health, and economic opportunities.
Low GDI Countries
Nations with low GDI values, such as **Afghanistan**, **Yemen**, and **Chad**, face significant gender disparities due to cultural, economic, and institutional barriers.
Applications of GDI

1. **Policy Formulation**

   - Governments use GDI to design and implement gender-sensitive policies, such as initiatives to increase female participation in education and employment.

2. **International Comparisons**

   - The GDI allows global organizations to compare gender disparities across countries and regions, identifying areas requiring targeted interventions.

3. **Progress Monitoring**

   - The GDI serves as a benchmark for tracking progress toward gender equality, aligning with global goals like the **Sustainable Development Goals (SDGs)**.

Advantages of GDI

1. **Focus on Gender Equality**

   - The GDI highlights disparities that traditional indices like HDI might overlook, emphasizing the importance of addressing gender-specific challenges.

2. **Comparative Tool**

   - It facilitates cross-country and regional comparisons, enabling the identification of best practices and areas needing improvement.

3. **Multi-Dimensional Analysis**

   - By including health, education, and income dimensions, the GDI provides a holistic view of gender disparities.

Limitations of GDI

1. **Aggregation Issues**

   - The GDI aggregates data at the national level, potentially masking intra-country disparities, such as differences across rural and urban areas.

2. **Focus on Outcomes, Not Processes**

   - The GDI measures outcomes but does not provide insights into the systemic causes of gender inequality, such as discrimination or social norms.

3. **Exclusion of Non-Monetary Aspects**

   - The GDI does not capture other critical dimensions of gender inequality, such as political participation or unpaid domestic work.

Complementary Gender Indices

1. **Gender Inequality Index (GII)**

   - Focuses on reproductive health, empowerment, and labor market participation to provide a more detailed picture of gender disparities.

2. **Global Gender Gap Index (GGGI)**

   - Published by the World Economic Forum, it measures gender equality in economic participation, educational attainment, health, and political empowerment.

3. **Multidimensional Poverty Index (MPI)**

   - Offers a gender-disaggregated view of poverty by assessing deprivation across multiple dimensions, including health, education, and living standards.

Real-World Applications of GDI

1. **Education Policies in Developing Countries**

   - Countries like India use GDI to evaluate and improve gender-specific educational initiatives such as **Beti Bachao, Beti Padhao.**

2. **Global Gender Equality Campaigns**

   - International organizations use GDI data to advocate for gender equality and direct funding to regions with significant disparities.

3. **Healthcare Interventions**

   - Programs addressing maternal health in low-GDI countries rely on insights from GDI to allocate resources effectively.

Case Study: India
India's GDI Trends
India has made strides in reducing gender disparities in education and health, but significant gaps remain in income and labor force participation. GDI has been instrumental in highlighting areas where gender-focused policies are most needed.
Policy Implications

- Expanding access to secondary and higher education for girls.
- Implementing skill development programs to increase female labor force participation.
- Enhancing maternal and child healthcare facilities in rural areas.

10.3.2 Multidimensional Poverty Index (MPI)

The **Multidimensional Poverty Index (MPI)** is a comprehensive measure of poverty that goes beyond traditional income-based metrics to capture the multiple deprivations individuals face in their daily lives. Developed by the **Oxford Poverty and Human Development Initiative (OPHI)** in collaboration with the **United Nations Development Programme (UNDP)**, the MPI provides a nuanced understanding of poverty by considering factors such as health, education, and living standards.

Understanding the MPI

Traditional poverty measures, like the poverty line, focus solely on income or consumption levels. However, poverty is multidimensional, encompassing various aspects of human well-being. The MPI addresses this by combining multiple indicators into a single index to identify and analyze the nature and intensity of poverty.

Key Dimensions and Indicators of MPI

The MPI evaluates poverty across three main dimensions, each represented by specific indicators:

1. Health

- **Nutrition**: Measures whether any household member is malnourished.
- **Child Mortality**: Accounts for the death of any child under the age of five in the household.

2. Education

- **Years of Schooling**: Considers whether any household member has completed at least six years of schooling.
- **School Attendance**: Tracks whether any school-aged child is not attending school.

3. Living Standards

- **Electricity**: Determines whether the household has access to electricity.
- **Sanitation**: Evaluates access to adequate sanitation facilities.

- **Drinking Water**: Assesses whether the household has access to safe drinking water.
- **Housing**: Measures the quality of housing materials used for walls, roof, and floor.
- **Cooking Fuel**: Considers whether the household relies on clean cooking fuel.
- **Assets**: Evaluates ownership of essential assets like a bicycle, radio, or refrigerator.

Calculation of MPI

The MPI identifies individuals as poor if they are deprived in at least **one-third of the weighted indicators**. The calculation involves the following steps:

1. **Identify Deprivations**

   - Each household is assessed for deprivations across the 10 indicators.

2. **Assign Weights**

   - Equal weights are assigned to each dimension (one-third for health, education, and living standards). Indicators within a dimension are weighted equally.

3. **Calculate Deprivation Score**

   - For each household, a deprivation score is calculated by summing the weighted indicators where deprivation occurs.

4. **Define Poverty Threshold**

   - A household is considered multidimensionally poor if its deprivation score is $\geq$ **33%**.

5. **Aggregate MPI**

   The MPI is calculated by multiplying two components
   MPI=H×A

Where:

- **H**: Headcount ratio (proportion of the population identified as poor)
- **A:** Average intensity of poverty (average proportion of deprivations experienced by the poor).

Interpreting the MPI

The MPI provides insights into both the **prevalence** and **intensity** of poverty:

- **Prevalence**: The proportion of the population identified as poor (HHH).
- **Intensity**: The average proportion of deprivations experienced by poor individuals (AAA).

A high MPI value indicates severe and widespread poverty, while a low MPI value reflects fewer and less intense deprivations.

Applications of MPI

1. **Policy Design and Targeting**

   - The MPI identifies specific areas and population groups most affected by poverty, enabling targeted interventions.

2. **Monitoring and Evaluation**

   - Governments and international organizations use MPI to track progress toward poverty reduction goals, such as the **Sustainable Development Goals (SDGs).**

3. **Comparative Analysis**

   - The MPI facilitates comparisons of poverty levels across countries, regions, and demographic groups.

Global Trends in MPI
High MPI Countries

Countries like Niger, Chad, and South Sudan have high MPI values, reflecting widespread poverty and deprivations in health, education, and living standards.

Low MPI Countries

Countries like Norway, Switzerland, and Germany have low MPI values due to well-developed infrastructure, universal healthcare, and high-quality education systems.

Advantages of MPI

1. **Multidimensional Perspective**

   - Unlike income-based measures, the MPI captures the diverse and interconnected aspects of poverty.

2. **Actionable Insights**

   - By disaggregating data by region, ethnicity, or gender, the MPI provides specific information to guide policy interventions.

3. **Cross-Country Comparability**

   - The standardized methodology allows for global comparisons while considering local contexts.

4. **Focus on Intensity**

   - The MPI highlights not just the prevalence but also the intensity of poverty, providing a more comprehensive view.

Limitations of MPI

1. **Data Dependency**

   - Reliable and up-to-date data are essential for accurate MPI calculations, which may be challenging in resource-constrained regions.

2. **Weighting Subjectivity**

- The equal weighting of dimensions and indicators may not reflect their relative importance in different cultural or economic contexts.

3. **Static Snapshot**

- The MPI provides a snapshot of poverty at a given time but may not capture its dynamic nature.

4. **Exclusion of Certain Factors**

- The MPI does not include aspects like political freedom, social inclusion, or psychological well-being.

Real-World Applications of MPI

1. **India's MPI**

- India uses MPI data to target welfare schemes like **PMAY** (housing), **Swachh Bharat Mission** (sanitation), and **Poshan Abhiyaan** (nutrition).
- Recent trends show significant reductions in poverty due to improved access to sanitation, electricity, and education.

2. **Sub-Saharan Africa**

- Countries like Nigeria and Ethiopia utilize MPI to guide international aid programs and prioritize investments in healthcare and education.

3. **Latin America**

- Nations such as Colombia and Mexico integrate MPI into social programs like **Familias en Acción**, improving living standards for vulnerable populatio

Aspect	Structural Unemployment	Frictional Unemployment	Cyclical Unemployment
Nature	Long-term	Short-term	Medium-term
Cause	Skill mismatch, industry shifts	Job transitions, workforce entry	Economic downturns
Impact	Persistent unemployment	Minimal	Severe during recessions
Solution	Reskilling, diversification	Job-matching platforms	Stimulus and monetary policies

Comparison with Other Poverty Measures

ELEVEN

SUSTAINABLE DEVELOPMENT AND ENVIRONMENTAL ECONOMICS

Sustainable development and environmental economics explore the interplay between economic growth, social inclusivity, and environmental sustainability. In the context of global challenges like climate change, resource depletion, and inequality, fostering inclusive growth becomes a critical objective. Inclusive growth ensures that the benefits of economic progress are widely shared across all sections of society, while aligning with the principles of sustainability.

11.1 Inclusive Growth

Concept of Inclusive Growth

Inclusive Growth refers to an economic growth strategy that not only increases the overall wealth of a nation but also ensures that the benefits are equitably distributed across various demographic, social, and geographic groups. It emphasizes creating opportunities for all, reducing inequality, and providing access to basic services and economic resources.

Inclusive growth goes beyond **economic efficiency** to focus on **equity**, **participation**, and **sustainability**, making it central to long-term development strategies.

Key Principles of Inclusive Growth

1. Equity in Opportunity

- Ensuring equal access to education, healthcare, employment, and financial services for all segments of society.
- Bridging disparities in income, gender, and geography.

2. Economic Participation

- Encouraging active involvement of marginalized groups in the economic process by removing barriers like discrimination or lack of skills.

3. Sustainability

- Balancing economic progress with environmental stewardship to ensure resources are available for future generations.

4. Social Safety Nets

- Protecting vulnerable populations from economic shocks through policies like unemployment benefits, pensions, and food security programs.

Dimensions of Inclusive Growth

1. Economic Growth

- Achieving sustained and broad-based economic growth that generates employment and raises living standards.

2. Income Equality

- Reducing income disparities through progressive taxation, minimum wage policies, and wealth redistribution.

3. Social Inclusion

- ○ Promoting gender equality, empowering marginalized communities, and fostering participation in decision-making.

4. **Environmental Sustainability**

- ○ Adopting green technologies, renewable energy, and sustainable agricultural practices to reduce ecological harm.

Policy Implications of Inclusive Growth

To achieve inclusive growth, governments, businesses, and international organizations must implement policies that address systemic barriers and promote equitable access to opportunities.

1. Education and Skill Development

Rationale

Education is a cornerstone of inclusive growth, enabling individuals to acquire skills and participate in the economy.

Policy Measures

- Universal access to quality primary and secondary education.
- Vocational training programs to enhance employability.
- Scholarships and financial aid to reduce educational disparities.

Example: India's **Skill India Mission** aims to train millions of youth, empowering them with employable skills.

2. Employment Generation

Rationale

Inclusive growth requires creating jobs that provide decent wages and working conditions.

Policy Measures

- Investments in labor-intensive industries like construction, agriculture, and manufacturing.
- Encouraging entrepreneurship through microfinance and startup incentives.
- Promoting formalization of informal sector jobs.

Example: The **Mahatma Gandhi National Rural Employment Guarantee Act (MGNREGA)** provides guaranteed employment to rural households in India.

3. Financial Inclusion

Rationale

Access to financial services enables individuals and businesses to save, invest, and grow, reducing economic disparities.

Policy Measures

- Expanding access to banking, credit, and insurance in underserved areas.
- Digital payment systems to promote financial literacy and inclusion.
- Supporting small and medium enterprises (SMEs) through low-interest loans.

Example: Kenya's **M-Pesa** mobile banking platform has revolutionized financial access for rural populations.

4. Infrastructure Development

Rationale

Robust infrastructure facilitates economic activity and improves access to basic services.

Policy Measures

- Investments in transportation, energy, and communication networks.
- Building affordable housing and sanitation facilities in urban and rural areas.
- Expanding access to clean water and renewable energy.

Example: China's investments in rural infrastructure have significantly reduced urban-rural disparities.

5. Social Protection Programs

Rationale

Social safety nets mitigate the effects of poverty and inequality, ensuring no one is left behind.

Policy Measures

- Universal healthcare systems to provide affordable medical care.
- Food security programs to address malnutrition.
- Pensions and unemployment benefits for vulnerable groups.

Example: Brazil's **Bolsa Família** program provides cash transfers to low-income families, conditional on education and health requirements.

6. Promoting Gender Equality

Rationale

Empowering women is integral to achieving inclusive growth, as gender inequality hinders overall development.

Policy Measures

- Equal pay legislation and workplace protections for women.
- Maternity and childcare support to enable workforce participation.
- Leadership programs to increase female representation in politics and business.

Example: Rwanda has one of the highest proportions of women in parliament globally, reflecting successful gender-focused policies.

7. Environmental Sustainability

Rationale

Economic growth that depletes natural resources or harms the environment is unsustainable in the long term.

Policy Measures

- Incentives for adopting renewable energy and green technologies.
- Sustainable agricultural practices to combat deforestation and soil degradation.
- Carbon pricing to reduce greenhouse gas emissions.

Example: Germany's **Energiewende** (energy transition) program promotes renewable energy and energy efficiency.

Challenges to Inclusive Growth

1. **Structural Barriers**

   - Inequality in land ownership, discriminatory practices, and lack of access to education or healthcare create systemic disadvantages.

2. **Economic Shocks**

- Global financial crises, pandemics, or natural disasters disproportionately affect vulnerable populations.

3. **Urban-Rural Divide**

- Disparities in infrastructure and opportunities between urban and rural areas hinder balanced development.

4. **Political and Institutional Weaknesses**

- Corruption, weak governance, and inefficient implementation of policies impede progress.

5. **Climate Change**

- Environmental degradation exacerbates poverty and inequality, particularly in resource-dependent economies.

Benefits of Inclusive Growth

1. **Economic Stability**

- Reducing inequality fosters social cohesion and minimizes risks of unrest or conflict.

2. **Enhanced Productivity**

- Empowering all sections of society improves human capital, boosting economic output.

3. **Sustainability**

- Inclusive policies ensure resources are utilized efficiently, balancing economic progress with environmental preservation.

4. **Global Competitiveness**

- Economies that reduce inequality attract more investment, trade, and innovation.

11.2 Environmental Sustainability

Environmental sustainability is integral to sustainable development, ensuring that economic progress does not come at the expense of environmental health. Traditional economic measures like Gross Domestic Product (GDP) often overlook environmental costs, leading to unsustainable practices. To address this gap, concepts like **Green GDP** have emerged, offering a more holistic approach to measuring economic growth.

11.2.1 Green GDP

Green GDP is an economic measure that accounts for the environmental costs of economic activities, such as resource depletion, pollution, and ecosystem degradation. It adjusts the traditional GDP by subtracting the monetary value of environmental damage, providing a more accurate representation of a nation's true wealth and sustainability.

Concept of Green GDP

The traditional GDP focuses on the market value of all goods and services produced in a country but ignores the negative externalities of production and consumption. This can lead to a false perception of prosperity, especially in economies reliant on activities that degrade natural resources.

Green GDP, on the other hand:

- **Subtracts environmental degradation** from the GDP.
- **Adds the economic value of ecosystem services**, such as clean air, water, and biodiversity.

By integrating environmental factors, Green GDP shifts the focus from short-term growth to long-term sustainability.

Calculation of Green GDP

The formula for Green GDP is:

Green GDP=Traditional GDP−Environmental Costs

Where:

- **Environmental Costs** include the monetary value of resource depletion, pollution, and ecological damage.

Example Calculation:

1. Traditional GDP = $1 trillion.
2. Environmental costs (pollution, deforestation, etc.) = $100 billion.
3. Green GDP = $1 trillion - $100 billion = $900 billion.

This adjustment provides a more realistic view of economic health.
Components of Green GDP

1. Costs of Resource Depletion

    ◦ Accounts for the exploitation of non-renewable resources like minerals, oil, and forests.
    ◦ Example: Overfishing reduces the future availability of fish stocks.

2. Pollution Costs

    ◦ Includes the economic damage caused by air, water, and soil pollution.
    ◦ Example: Healthcare costs arising from air pollution-related illnesses.

3. Loss of Ecosystem Services

    ◦ Quantifies the value of services lost due to deforestation, biodiversity loss, or wetland destruction.
    ◦ Example: Reduced carbon sequestration due to deforestation.

4. Climate Change Impacts

    ◦ Incorporates the economic costs of climate-related disasters, such as floods or droughts.

Policy Implications of Green GDP

1. Incentivizing Sustainable Practices

    ◦ Governments can promote green technologies and renewable energy to reduce environmental costs.

- Example: Subsidies for solar energy installations.

2. Redefining Development Goals

   - Policies can focus on sustainable development rather than purely economic growth.
   - Example: Including environmental metrics in national development plans.

3. Integrating Environmental Accounting

   - Regular Green GDP reporting can help countries assess the trade-offs between growth and environmental health.

4. Taxation and Regulation

   - Imposing taxes on activities that degrade the environment (e.g., carbon taxes) aligns economic incentives with sustainability.

Global Examples of Green GDP

1. China

   - China introduced Green GDP in 2004 to assess the environmental costs of its rapid industrialization. While initial results showed significant ecological losses, the initiative highlighted the need for stricter environmental regulations.

2. Norway

   - Norway incorporates environmental accounting into its national statistics, emphasizing sustainable management of its oil and natural gas resources.

3. India

   - The Ministry of Statistics and Programme Implementation (MoSPI) has developed a framework for environmental accounting, focusing on forests, water, and air quality as part of its Green GDP initiative.

Advantages of Green GDP

1. Holistic Measurement

   - Provides a comprehensive view of economic progress by integrating environmental costs.

2. Policy Guidance

   - Helps policymakers prioritize sustainable practices and investments.

3. Public Awareness

   - Highlights the environmental impact of economic activities, fostering public support for conservation.

4. Global Comparability

   - Enables countries to benchmark their sustainability efforts against others.

Limitations of Green GDP

1. Valuation Challenges

   - Assigning monetary value to environmental goods and services, like clean air or biodiversity, is complex and subjective.

2. Data Limitations

   - Accurate Green GDP calculations require extensive environmental data, which may not be available in all countries.

3. Potential Policy Resistance

- Highlighting environmental costs may discourage investments in resource-intensive industries, facing pushback from stakeholders.

4. Focus on Monetary Metrics

- Green GDP still relies on monetary valuation, which may not fully capture the intrinsic value of nature.

Role of Green GDP in Sustainable Development

1. Promoting Environmental Accountability

- Green GDP encourages businesses and governments to account for environmental costs in their decisions.

2. Achieving SDGs

- Aligns with the Sustainable Development Goals (SDGs), particularly Goal 12 (Responsible Consumption and Production) and Goal 13 (Climate Action).

3. Transitioning to Green Economies

- Provides a roadmap for transitioning from resource-intensive growth models to sustainable economies.

4. Highlighting Trade-Offs

- Shows the true cost of growth, enabling balanced decision-making between economic development and ecological preservation.

11.2.1 Sustainable Development Goals (SDGs)

The Sustainable Development Goals (SDGs) are a set of 17 global goals established by the United Nations in 2015 as part of the 2030 Agenda for Sustainable Development. These goals aim to address the most pressing social, economic, and environmental challenges, ensuring a better and sustainable future for all. The SDGs are universal, integrative, and transformative, calling for action from governments, private sectors, civil society, and individuals.

Overview of the SDGs

The SDGs build upon the successes of the Millennium Development Goals (MDGs), expanding their scope to include not just poverty eradication but also sustainability and inclusivity. They focus on balancing three dimensions of sustainable development:

- Economic Growth
- Social Inclusion
- Environmental Protection

The 17 SDGs

Each goal is interconnected, addressing diverse aspects of global development:

1. No Poverty: End poverty in all its forms everywhere.
2. Zero Hunger: End hunger, achieve food security, and promote sustainable agriculture.
3. Good Health and Well-being: Ensure healthy lives and promote well-being for all.
4. Quality Education: Ensure inclusive and equitable quality education.
5. Gender Equality: Achieve gender equality and empower all women and girls.
6. Clean Water and Sanitation: Ensure access to water and sanitation for all.
7. Affordable and Clean Energy: Ensure access to affordable, reliable, and sustainable energy.
8. Decent Work and Economic Growth: Promote sustained, inclusive, and sustainable economic growth.
9. Industry, Innovation, and Infrastructure: Build resilient infrastructure and foster innovation.
10. Reduced Inequalities: Reduce inequality within and among countries.
11. Sustainable Cities and Communities: Make cities and human settlements inclusive and sustainable.

12. Responsible Consumption and Production: Ensure sustainable consumption and production patterns.
13. Climate Action: Take urgent action to combat climate change and its impacts.
14. Life Below Water: Conserve and sustainably use oceans, seas, and marine resources.
15. Life on Land: Protect, restore, and promote sustainable use of terrestrial ecosystems.
16. Peace, Justice, and Strong Institutions: Promote peaceful and inclusive societies.
17. Partnerships for the Goals: Strengthen global partnerships for sustainable development.

Key Features of the SDGs

1. Universal Application

   - The SDGs apply to all countries, regardless of economic status, emphasizing collective responsibility.

2. Inclusivity

   - They prioritize marginalized and vulnerable groups to leave no one behind.

3. Integration

   - Each goal is interconnected, requiring a holistic approach to development.

4. Measurable Targets

   - The SDGs include 169 targets and 232 indicators to track progress and ensure accountability.

Importance of SDGs

1. Global Development Framework

   - The SDGs provide a common agenda for addressing global challenges, promoting peace, prosperity, and sustainability.

2. Focus on Sustainability

   - They emphasize the need to balance economic growth with environmental protection and social inclusion.

3. Driving Policy and Investment

   - Governments and organizations align their policies and resources to achieve these goals.

4. Monitoring Progress

   - The goals include measurable indicators to assess the success of development initiatives.

Challenges in Achieving the SDGs

1. Resource Constraints

   - Many countries face financial and technological barriers to implementing SDG initiatives.

2. Global Inequality

   - Disparities in resources and capacities hinder progress, particularly in developing countries.

3. Conflicting Priorities

○ Balancing economic growth with environmental sustainability remains a significant challenge.

4. Lack of Awareness

○ Limited public understanding of the SDGs reduces grassroots participation.

5. Pandemics and Crises

○ Global challenges like COVID-19 and geopolitical tensions disrupt progress.

Success Stories and Global Examples

1. No Poverty (Goal 1)

○ China lifted over 800 million people out of extreme poverty, aligning with SDG targets.

2. Quality Education (Goal 4)

○ Kenya's free primary education program significantly increased school enrollment.

3. Affordable and Clean Energy (Goal 7)

○ India's Ujjwala Yojana initiative provided clean cooking fuel to millions of households.

4. Climate Action (Goal 13)

○ Costa Rica is a global leader in renewable energy, meeting over 99% of its energy needs sustainably.

Role of Partnerships in Achieving the SDGs

Goal 17: Partnerships for the Goals emphasizes the importance of collaboration among:

- Governments: Aligning national policies with global targets.
- Private Sector: Driving innovation, technology, and investment for sustainable practices.
- Civil Society: Advocating for equitable and inclusive policies.
- International Organizations: Providing funding, technical support, and capacity building.

SDGs and Environmental Economics

1. Climate Action (Goal 13)

    ◦ Combating climate change is central to environmental sustainability, requiring global commitments like the Paris Agreement.

2. Life Below Water (Goal 14)

    ◦ Ensuring sustainable fisheries and marine conservation aligns with the principles of blue economy.

3. Life on Land (Goal 15)

    ◦ Addressing deforestation, biodiversity loss, and land degradation contributes to long-term ecological balance.

4. Sustainable Consumption and Production (Goal 12)

    ◦ Encourages reducing waste, improving resource efficiency, and adopting circular economy models.

Future Outlook and the Road Ahead

1. Leveraging Technology

   - Innovations like artificial intelligence, renewable energy, and biotechnology can accelerate progress toward SDGs.

2. Empowering Communities

   - Grassroots participation ensures that SDG initiatives are inclusive and locally relevant.

3. Global Accountability

   - Regular progress reports and peer reviews hold stakeholders accountable for their commitments.

4. Adaptability to Emerging Challenges

   - Addressing unforeseen issues like pandemics or geopolitical conflicts requires adaptive strategies.

11.3 Economic Models of Sustainability

Economic models of sustainability provide frameworks for understanding the relationship between economic growth, environmental degradation, and social well-being. These models guide policymakers in balancing development goals with ecological preservation. One of the most influential models in this context is the Kuznets Curve, which examines how income inequality and environmental degradation evolve with economic growth.

11.3.1 Kuznets Curve

The Kuznets Curve, proposed by economist Simon Kuznets in the 1950s, describes the relationship between economic development and inequality. Its environmental adaptation, the Environmental Kuznets Curve (EKC), explores the relationship between economic growth and environmental degradation.

Both forms of the curve hypothesize that this relationship follows an inverted U-shape:

- Early stages of growth: Economic expansion leads to increased inequality or environmental harm.
- Later stages of growth: Higher income levels lead to greater equality or reduced environmental degradation due to investments in social equity and cleaner technologies.

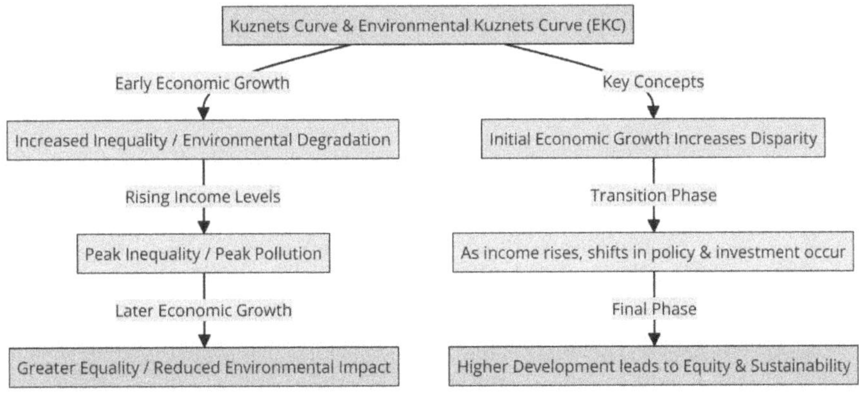

Kuznets Curve

Original Kuznets Curve (Income Inequality)

Hypothesis

Kuznets proposed that as an economy develops:

1. Initial Phase: Income inequality increases as urbanization and industrialization concentrate wealth among a small segment of the population.
2. Middle Phase: Inequality peaks as more individuals transition from low-income rural areas to higher-income urban sectors.
3. Final Phase: Inequality decreases as broader access to education, healthcare, and employment reduces disparities.

Graphical Representation

- X-axis: Economic growth (measured by GDP per capita).
- Y-axis: Income inequality (measured by Gini coefficient).
- Curve Shape: An inverted U, with inequality rising initially and falling as economies mature.

Environmental Kuznets Curve (EKC)

Hypothesis

The EKC extends the Kuznets Curve framework to environmental issues, suggesting that as income grows:

1. Initial Phase: Environmental degradation increases due to industrialization and unsustainable resource use.
2. Middle Phase: Degradation peaks as industrial activity intensifies without environmental safeguards.
3. Final Phase: Degradation declines as higher incomes enable investments in clean technologies, regulatory frameworks, and public awareness.

Graphical Representation

- X-axis: Economic growth (measured by GDP per capita).
- Y-axis: Environmental degradation (e.g., pollution levels, deforestation rates).
- Curve Shape: An inverted U, reflecting rising and then falling environmental harm.

Examples of Environmental Kuznets Curve

1. Air Pollution

   - Initial Phase: Industrialization increases emissions of pollutants like sulfur dioxide (SO_2) and nitrogen oxides (NO_x).
   - Later Phase: Economies invest in cleaner energy and pollution controls, reducing emissions.

Example: The United States and Western Europe experienced declining air pollution levels after reaching high-income thresholds.

1. Deforestation

   - Initial Phase: Expansion of agriculture and logging depletes forests.
   - Later Phase: Wealthier societies implement reforestation programs and sustainable forestry practices.

Example: Brazil has shown mixed trends, with efforts to reduce deforestation counterbalanced by economic pressures.

3. Water Quality

- Initial Phase: Industrial runoff and urbanization degrade water resources.
- Later Phase: Investments in wastewater treatment and regulations improve water quality.

Example: European countries have significantly reduced water pollution through strict environmental policies.

Criticisms and Limitations of the Kuznets Curve

1. Generalization

- The curve assumes a universal path of development, which may not apply to all countries or environmental indicators.

2. Rebound Effect

- Economic growth can lead to increased consumption and environmental impacts, counteracting gains from cleaner technologies.

3. Data Dependency

- Empirical evidence supporting the EKC is inconsistent, with variations across countries and environmental metrics.

4. Ignoring Irreversibility

- Some forms of environmental damage, such as biodiversity loss or climate change, may be irreversible, undermining the notion of recovery.

5. Focus on Growth

- The model prioritizes economic growth, often neglecting the need for systemic changes to consumption patterns and production systems.

Policy Implications of the Kuznets Curve

1. Early Interventions

   - Governments can adopt proactive policies to minimize environmental degradation during the early stages of economic growth, such as green industrial practices and environmental regulations.

2. Technological Innovation

   - Encouraging research and development in clean energy and sustainable technologies accelerates the transition to the downward slope of the EKC.

3. Global Cooperation

   - High-income countries can support low-income nations through technology transfer and funding for environmental initiatives.

4. Strengthening Institutions

   - Building robust regulatory frameworks ensures that economic growth does not come at the expense of environmental health.

5. Sustainable Development Goals (SDGs)

   - Aligning national policies with SDGs, particularly those related to climate action (Goal 13) and sustainable consumption (Goal 12), supports the principles of the Kuznets Curve.

Alternative Perspectives on Sustainability

1. Steady-State Economy

   - Advocates for limiting economic growth to achieve ecological balance and preserve finite resources.

2. Circular Economy

    ◦ Focuses on minimizing waste and maximizing resource efficiency through recycling and reuse.

3. Degrowth Movement

    ◦ Challenges the growth-centric paradigm, promoting reduced consumption and environmental restoration.

Aspect	Structural Unemployment	Frictional Unemployment	Cyclical Unemployment
Nature	Long-term	Short-term	Medium-term
Cause	Skill mismatch, industry shifts	Job transitions, workforce entry	Economic downturns
Impact	Persistent unemployment	Minimal	Severe during recessions
Solution	Reskilling, diversification	Job-matching platforms	Stimulus and monetary policies

Green GDP vs. Traditional GDP

TWELVE
BANKING INNOVATIONS AND FINANCIAL MARKETS

The banking sector is a vital component of the financial system, enabling capital allocation, credit creation, and economic growth. However, the performance and stability of banks can be undermined by the accumulation of **Non-Performing Assets (NPAs)**, which pose significant challenges to the financial ecosystem. Understanding the causes and impacts of NPAs is essential for developing effective strategies to manage and mitigate them.

12.1 Non-Performing Assets (NPAs)

Definition of NPAs

Non-Performing Assets (NPAs) refer to loans or advances for which the principal or interest payment has been overdue for a specified period, typically **90 days** in most banking systems. Once classified as an NPA, the loan ceases to generate income for the bank and is considered a liability.

Classification of NPAs

1. **Substandard Assets**

    - Loans overdue for **more than 90 days but less than 12 months.**
    - These carry higher credit risks but have the potential for recovery.

2. **Doubtful Assets**

   ○ Loans that remain in the substandard category for more than 12 months.
   ○ The probability of full recovery diminishes significantly.

3. **Loss Assets**

   ○ Loans identified by auditors or the Reserve Bank of India (RBI) as **non-recoverable**.
   ○ These are considered irretrievable and require full provisioning by the bank.

Causes of NPAs

The accumulation of NPAs is driven by several factors, often linked to macroeconomic conditions, sector-specific challenges, or operational inefficiencies within banks.

1. Economic Slowdown

- During periods of economic downturn, borrowers face reduced income and profitability, impacting their ability to repay loans.
  Example: The global financial crisis of 2008 led to widespread defaults in various sectors.

2. Poor Credit Appraisal

- Inadequate assessment of borrowers' repayment capacity during the loan sanctioning process increases the likelihood of default.
  Example: Loans extended without proper due diligence or based on inflated collateral valuations.

3. High Sectoral Exposure

- Over-reliance on specific industries or sectors, such as real estate or infrastructure, makes banks vulnerable to sectoral downturns.
  Example: The infrastructure sector in India has been a significant contributor to NPAs due to project delays and regulatory hurdles.

4. Wilful Defaults

- Some borrowers deliberately avoid repaying loans despite having the capacity to do so.
  Example: High-profile cases like Vijay Mallya and Nirav Modi in India highlighted the issue of wilful defaults.

5. Policy and Regulatory Issues

- Sudden policy changes, such as demonetization or changes in import/export tariffs, can disrupt businesses, leading to defaults.
  Example: Regulatory delays in environmental clearances for infrastructure projects in India.

6. External Shocks

- Events such as pandemics, natural disasters, or geopolitical conflicts can disrupt economic activities and repayment cycles.
  Example: The COVID-19 pandemic significantly increased NPAs globally as businesses faced prolonged closures.

7. Ineffective Recovery Mechanisms

- Delays in legal proceedings and the inefficiency of debt recovery tribunals impede timely resolution of stressed assets.
  Example: Cases lingering for years in courts reduce the chances of recovery.

Impacts of NPAs

The rise of NPAs has far-reaching implications for banks, the financial sector, and the broader economy.

1. Erosion of Profitability

- NPAs reduce interest income, which is a primary revenue source for banks.
- Banks must make provisions for bad loans, further straining their profits.
  Example: Indian public sector banks experienced significant profit

erosion due to high NPA levels between 2015 and 2020.

2. Capital Constraints

- High NPAs lead to reduced capital adequacy, limiting banks' ability to lend.
- Capital infusion may be required from the government, diverting funds from other developmental priorities.

3. Decline in Credit Growth

- The banking sector becomes risk-averse, reducing lending to productive sectors.
- This curtails investments and slows economic growth.

4. Loss of Public Confidence

- Persistent NPA issues erode trust in the banking system, prompting depositors to withdraw their funds.
  Example: Failures of cooperative banks in India have highlighted the risks associated with poor asset quality.

5. Impact on Economic Growth

- Stressed banking systems hinder the efficient allocation of credit, slowing down key sectors like agriculture, MSMEs, and infrastructure.
  Example: The ripple effects of the banking crisis in Greece significantly hampered the nation's economic recovery.

6. Increased Regulatory Oversight

- Regulatory bodies impose stricter norms, increasing compliance costs for banks.
- Enhanced monitoring also diverts resources from growth-oriented activities.

Strategies to Mitigate NPAs

1. **Strengthening Credit Appraisal Processes**

   - Implement robust credit risk assessment tools to evaluate borrowers' repayment capacity accurately.

2. **Diversifying Loan Portfolios**

   - Reduce concentration in high-risk sectors and diversify lending across industries.

3. **Prompt Resolution Mechanisms**

   - Expedite the resolution of stressed assets through mechanisms like the Insolvency and Bankruptcy Code (IBC).
     Example: The IBC in India has streamlined the recovery process for banks.

4. **Encouraging Digital Lending Platforms**

   - Use advanced analytics and AI to improve loan underwriting and reduce defaults.

5. **Addressing Wilful Defaults**

   - Strengthen legal frameworks to penalize wilful defaulters and recover dues efficiently.

6. **Public Awareness Campaigns**

   - Educate borrowers about financial literacy and the consequences of defaulting on loans.

Government Initiatives to Address NPAs

1. **Recapitalization of Banks**

   - Infusion of capital into public sector banks to strengthen their balance sheets.

Example: The Indian government allocated ₹2.11 trillion for bank recapitalization in 2017.

2. **Asset Reconstruction Companies (ARCs)**

   - ARCs acquire bad loans from banks, allowing them to focus on core banking activities.
   Example: The **National Asset Reconstruction Company Limited (NARCL)** in India.

3. **SARFAESI Act (2002)**

   - Empowered banks to recover dues by auctioning defaulters' assets without court intervention.

4. **Insolvency and Bankruptcy Code (IBC)**

   - Provides a time-bound resolution framework for stressed assets.

12.2 Basel Norms

The **Basel Norms** are a set of international banking regulations established by the **Basel Committee on Banking Supervision (BCBS)** to ensure financial stability and improve risk management practices in the global banking system. These norms provide a framework for banks to maintain adequate capital and manage risks effectively, thereby reducing the likelihood of financial crises.

The Basel Norms have evolved over time, with **Basel I**, **Basel II**, and **Basel III** representing successive enhancements to address emerging challenges in the financial sector.

12.2.1 Basel I

Introduction

Introduced in **1988**, **Basel I** was the first international framework for banking regulation. Its primary focus was on credit risk, requiring banks to maintain sufficient capital to absorb potential losses. The norms aimed to strengthen the soundness and stability of the international banking system by promoting a minimum capital adequacy standard.

Key Features

1. **Capital Adequacy Ratio (CAR)**

   - Basel I introduced the concept of the **Capital Adequacy Ratio (CAR)**, requiring banks to hold capital equal to at least **8% of their risk-weighted assets (RWA)**.
   - **Formula:**

$$CAR = \frac{Capital}{Risk\text{-}Weighted\ Assets} \times 100$$

1. **Risk Categorization**

   - Assets were categorized into four risk weights: **0%, 20%, 50%, and 100%,** based on the credit risk associated with each type of asset.
   - For example:

     - Government securities: **0% risk weight.**
     - Residential mortgages: **50% risk weight.**
     - Commercial loans: **100% risk weight.**

2. **Focus on Credit Risk**

   - Basel I primarily addressed **credit risk**, the risk of loss due to a borrower's failure to repay.

Impact

- Basel I laid the foundation for global banking regulation, ensuring minimum capital requirements.
- However, it was criticized for its simplistic risk-weighting system, which did not adequately address other types of risks, such as operational and market risks.

12.2.2 Basel II

Introduction

Introduced in **2004, Basel II** was designed to address the limitations of Basel I by incorporating a broader range of risks and improving the risk sensitivity of the framework. It aimed to strengthen risk management practices and align regulatory capital requirements more closely with the underlying risks.

Key Features

Basel II was structured around three pillars:

1. Pillar 1: Minimum Capital Requirements

- Banks were required to maintain capital for **three types of risks**:

  - **Credit Risk**: Enhanced risk-weighting methods based on credit ratings.
  - **Market Risk**: Risk of losses due to fluctuations in market prices.
  - **Operational Risk**: Risk of losses due to inadequate internal processes or external events.

2. Pillar 2: Supervisory Review Process

- Emphasized the need for banks to assess their risk profiles and maintain capital beyond the minimum regulatory requirements.
- Encouraged regulators to evaluate banks' internal risk management processes.

3. Pillar 3: Market Discipline

- Required banks to disclose information on their risk exposures, capital adequacy, and risk management practices to promote transparency and accountability.

Improvements Over Basel I

1. **Advanced Risk Assessment**

   - Introduced **Internal Ratings-Based (IRB) Approach**, allowing banks to use their internal models to calculate credit risk.

2. **Operational Risk Management**

   - For the first time, operational risk was explicitly included in capital requirements.

3. **Emphasis on Transparency**

   - Market discipline ensured that stakeholders could assess a bank's financial health and risk management practices.

Impact

- Basel II improved the alignment of capital requirements with risks.
- However, its reliance on external credit ratings and complex models drew criticism during the **2008 global financial crisis**, as it failed to account for systemic risks and market interconnectedness.

12.2.3 Basel III

Introduction

In response to the shortcomings exposed by the **2008 financial crisis**, **Basel III** was introduced in **2010**. It aimed to strengthen the resilience of the banking system by enhancing capital requirements, introducing liquidity standards, and addressing systemic risks.

Key Features

1. **Enhanced Capital Requirements**

   - Increased the minimum **CAR** to **10.5%**, including a **Capital Conservation Buffer** of 2.5% to absorb losses during periods of stress.
   - Introduced **Tier 1 Capital** and **Common Equity Tier 1 (CET1)** as key components of high-quality capital.

2. **Leverage Ratio**

   - Introduced a **Leverage Ratio** to limit excessive borrowing by banks

$$\text{Leverage Ratio} = \frac{\text{Tier 1 Capital}}{\text{Total Assets}} \times 100$$

Minimum leverage ratio: **3%.**

1. **Liquidity Standards**

   - Introduced two liquidity ratios to ensure short-term and long-term resilience:

       - **Liquidity Coverage Ratio (LCR)**: Banks must hold high-quality liquid assets (HQLA) sufficient to cover net cash outflows for 30 days.
       - **Net Stable Funding Ratio (NSFR)**: Encourages stable funding over a one-year horizon.

2. **Counter-Cyclical Capital Buffer**

   - Requires banks to build additional capital buffers during economic booms to absorb potential losses during downturns.

3. **Systemically Important Banks (SIBs)**

   - Identified **Global Systemically Important Banks (G-SIBs)** that must maintain additional capital to reduce systemic risks.

Impact

- Basel III significantly enhanced the banking sector's ability to absorb shocks, reducing systemic risks.
- However, its stringent requirements posed challenges for smaller banks, which struggled to meet the higher capital and liquidity thresholds.

12.4 Modern Financial Instruments

Modern financial instruments have revolutionized investment and risk management practices, offering investors and institutions a wide range of tools to diversify portfolios, manage risks, and achieve financial goals. Among these instruments, **Derivatives**, **Mutual Funds**, and **Exchange-Traded Funds (ETFs)** stand out for their versatility, accessibility, and role in shaping global financial markets.

12.4.1 Derivatives

Definition

Derivatives are financial instruments whose value is derived from an underlying asset, such as stocks, bonds, commodities, currencies, or indices. They are primarily used for hedging, speculation, and arbitrage.

Types of Derivatives

1. Futures

- A **futures contract** obligates the buyer to purchase, and the seller to sell, the underlying asset at a predetermined price on a specific date.
- Traded on organized exchanges, futures are standardized and regulated.
  Example: Commodity futures for crude oil, gold, or agricultural products.

2. Options

- An **options contract** gives the holder the right, but not the obligation, to buy (call option) or sell (put option) the underlying asset at a specified price before or on a specific date.
  Example: Stock options to hedge against price fluctuations.

3. Swaps

- A **swap** is a contract in which two parties exchange cash flows based on underlying assets or interest rates.
  Example: Interest rate swaps where fixed-rate payments are exchanged

for floating-rate payments.

4. Forwards

- Similar to futures but traded over-the-counter (OTC), **forward contracts** are customized agreements between two parties to buy or sell an asset at a future date.
  Example: Currency forwards used to hedge against exchange rate risks.

Applications of Derivatives

1. **Hedging**

   - Protects investors and companies from adverse price movements in underlying assets.
     Example: An airline company uses fuel futures to lock in fuel costs.

2. **Speculation**

   - Traders use derivatives to profit from anticipated price movements.
     Example: Speculators buy stock options betting on future price increases.

3. **Arbitrage**

   - Exploiting price differences between markets to earn risk-free profits.
     Example: Arbitrageurs buy gold in one market and sell it in another where prices are higher.

Risks and Challenges

- **Market Risk**: Sudden price movements can lead to significant losses.
- **Leverage**: Derivatives are highly leveraged, amplifying gains and losses.
- **Counterparty Risk**: In OTC derivatives, the risk of the counterparty defaulting is a concern.
- **Complexity**: Derivatives require expertise to understand and manage effectively.

12.4.2 *Mutual Funds*

Definition

A **mutual fund** is a pooled investment vehicle that collects money from multiple investors to invest in a diversified portfolio of securities, such as stocks, bonds, or money market instruments. Managed by professional fund managers, mutual funds provide retail investors access to diversified investments.

Types of Mutual Funds

1. Equity Funds

- Invest primarily in stocks, offering high returns with higher risk.
  Example: Large-cap equity funds focused on established companies.

2. Debt Funds

- Invest in fixed-income securities like bonds and treasury bills, offering stability and regular income.
  Example: Government bond funds.

3. Hybrid Funds

- Combine equity and debt investments to balance risk and return.
  Example: Balanced funds with a 60:40 equity-to-debt ratio.

4. Index Funds

- Track a specific market index, such as the **S&P 500** or **NIFTY 50**, providing passive investment opportunities.

5. Money Market Funds

- Invest in short-term, high-quality debt instruments like certificates of deposit and commercial paper.

Advantages of Mutual Funds

1. **Diversification**

   ◦ Reduces risk by spreading investments across multiple securities.

2. **Professional Management**

   ◦ Experienced fund managers make investment decisions on behalf of investors.

3. **Liquidity**

   ◦ Mutual fund units can be redeemed on any business day.

4. **Accessibility**

   ◦ Retail investors can participate with low initial investment amounts.

Risks and Challenges

- **Market Risk**: Mutual funds are subject to fluctuations in market conditions.
- **Fees and Expenses**: Management fees can reduce net returns.
- **Lack of Control**: Investors rely entirely on the fund manager's decisions.

12.4.3 Exchange-Traded Funds (ETFs)

Definition

Exchange-Traded Funds (ETFs) are investment funds traded on stock exchanges, similar to stocks. They track the performance of an index, sector, commodity, or asset class. ETFs combine the benefits of mutual funds (diversification) and stocks (real-time trading).

Types of ETFs
1. Equity ETFs

- Track stock market indices or sectors.
  Example: SPDR S&P 500 ETF.

2. Bond ETFs

- Invest in fixed-income securities like government or corporate bonds.

3. Commodity ETFs

- Track commodity prices, such as gold or crude oil.
  Example: Gold ETFs.

4. Sector and Thematic ETFs

- Focus on specific sectors (e.g., technology) or themes (e.g., ESG investing).

5. International ETFs

- Provide exposure to foreign markets.
  Example: ETFs tracking emerging markets.

Advantages of ETFs

1. **Low Costs**

   - ETFs typically have lower expense ratios compared to mutual funds.

2. **Liquidity**

   - Real-time trading allows investors to buy and sell ETFs during market hours.

3. **Transparency**

   - Holdings are disclosed daily, offering investors clarity on underlying assets.

4. **Tax Efficiency**

   - ETFs are more tax-efficient due to their unique creation and redemption process.

Risks and Challenges

- **Market Volatility**: ETFs are subject to market fluctuations.
- **Tracking Error**: ETFs may not perfectly replicate the performance of their benchmark index.
- **Liquidity Risk**: Thinly traded ETFs may have wider bid-ask spreads.

Modern Financial Instruments: Opportunities and Challenges
Opportunities

1. **Diversification**: Investors can spread risk across multiple asset classes.
2. **Accessibility**: Even retail investors can access complex instruments like derivatives and ETFs.
3. **Innovation**: Tailored instruments cater to specific investment needs and strategies.

Challenges

1. **Complexity**: Requires financial literacy and expertise to make informed decisions.
2. **Regulation**: Striking a balance between innovation and oversight is challenging.
3. **Volatility**: Modern instruments often amplify market fluctuations.

Aspect	Structural Unemployment	Frictional Unemployment	Cyclical Unemployment
Nature	Long-term	Short-term	Medium-term
Cause	Skill mismatch, industry shifts	Job transitions, workforce entry	Economic downturns
Impact	Persistent unemployment	Minimal	Severe during recessions
Solution	Reskilling, diversification	Job-matching platforms	Stimulus and monetary policies

Comparison: Mutual Funds vs. ETFs

Aspect	Structural Unemployment	Frictional Unemployment	Cyclical Unemployment
Nature	Long-term	Short-term	Medium-term
Cause	Skill mismatch, industry shifts	Job transitions, workforce entry	Economic downturns
Impact	Persistent unemployment	Minimal	Severe during recessions
Solution	Reskilling, diversification	Job-matching platforms	Stimulus and monetary policies

Digital Banking and Shadow Banking: Comparative Insights

Aspect	Structural Unemployment	Frictional Unemployment	Cyclical Unemployment
Nature	Long-term	Short-term	Medium-term
Cause	Skill mismatch, industry shifts	Job transitions, workforce entry	Economic downturns
Impact	Persistent unemployment	Minimal	Severe during recessions
Solution	Reskilling, diversification	Job-matching platforms	Stimulus and monetary policies

Comparison of Basel I, II, and III

THIRTEEN

EMPLOYMENT AND UNEMPLOYMENT

Understanding the dynamics of employment and unemployment is crucial for assessing the health of an economy. Unemployment, a situation where individuals capable of working and actively seeking work are unable to find employment, has various forms, each with distinct causes and implications. This section explores the key types of unemployment—**Structural, Frictional**, and **Cyclical Unemployment**—and their relevance in economic policymaking.

13.1 Types of Unemployment

Definition of Unemployment

Unemployment occurs when individuals who are willing and able to work at prevailing wage rates cannot secure employment. Economists classify unemployment into various categories based on its causes, duration, and impact on the economy.

Structural Unemployment

Definition

Structural unemployment arises when there is a mismatch between the skills of workers and the demands of the labor market. It is caused by long-term shifts in the economy, such as technological advancements, changes in consumer preferences, or globalization.

Key Characteristics

- Persistent and long-term in nature.

- Often requires retraining or reskilling of workers.
- Linked to structural changes in industries or regions.

Causes

1. **Technological Advancements**

   - Automation and artificial intelligence replace jobs, leaving workers with outdated skills.
     Example: The decline in manufacturing jobs due to the rise of automated assembly lines.

2. **Globalization**

   - Industries relocate to regions with lower production costs, leaving workers in high-cost regions unemployed.
     Example: Outsourcing of customer service jobs to countries with lower labor costs.

3. **Sectoral Shifts**

   - Economic transitions from primary (agriculture) to secondary (manufacturing) and tertiary (services) sectors.
     Example: Decline of coal mining jobs due to the transition to renewable energy sources.

Impact

- Leads to regional disparities in employment.
- Can result in long-term economic inefficiencies if not addressed.

Solutions

- **Retraining Programs**: Governments and organizations can provide skill enhancement courses.
- **Education Reform**: Aligning curricula with future industry demands.
- **Economic Diversification**: Promoting new industries in affected regions.

Frictional Unemployment

Definition

Frictional unemployment occurs when workers are temporarily unemployed while transitioning between jobs, entering the workforce, or re-entering after a break. It reflects the time taken to match workers with suitable job opportunities.

Key Characteristics

- Short-term and voluntary in nature.
- Considered a normal aspect of a dynamic economy.

Causes

1. **Job Transitioning**

   - Workers leave one job to find another that better suits their skills or preferences.
   Example: A software engineer switching companies for better career growth.

2. **New Entrants**

   - Fresh graduates or individuals re-entering the workforce after a hiatus experience delays in securing employment.
   Example: A recent college graduate searching for their first job.

3. **Geographic Mobility**

   - Workers relocating to different regions may experience temporary unemployment.

Impact

- Typically has minimal adverse effects on the economy.
- Indicates a healthy labor market where workers seek optimal job matches.

Solutions

- **Improved Job Matching**: Platforms like job portals and recruitment agencies reduce the time taken for matching.
- **Career Guidance**: Assisting workers in identifying opportunities aligned with their skills and aspirations.

Cyclical Unemployment
Definition
Cyclical unemployment is caused by economic fluctuations and reflects the decline in labor demand during periods of economic slowdown or recession. It is closely tied to the business cycle.
Key Characteristics

- Directly proportional to economic activity levels.
- Rises during recessions and falls during economic booms.

Causes

1. **Economic Downturns**

   - Reduced consumer demand leads to lower production, prompting firms to lay off workers.
   Example: Job losses during the 2008 global financial crisis.

2. **Demand-Supply Imbalances**

   - Overproduction during economic booms can lead to subsequent cutbacks in employment during slowdowns.

3. **Global Crises**

   - Pandemics, wars, or trade disruptions can trigger widespread layoffs.
   Example: Mass unemployment during the COVID-19 pandemic due to lockdowns and reduced economic activity.

Impact

- Can lead to severe economic consequences, including reduced income, lower consumer spending, and prolonged recessions.

- Increases government expenditure on unemployment benefits and stimulus packages.

Solutions

- **Stimulus Measures**: Governments can boost demand through fiscal policies, such as tax cuts or increased public spending.
- **Monetary Easing**: Central banks can lower interest rates to encourage investment and consumption.
- **Work-Sharing Programs**: Temporary reduction of working hours to retain employees during downturns.

Implications for Policy and Economy

1. **Economic Stability**

   - High levels of cyclical unemployment signal economic instability, necessitating immediate intervention.

2. **Labor Market Flexibility**

   - Frictional unemployment highlights the need for efficient job markets and employment services.

3. **Workforce Resilience**

   - Structural unemployment underscores the importance of lifelong learning and adaptability in a changing economy.

4. **Global Competitiveness**

   - Addressing unemployment effectively can enhance a country's productivity and economic growth.

13.2 Employment Policies

The role of government in addressing unemployment and fostering employment is pivotal for economic growth and social stability. Governments implement various **employment policies** and programs to promote job creation, reduce unemployment, and support the workforce in adapting to changing economic demands. These initiatives aim to ensure inclusive growth by targeting vulnerable sections of society, fostering entrepreneurship, and aligning labor market needs with skills development.

Government Initiatives for Job Creation

Governments worldwide adopt diverse strategies to create jobs and stimulate employment. These include infrastructure development, promoting entrepreneurship, enhancing skill development, and implementing targeted welfare schemes. In this section, we explore prominent initiatives undertaken by governments, with a focus on examples from India and global best practices.

1. Infrastructure Development

Rationale

Investment in infrastructure projects, such as roads, railways, energy, and housing, generates direct employment opportunities and boosts economic activity in related sectors.

Government Initiatives

- **India: Pradhan Mantri Gram Sadak Yojana (PMGSY)**

    ○ Aims to connect rural areas with all-weather roads, creating jobs in construction and allied industries.

- **Global: The New Deal (USA)**

    ○ Introduced during the Great Depression, it focused on large-scale public works projects to reduce unemployment.

2. Promoting Entrepreneurship

Rationale

Encouraging entrepreneurship creates self-employment opportunities and fosters innovation, which drives job creation in the long term.
Government Initiatives

- **India: Startup India**

  - Provides tax incentives, financial support, and simplified regulatory processes to encourage startups.

- **Global: Small Business Administration (USA)**

  - Offers funding and technical support to small businesses, promoting job creation in local communities.

3. Skill Development Programs
Rationale
Skill development bridges the gap between the labor market's demands and the workforce's capabilities, ensuring employability across sectors.
Government Initiatives

- **India: Skill India Mission**

  - Aims to train over 40 crore individuals in market-relevant skills by 2022 through programs like Pradhan Mantri Kaushal Vikas Yojana (PMKVY).

- **Global: Germany's Dual Training System**

  - Combines on-the-job training with classroom instruction to create a highly skilled workforce.

4. Rural Employment Schemes
Rationale
Rural employment schemes focus on creating sustainable livelihoods in rural areas, reducing migration to urban centers and addressing regional disparities.
Government Initiatives

- **India: Mahatma Gandhi National Rural Employment Guarantee Act (MGNREGA)**

  - Guarantees 100 days of wage employment annually to rural households, creating jobs in public works and infrastructure.

- **Global: Bolsa Verde (Brazil)**

  - Provides payments to rural workers engaged in sustainable environmental conservation activities.

5. Support for Informal Sector Workers
Rationale
The informal sector is a significant source of employment in many developing economies. Targeted interventions ensure social security and income stability for these workers.
Government Initiatives

- **India: E-Shram Portal**

  - A national database for unorganized workers to provide social security benefits and improve their working conditions.

- **Global: Social Security for Informal Workers (South Africa)**

  - Implements pension schemes and healthcare benefits for informal sector workers.

6. Job Creation Through Technology and Innovation
Rationale
Investments in technology-intensive sectors, such as renewable energy, information technology, and artificial intelligence, generate high-value jobs and drive economic growth.
Government Initiatives

- **India: Digital India**

- Promotes IT-based solutions and infrastructure to create jobs in technology and digital services.

- **Global: Green Jobs Initiative (UNEP)**

  - Focuses on employment opportunities in renewable energy and sustainable industries.

7. Women's Employment Initiatives
Rationale

Encouraging women's participation in the workforce enhances economic productivity and reduces gender disparities.

Government Initiatives

- **India: Support to Training and Employment Program (STEP)**

  - Provides skill development and financial assistance to women for self-employment.

- **Global: Women in Work Program (OECD)**

  - Focuses on policies that promote gender equality and work-life balance.

8. Export-Oriented Employment
Rationale

Promoting exports creates jobs in manufacturing, agriculture, and services sectors while boosting foreign exchange earnings.

Government Initiatives

- **India: Make in India**

  - Encourages investment in manufacturing and exports, creating jobs across sectors.

- **Global: Special Economic Zones (China)**

- SEZs attract foreign investment and create large-scale employment in export-oriented industries.

9. Youth Employment Programs
Rationale

Youth unemployment is a critical issue globally. Targeted programs aim to integrate young people into the workforce through internships, apprenticeships, and skill training.

Government Initiatives

- **India: National Career Service (NCS)**

  - Provides career counseling, job matching, and vocational training for youth.

- **Global: Youth Guarantee Program (EU)**

  - Ensures young people under 25 receive a quality job offer, education, or training within four months of unemployment.

10. Fiscal and Monetary Policies
Rationale

Governments use fiscal and monetary tools to stimulate job creation by encouraging investments and consumer spending.

Government Initiatives

- **India: Atmanirbhar Bharat Package**

  - Economic stimulus package to revive businesses and protect jobs during the COVID-19 pandemic.

- **Global: Quantitative Easing (USA)**

  - Injected liquidity into the economy post-2008 financial crisis to encourage lending and job creation.

Impact of Employment Policies

1. **Economic Growth**

   - Job creation drives consumer spending, boosts productivity, and fosters economic stability.

2. **Social Inclusion**

   - Employment policies reduce income inequality and empower marginalized communities.

3. **Skill Enhancement**

   - Workforce development ensures adaptability to changing market demands.

4. **Reduction in Poverty**

   - Sustainable employment programs directly contribute to poverty alleviation.

5. **Gender Equality**

   - Targeted initiatives improve women's participation in the workforce, fostering inclusive growth.

Challenges in Implementation

1. **Regional Disparities**

   - Uneven development leads to unequal access to employment opportunities.

2. **Informal Economy**

   - The dominance of informal jobs limits the reach of formal employment policies.

3. **Skill Mismatch**

- Gaps between industry needs and workforce skills hinder effective job placement.

4. Funding Constraints

- Insufficient financial resources impede large-scale program implementation.

5. Monitoring and Evaluation

- Lack of robust mechanisms to assess the impact of policies reduces accountability.

Aspect	Structural Unemployment	Frictional Unemployment	Cyclical Unemployment
Nature	Long-term	Short-term	Medium-term
Cause	Skill mismatch, industry shifts	Job transitions, workforce entry	Economic downturns
Impact	Persistent unemployment	Minimal	Severe during recessions
Solution	Reskilling, diversification	Job-matching platforms	Stimulus and monetary policies

Comparison of Structural, Frictional, and Cyclical Unemployment

FOURTEEN

CASE STUDIES IN ECONOMICS

Economic case studies provide valuable insights into the causes, dynamics, and consequences of major economic events, offering lessons for policymakers and stakeholders to navigate future challenges. One of the most significant events in modern economic history is the **Global Financial Crisis of 2008**, a crisis that originated in the financial sector but rippled across the global economy, leaving lasting impacts.

14.1 The Global Financial Crisis of 2008

The **Global Financial Crisis (GFC)** of 2008 was a severe worldwide economic downturn triggered by the collapse of the U.S. housing market and the subsequent failure of major financial institutions. Its causes were multifaceted, rooted in systemic vulnerabilities, risky financial practices, and regulatory lapses.

Causes of the Global Financial Crisis

1. Housing Market Bubble

- **Subprime Mortgage Loans**: Banks issued high-risk loans to borrowers with poor credit histories, betting on continuous housing price appreciation.
- **Rising Housing Prices**: Excessive demand, speculative investments, and easy credit led to inflated housing prices, creating a bubble.

2. Financial Innovation and Risk Mismanagement

- **Securitization of Mortgages**: Banks bundled subprime mortgages into complex financial products, such as **mortgage-backed securities (MBS)** and **collateralized debt obligations (CDOs)**, which were sold to investors globally.
- **Credit Default Swaps (CDS)**: Insurance-like derivatives designed to protect against loan defaults amplified systemic risks.

3. Regulatory Lapses

- **Lax Oversight**: Inadequate regulation allowed financial institutions to engage in risky behavior without sufficient safeguards.
- **Shadow Banking System**: Non-bank financial institutions operated outside traditional regulatory frameworks, creating opaque risk exposure.

4. Over-Leverage and Excessive Risk-Taking

- **High Leverage Ratios**: Financial institutions borrowed heavily to fund speculative investments, magnifying losses when asset values declined.
- **Moral Hazard**: Belief in government bailouts encouraged reckless behavior by financial firms.

5. Liquidity Crunch

- As defaults on subprime mortgages increased, banks and financial institutions faced significant losses, leading to a freeze in credit markets.

Example: The collapse of Lehman Brothers in September 2008 marked a turning point, triggering widespread panic and a global liquidity crisis.

Impact of the Global Financial Crisis

1. Economic Recession

- The GFC caused a sharp contraction in economic activity globally, with GDP declines in major economies.

Example: The U.S. GDP contracted by 4.3% in 2009, the steepest drop since World War II.

2. Unemployment

- Millions of jobs were lost as businesses faced declining revenues and cut costs.
  Example: U.S. unemployment peaked at 10% in October 2009.

3. Bank Failures

- Major financial institutions either collapsed or required government bailouts.
  Example: Bear Stearns and Lehman Brothers collapsed, while AIG and Citigroup received substantial government support.

4. Housing Market Collapse

- Housing prices plummeted, leading to widespread foreclosures and loss of wealth for homeowners.
  Example: In the U.S., housing prices declined by approximately 30% from their peak.

5. Global Trade and Investment Decline

- The crisis disrupted international trade and reduced foreign direct investment, particularly in emerging economies.

6. Widening Inequality

- The recovery period saw uneven benefits, with low-income groups bearing the brunt of job losses and foreclosures, while financial markets rebounded quickly.

7. Policy Responses

- Central banks and governments implemented unprecedented measures to stabilize the economy, including:

  - **Monetary Policies**: The U.S. Federal Reserve and other central banks reduced interest rates to near zero.
  - **Fiscal Stimulus**: Governments launched stimulus packages to boost spending and revive demand.

Example: The American Recovery and Reinvestment Act (ARRA) of 2009 allocated \$831 billion for infrastructure, education, and health care.

Lessons from the Global Financial Crisis
1. Importance of Financial Regulation

- Strengthened oversight of financial institutions is critical to prevent excessive risk-taking.
  Post-GFC Measures:

  - Introduction of the **Dodd-Frank Act** in the U.S., which imposed stricter regulations on banks and financial institutions.
  - **Basel III Norms**: Enhanced capital and liquidity requirements for banks globally.

2. Systemic Risk Awareness

- The interconnectedness of financial institutions underscores the need for monitoring systemic risks.
  Example: Regular stress testing of banks to assess their ability to withstand economic shocks.

3. Risk Management and Transparency

- Complex financial products must be transparent and better understood by regulators and investors.

4. Role of Central Banks

- Central banks play a critical role in maintaining liquidity and preventing panic during crises.
  Example: The Federal Reserve's quantitative easing (QE) program injected liquidity into the economy.

5. Consumer Protection

- Enhanced consumer protection laws are essential to prevent predatory lending and ensure financial literacy.

6. Need for Global Cooperation

- Coordinated efforts among countries are necessary to address cross-border financial challenges.
  Example: The G20 Summit in 2009 led to agreements on financial reforms and fiscal coordination.

Global Case Studies
1. The U.S.

- The epicenter of the crisis, driven by the collapse of subprime mortgages and the failure of major financial institutions.

2. Europe

- Many European countries faced sovereign debt crises due to the GFC, particularly Greece, Ireland, and Spain.

3. Emerging Economies

- Countries like India and China experienced slower growth but avoided major financial disruptions due to their relatively insulated banking systems.

14.2 Indian Economic Reforms

India has undertaken significant economic reforms to foster growth, enhance fiscal responsibility, and promote financial inclusion. Among these reforms, the introduction of the **Goods and Services Tax (GST)**, the enactment of the **Fiscal Responsibility and Budget Management (FRBM) Act**, and various initiatives aimed at **financial inclusion** have played transformative roles in reshaping the Indian economy.

14.2.1 Goods and Services Tax (GST)

Introduction

The **Goods and Services Tax (GST)**, implemented on **July 1, 2017**, is one of the most significant tax reforms in India's history. It replaced a complex system of multiple indirect taxes with a unified tax regime, streamlining taxation and promoting ease of doing business.

Key Features of GST

1. **Comprehensive Coverage**

   - GST subsumes multiple indirect taxes, including VAT, excise duty, and service tax, into a single tax structure.

2. **Dual Structure**

   - GST operates under a dual system:

     - **Central GST (CGST)**: Levied by the central government.
     - **State GST (SGST)**: Levied by state governments.
     - **Integrated GST (IGST)**: Levied on inter-state transactions.

3. **Destination-Based Taxation**

   - GST is collected at the point of consumption rather than production, ensuring equitable tax distribution.

4. **Input Tax Credit (ITC)**

   - Businesses can claim credit for taxes paid on inputs, reducing cascading effects.

5. **Simplified Tax Filing**

   - The **GST Network (GSTN)** facilitates online filing, payment, and reconciliation.

Impact of GST

Economic Benefits

- **Unified Market**: Eliminated inter-state tax barriers, creating a seamless national market.
- **Increased Compliance**: Simplified tax structure incentivized businesses to formalize operations.
- **Boost to Exports**: Zero-rated exports under GST improved India's competitiveness in global markets.

Challenges

- **Initial Transition**: Businesses faced difficulties adapting to new tax filing procedures.
- **Rate Rationalization**: Multiple tax slabs created confusion and required periodic adjustments.

Real-World Example

The introduction of GST significantly reduced logistics costs, as goods could move across states without delays caused by inter-state taxes and checkpoints. For instance, transport time for goods like FMCG products reduced by **20-30%** post-GST.

14.2.2 *Fiscal Responsibility and Budget Management (FRBM) Act*

Introduction

The **FRBM Act**, enacted in **2003**, aims to institutionalize fiscal discipline and reduce fiscal deficits to ensure long-term economic stability. The Act sets targets for fiscal consolidation and mandates transparency in fiscal operations.

Key Objectives of the FRBM Act

1. **Reduction of Fiscal Deficit**

   - Targets a fiscal deficit of **3% of GDP**.

2. **Reduction of Revenue Deficit**

- ◦ Aims to eliminate revenue deficits to ensure public expenditure is directed toward asset creation rather than consumption.

3. **Public Debt Management**

- ◦ Limits government borrowings to sustainable levels to reduce interest burden.

4. **Transparency and Accountability**

- ◦ Mandates regular fiscal updates to Parliament and ensures public disclosure of fiscal data.

Amendments and Modifications

- **FRBM Review Committee (2017)**: Recommended more flexible fiscal targets based on economic conditions, introducing an **escape clause** to allow deviations during crises (e.g., pandemics or recessions).
- **Debt Target**: Introduced a target to limit government debt to **60% of GDP** (40% for the central government and 20% for states).

Impact of the FRBM Act
Achievements

- Improved fiscal discipline, reducing the fiscal deficit from **5.9% of GDP (2003)** to **3.3% (2008)**.
- Increased investor confidence due to predictable fiscal policies.

Challenges

- Achieving targets became difficult during economic slowdowns, necessitating deviations.
- Public investment in infrastructure was constrained due to strict deficit limits.

Example of Implementation

During the COVID-19 pandemic, India invoked the FRBM Act's escape clause, allowing the fiscal deficit to rise beyond the stipulated limit to accommodate increased healthcare and stimulus spending.

14.2.3 Financial Inclusion

Introduction

Financial inclusion refers to providing affordable access to financial services, such as banking, credit, insurance, and pensions, to underserved and unbanked populations. In India, financial inclusion has been a critical policy focus, aimed at reducing poverty and promoting equitable growth.

Key Initiatives for Financial Inclusion

1. Pradhan Mantri Jan Dhan Yojana (PMJDY)

- Launched in **2014**, this flagship scheme aims to provide universal access to banking services.
- Achievements:

  - Over **48 crore** bank accounts opened (as of 2023).
  - Total deposits under PMJDY exceeded ₹**2 lakh crore**.

2. Aadhaar-Linked Services

- Aadhaar-enabled payment systems (AEPS) facilitate direct benefit transfers (DBT) to reduce leakages in subsidy distribution.

3. Digital Payment Systems

- Unified Payments Interface (UPI) has revolutionized digital payments, enabling instant and cost-effective transactions.
- **Example**: UPI processed **74 billion transactions** worth ₹125.94 lakh crore in 2022-23.

4. Microfinance and Self-Help Groups (SHGs)

- Programs like the **National Rural Livelihood Mission (NRLM)** empower women through microcredit and SHG-based financing.

5. Small Finance Banks and Payment Banks

- These specialized institutions cater to the credit and savings needs of small businesses, farmers, and low-income groups.

6. Pradhan Mantri Suraksha Bima Yojana (PMSBY) and Pradhan Mantri Jeevan Jyoti Bima Yojana (PMJJBY)

- Provide affordable insurance coverage to low-income populations.

Impact of Financial Inclusion
Economic Benefits

- Enhanced savings and investments among low-income households.
- Increased credit access for micro and small enterprises.
- Boosted consumption and economic activity in rural areas.

Social Benefits

- Empowered marginalized groups, especially women and rural populations.
- Reduced dependence on informal and high-interest money lenders.

Challenges in Financial Inclusion

1. **Digital Divide**

   - Limited access to digital infrastructure in rural and remote areas.

2. **Financial Literacy**

   - Lack of awareness about financial products hinders effective utilization.

3. **Operational Barriers**

   - High operational costs and low profitability in servicing remote areas.

Example of Success

The **PMJDY scheme** significantly improved financial inclusion in India, with over **67% of accounts** belonging to rural areas and **56%** held by women, promoting gender and regional equity.

Aspect	Pre-GFC	Post-GFC
Regulation	Lax and fragmented	Stricter and globally harmonized
Risk Awareness	Limited	Increased focus on systemic risks
Capital Requirements	Lower (Basel II)	Higher (Basel III)
Transparency	Limited disclosure of derivatives	Enhanced reporting and disclosure
Consumer Protection	Weak	Strengthened through new laws

Comparison: Pre- and Post-GFC Banking Environment

FIFTEEN
FUTURE OF ECONOMICS

The rapid evolution of technology, particularly **Artificial Intelligence (AI)**, is reshaping the field of economics. From data analysis to forecasting, AI is enabling economists to gain deeper insights, make accurate predictions, and develop innovative solutions to complex economic problems. This chapter explores the transformative role of AI in economics, with a focus on its applications in **economic forecasting**.

15.1 Artificial Intelligence in Economics

Introduction to Artificial Intelligence in Economics

Artificial Intelligence refers to the simulation of human intelligence in machines that can learn, analyze, and make decisions based on data. In economics, AI encompasses a range of technologies such as **machine learning (ML)**, **natural language processing (NLP)**, and **predictive analytics** that enable better understanding and forecasting of economic trends.

Economic systems generate vast amounts of data, and AI tools are uniquely positioned to process and analyze this information efficiently. By identifying patterns, predicting future outcomes, and automating processes, AI is revolutionizing how economists approach problems and formulate policies.

Role of AI in Economic Forecasting

Economic forecasting involves predicting future economic conditions, such as GDP growth, inflation, unemployment, and trade flows, based on historical and real-time data. Traditional forecasting methods rely on econometric models and statistical techniques, which, while robust, are limited by their linearity and assumptions. AI overcomes these limitations by handling complex, nonlinear relationships and large datasets with greater precision.

Key Applications of AI in Economic Forecasting

1. Data Analysis and Pattern Recognition

AI algorithms excel at processing vast amounts of structured and unstructured data. By identifying hidden patterns, trends, and anomalies in economic data, AI enhances the accuracy of forecasts.

Example: Predicting GDP growth using satellite imagery of economic activity, such as night-time lights or traffic patterns.

2. Real-Time Forecasting

AI enables real-time analysis of economic conditions by integrating diverse data sources, such as stock market indices, trade data, and social media sentiment. This helps policymakers respond swiftly to emerging economic challenges.

Example: Analyzing supply chain disruptions during the COVID-19 pandemic using real-time shipping data.

3. Predictive Analytics

Using historical data, AI models forecast key economic indicators like inflation, unemployment rates, and currency fluctuations. These predictions guide businesses and governments in decision-making.

Example: AI-powered models by the International Monetary Fund (IMF) forecast commodity prices based on weather patterns and geopolitical factors.

4. Scenario Analysis

AI facilitates scenario planning by simulating multiple economic outcomes under different assumptions. This helps policymakers evaluate the impact of various policies or external shocks.

Example: Assessing the economic impact of climate change on agricultural output using AI-based models.

5. Natural Language Processing (NLP) for Sentiment Analysis

AI tools use NLP to analyze economic sentiment from news articles, social media, and financial reports. Sentiment analysis provides insights into consumer confidence and market trends.

Example: Predicting stock market movements based on sentiment extracted from financial news and tweets.

6. Forecasting Global Trade and Supply Chains

AI models predict trade flows and supply chain disruptions by analyzing global shipping data, trade agreements, and geopolitical developments. **Example**: Monitoring port congestion and its impact on international trade during global crises.

Advantages of AI in Economic Forecasting

1. **Accuracy**

   - AI models improve forecasting accuracy by incorporating nonlinear relationships and complex interactions among variables.

2. **Scalability**

   - AI processes large datasets from diverse sources, including economic reports, satellite data, and social media.

3. **Speed**

   - AI delivers faster results compared to traditional econometric models, enabling timely decision-making.

4. **Adaptability**

   - Machine learning algorithms learn from new data, refining their predictions over time.

5. **Customization**

   - AI systems can be tailored to specific industries, regions, or economic indicators.

Challenges and Limitations

1. **Data Quality and Bias**

   - AI models are only as good as the data they are trained on. Incomplete or biased datasets can lead to inaccurate forecasts.

2. **Complexity of Economic Systems**

   - While AI models are powerful, they may struggle to fully capture the complexities of global economic systems and human behavior.

3. **Ethical Concerns**

   - Over-reliance on AI could lead to opaque decision-making processes, raising accountability issues.

4. **Resource Intensive**

   - Developing and maintaining AI models requires significant computational resources and expertise.

Case Studies: AI in Economic Forecasting
1. Central Banks and Inflation Forecasting

- Central banks, such as the Federal Reserve and the European Central Bank, use AI models to forecast inflation and guide monetary policy. These models integrate diverse datasets, including labor market conditions, consumer spending, and global commodity prices.

2. Predicting Recessions

- AI models like Google's **DeepMind** analyze macroeconomic indicators to predict the likelihood of economic recessions, enabling governments to implement preemptive measures.

3. Agriculture and Commodity Prices

- AI-based systems predict crop yields and commodity prices using weather data, soil conditions, and market trends.
  Example: India's use of AI to forecast monsoon patterns and their impact on agricultural production.

Future Outlook: AI in Economics

1. **Integration with Big Data**

   - Combining AI with big data analytics will enhance forecasting accuracy by incorporating diverse and real-time data sources.

2. **AI-Driven Policy Design**

   - Policymakers will increasingly rely on AI to simulate the impact of fiscal and monetary policies before implementation.

3. **Personalized Economic Insights**

   - AI tools will provide tailored economic insights to businesses and individuals, democratizing access to economic intelligence.

4. **Collaboration Across Disciplines**

   - The integration of AI with behavioral economics, climate science, and geopolitics will expand its applicability.

15.2 Blockchain and Cryptocurrencies

The advent of **blockchain technology** and **cryptocurrencies** has introduced transformative changes to financial systems worldwide. Blockchain's decentralized and secure ledger technology, combined with cryptocurrencies as digital assets, offers innovative solutions to long-standing challenges in traditional financial systems, such as inefficiencies, lack of transparency, and high transaction costs.

Blockchain Technology in Financial Systems

Definition of Blockchain

A **blockchain** is a decentralized, distributed ledger that records transactions across a network of computers. Each transaction is stored in a "block" and linked to previous blocks through cryptographic hashes, forming a secure and immutable chain.

Key Features of Blockchain

1. **Decentralization**

○ No single authority controls the ledger, making it transparent and resistant to manipulation.

2. **Transparency**

   ○ All transactions are recorded in a public ledger, ensuring accountability.

3. **Immutability**

   ○ Transactions, once added to the blockchain, cannot be altered or deleted.

4. **Security**

   ○ Cryptographic techniques protect data integrity and prevent unauthorized access.

5. **Smart Contracts**

   ○ Self-executing contracts automate processes based on predefined conditions.

Applications in Financial Systems
1. Payment Systems and Cross-Border Transactions

· Blockchain enables fast and cost-effective cross-border payments by eliminating intermediaries.
Example: Ripple (XRP) facilitates near-instantaneous international payments.

2. Trade Finance

· Blockchain reduces paperwork, automates processes, and enhances transparency in trade finance.
Example: HSBC and IBM use blockchain platforms for trade settlements.

3. Securities Trading

- Blockchain streamlines the trading of stocks, bonds, and derivatives by enabling real-time settlement and reducing counterparty risk.
  Example: The Australian Securities Exchange (ASX) is transitioning to a blockchain-based clearing and settlement system.

4. Fraud Prevention

- Immutable records and transparent transactions reduce the risk of financial fraud and improve trust.
  Example: Blockchain ensures the authenticity of financial transactions and prevents double-spending.

5. Decentralized Finance (DeFi)

- DeFi platforms use blockchain to provide financial services like lending, borrowing, and trading without traditional intermediaries.
  Example: Platforms like **Uniswap** and **Aave** enable peer-to-peer financial interactions.

Cryptocurrencies in Financial Systems
Definition of Cryptocurrencies
Cryptocurrencies are digital or virtual currencies that use cryptography for security and operate on blockchain technology. Unlike fiat currencies, they are decentralized and not governed by any central authority.
Examples of Cryptocurrencies

1. **Bitcoin (BTC)**

   - The first and most well-known cryptocurrency, designed as a decentralized digital currency for peer-to-peer transactions.

2. **Ethereum (ETH)**

   - Enables the execution of smart contracts and decentralized applications (DApps) on its blockchain.

3. **Stablecoins**

- ○ Cryptocurrencies pegged to stable assets like the U.S. dollar to reduce volatility.
  Example: Tether (USDT).

4. **Central Bank Digital Currencies (CBDCs)**

- ○ Digital currencies issued and regulated by central banks, combining blockchain's efficiency with central oversight.
  Example: China's **Digital Yuan.**

Impact of Cryptocurrencies on Financial Systems
1. Financial Inclusion

- Cryptocurrencies enable access to financial services for the unbanked population by eliminating reliance on traditional banks.
  Example: Mobile wallets powered by cryptocurrencies are widely used in Africa for remittances.

2. Reduced Transaction Costs

- By removing intermediaries, cryptocurrencies lower the costs of transactions, especially for international payments.

3. Enhanced Security and Privacy

- Blockchain's cryptographic techniques ensure secure transactions while offering pseudonymity to users.

4. Volatility Risks

- High price volatility makes cryptocurrencies unsuitable for stable transactions or long-term investments.
  Example: Bitcoin's value fluctuates significantly over short periods.

5. Regulatory Challenges

- Cryptocurrencies' decentralized nature complicates regulation, raising concerns about money laundering and tax evasion.

6. Alternative Investment Assets

- Cryptocurrencies have emerged as an asset class, attracting investors seeking high returns.
  Example: Bitcoin is often referred to as "digital gold" for its store-of-value properties.

Impact on Financial Systems
1. Decentralization of Financial Services
Blockchain and cryptocurrencies reduce reliance on traditional financial institutions, empowering individuals and fostering peer-to-peer interactions.
2. Improved Transparency and Accountability

- Blockchain's transparent ledger ensures that all transactions are publicly verifiable, reducing corruption and fraud in financial systems.

3. Cost and Time Efficiency

- Automated processes and the elimination of intermediaries significantly reduce transaction costs and processing times, particularly in cross-border payments.

4. Financial Innovation

- Cryptocurrencies and blockchain have spurred innovation in financial products, such as tokenized assets, decentralized exchanges, and yield farming.

5. Risks to Traditional Financial Institutions

- Cryptocurrencies challenge traditional banking systems by offering alternatives to fiat currencies and centralized payment networks.

6. Systemic Risks

- The unregulated nature of cryptocurrencies poses systemic risks to financial stability, particularly during speculative bubbles and market crashes.

Challenges and Limitations

1. **Regulatory Uncertainty**

   - Governments worldwide struggle to regulate cryptocurrencies without stifling innovation.
   Example: India has debated implementing a cryptocurrency ban while exploring a CBDC.

2. **Energy Consumption**

   - Blockchain networks like Bitcoin consume significant energy for mining, raising environmental concerns.

3. **Security Risks**

   - While blockchain itself is secure, associated platforms like cryptocurrency exchanges are vulnerable to hacking.
   Example: The 2014 **Mt. Gox** hack resulted in the loss of 850,000 Bitcoins.

4. **Volatility**

   - Extreme price swings deter mainstream adoption of cryptocurrencies for everyday transactions.

5. **Scalability Issues**

   - Popular blockchains face challenges in handling a high volume of transactions efficiently.
   Example: Ethereum's high gas fees during network congestion.

Future Outlook

1. **Mainstream Adoption**

- Increasing adoption of blockchain and cryptocurrencies in banking, trade, and supply chain management.

2. **Regulatory Evolution**

- Governments are likely to establish clearer frameworks, balancing innovation with consumer protection.

3. **Integration with Traditional Finance**

- Financial institutions are exploring blockchain for efficient operations and cryptocurrencies as investment products.

4. **Environmental Sustainability**

- Transition to energy-efficient consensus mechanisms like **Proof of Stake (PoS)**.

5. **Growth of Decentralized Finance (DeFi)**

- DeFi is expected to challenge traditional financial systems by offering borderless and permissionless financial services.

15.3 Emerging Trends in Global Trade and Finance

Global trade and finance are undergoing transformative changes driven by technological advancements, evolving geopolitical dynamics, and shifts in consumer behavior. These emerging trends present significant **opportunities** for innovation, efficiency, and growth but also pose **challenges** that require proactive policymaking and adaptive strategies.

Emerging Trends in Global Trade

1. Digitalization of Trade

Opportunities

- **Streamlined Processes**: Technologies like blockchain, artificial intelligence (AI), and Internet of Things (IoT) optimize supply chains, reduce paperwork, and improve efficiency.
- **E-commerce Growth**: Platforms like Amazon and Alibaba enable small businesses to access global markets, fostering inclusivity in trade.

Example: Blockchain-based trade finance platforms like TradeLens enhance transparency in cross-border transactions.

Challenges

- **Digital Divide**: Developing countries face challenges in adopting digital trade due to inadequate infrastructure and skills.
- **Cybersecurity Risks**: Increased reliance on digital systems exposes global trade to hacking and data breaches.

2. Regional Trade Agreements (RTAs)
Opportunities

- **Enhanced Market Access**: RTAs like the Comprehensive and Progressive Agreement for Trans-Pacific Partnership (CPTPP) and the African Continental Free Trade Area (AfCFTA) open new avenues for trade.
- **Standardization**: Harmonized regulations reduce trade barriers and improve efficiency.

Challenges

- **Fragmentation**: Overlapping agreements can complicate global trade dynamics.
- **Exclusion of Non-Members**: Countries outside RTAs may face disadvantages, exacerbating inequalities.

3. Sustainability in Trade
Opportunities

- **Green Trade Initiatives**: Growing emphasis on environmentally sustainable trade practices, including low-carbon logistics and renewable energy-powered supply chains.
Example: Carbon border adjustment mechanisms in the EU incentivize sustainable production.

Challenges

- **Cost Pressures**: Transitioning to sustainable trade practices involves high upfront costs.
- **Regulatory Complexity**: Differing environmental standards across countries complicate compliance.

4. Reshoring and Nearshoring
Opportunities

- **Resilient Supply Chains**: Companies are diversifying supply chains to reduce reliance on single regions, fostering regional trade hubs.
  Example: Nearshoring in Mexico for U.S. markets to reduce dependency on Asia.

Challenges

- **Cost Increases**: Reshoring may raise production costs compared to outsourcing to low-cost regions.
- **Geopolitical Tensions**: Trade realignments can strain international relations.

5. Geopolitical Influences on Trade
Opportunities

- **Strategic Alliances**: Countries can leverage trade partnerships to strengthen geopolitical ties.
  Example: India's focus on Quad partnerships for economic and strategic collaboration.

Challenges

- **Trade Wars**: Tariff impositions and retaliatory measures disrupt global supply chains.
  Example: U.S.-China trade tensions affected technology and agricultural markets.

Emerging Trends in Global Finance
1. Fintech Revolution
Opportunities

- **Increased Financial Inclusion**: Digital wallets and mobile banking provide access to underserved populations.
  Example: M-Pesa in Kenya has revolutionized mobile-based payments.
- **Efficiency**: Technologies like blockchain reduce transaction costs and processing times.

Challenges

- **Regulatory Gaps**: Fintech innovations often outpace existing regulations, leading to risks in consumer protection and systemic stability.
- **Cyber Threats**: Increasing reliance on digital platforms exposes the financial system to hacking.

2. Green Finance
Opportunities

- **Investment in Sustainability**: Green bonds and ESG (Environmental, Social, and Governance) investments direct capital towards sustainable projects.
  Example: The issuance of green bonds exceeded $1 trillion globally in 2022.
- **Corporate Responsibility**: Companies benefit from aligning with sustainability goals.

Challenges

- **Greenwashing**: Misrepresentation of sustainability credentials can erode trust in green finance instruments.
- **Limited Standardization**: Lack of universal standards complicates the evaluation of ESG investments.

3. Digital Currencies
Opportunities

- **Central Bank Digital Currencies (CBDCs)**: Governments are exploring CBDCs to enhance payment systems and reduce reliance on cash.
  Example: China's Digital Yuan pilot has expanded to millions of users.

- **Cryptocurrencies**: Decentralized currencies like Bitcoin provide alternatives to traditional finance, promoting financial innovation.

Challenges

- **Volatility**: Cryptocurrencies experience significant price fluctuations, limiting their adoption as stable payment methods.
- **Regulation**: Balancing innovation with oversight remains a key challenge.

4. Globalization of Capital Markets
Opportunities

- **Cross-Border Investments**: Technology and deregulation facilitate investments across borders, increasing portfolio diversification.
  Example: Foreign portfolio investments in emerging markets like India and Brazil.
- **Access to Capital**: Companies in developing countries can access global markets for funding.

Challenges

- **Volatility**: Capital flows are sensitive to global economic conditions, leading to risks for emerging markets.
- **Currency Risk**: Exchange rate fluctuations can erode returns on cross-border investments.

5. Decentralized Finance (DeFi)
Opportunities

- **Innovative Financial Products**: DeFi platforms offer lending, borrowing, and trading services without intermediaries.
  Example: Platforms like Uniswap and Compound enable peer-to-peer financial transactions.
- **Inclusion**: DeFi expands access to financial services for underserved populations.

Challenges

- **Security Risks**: DeFi platforms are vulnerable to hacks and exploits.
- **Regulatory Uncertainty**: The lack of clear legal frameworks complicates adoption.

Opportunities and Challenges of Emerging Trends
Opportunities

1. **Economic Growth**

   - Emerging trends drive innovation, efficiency, and access, fostering global economic expansion.

2. **Inclusivity**

   - Fintech and decentralized finance bridge gaps in financial inclusion, particularly in developing economies.

3. **Sustainability**

   - Green finance and sustainable trade practices align economic growth with environmental goals.

Challenges

1. **Regulatory Adaptation**

   - Policymakers must balance innovation with oversight to ensure systemic stability.

2. **Technological Risks**

   - Cybersecurity threats and the digital divide can impede the adoption of emerging technologies.

3. **Geopolitical Uncertainty**

   - Trade wars and protectionist policies can disrupt global supply chains and financial markets.

Future Outlook

1. Integration of Technology

- Digitalization in trade and finance will continue to redefine global interactions, fostering efficiency and connectivity.

2. Focus on Sustainability

- Green finance and trade policies will gain prominence as countries commit to reducing carbon footprints.

3. Evolving Regulatory Frameworks

- Governments and international bodies will work to develop standardized regulations to address challenges like cybersecurity, greenwashing, and cross-border trade complexities.

4. Geopolitical Realignments

- Strategic partnerships and regional trade blocs will shape the future of global trade and finance.